LAROUSSE
GASTRONOMIQUE

FISH & SEAFOOD

LAROUSSE
GASTRONOMIQUE

FISH & SEAFOOD

With the assistance of the Gastronomic Committee
President Joël Robuchon

First published in Great Britain in 2004 by
Hamlyn, a division of Octopus Publishing Group Ltd

This edition published in 2011 by Bounty Books,
a division of Octopus Publishing Group Ltd
Endeavour House, 189 Shaftesbury Avenue, London WC2H 8JY
www.octopusbooks.co.uk

An Hachette UK Company
www.hachette.co.uk

ISBN: 978-0-753721-42-1

A CIP catalogue record for this book is available from the British Library

Printed and bound in China

Gastronomic Committee

President

Joël Robuchon

Members of the Committee

Michel Creignou, *Journalist*

Jean Delaveyne, *Chef, founder of Restaurant Le Camélia, Bougival*

Éric Frachon, *Honorary president, Evian Water SA*

Michel Guérard, *Chef, Restaurant Les Prés d'Eugénie, Eugénie-les-Bains*

Pierre Hermé, *Confectioner, Paris*

Robert Linxe, *Founder, The House of Chocolate, Paris and New York*

Élisabeth de Meurville, *Journalist*

Georges Pouvel, *Professor of cookery; consultant on cookery techniques*

Jean-François Revel, *Writer*

Pierre Troisgros, *Chef, Restaurant Pierre Troisgros, Roanne*

Alain Weill, *Art expert; member of the National Council of Gastronomy*

Contributors

Marie-Paule Bernardin
Archivist

Geneviève Beullac
Editor

Jean Billault
*Member of the College of
Butchery*

Christophe Bligny
Paris College of Catering

Thierry Borghèse
*Chief Inspector of Consumer
Affairs*

Francis Boucher
Confectioner

Pascal Champagne
*Barman, Hotel Lutetia;
Member, French Association
of Barmen*

Frédéric Chesneau
Project manager

Marcel Cottenceau
*Former technical director,
College of Butchery*

Robert Courtine
President, Marco-Polo Prize

Philippe Dardonville
*Secretary-general, National
Union of Producers of Fruit
Juice*

Bertrand Debatte
*Officer of the Bakery,
Auchamps*

Jean Dehillerin
*President and managing
director, E. Dehillerin SA
(manufacturers of kitchen
equipment)*

Gilbert Delos
Writer and journalist

Christian Flacelière
Journalist

Jean-Louis Flandrin
*Professor emeritus,
University of Paris VII;
Director of studies,*

*E.H.E.S.S. (College of Social
Sciences)*

Dr André Fourel
Economist

Dominique Franceschi
Journalist

Dr Jacques Fricker
Nutritionist

Jean-Pierre Gabriel
Journalist

Thierry Gaudillère
*Editor, Bourgogne
Aujourd'hui (Burgundy
Today)*

Ismène Giachetti
*Director of research, C.N.R.S.
(National Centre for
Scientific Research)*

Sylvie Girard
Cookery writer

Catherine Goavec-Bouvard
Agribusiness consultant

Jo Goldenberg
Restaurateur

Catherine Gomy
*Agribusiness certification
officer,
French Association of
Standardization*

Bruno Goussault
*Scientific director, C.R.E.A.
(Centre of Food and
Nutrition Studies)*

Jacques Guinberteau
*Mycologist; Director of
studies, I.N.R.A. (National
Institute of Agriculture)*

Joseph Hossenlopp
*Director of studies, Cemagref
(Institute of Research for
Agricultural and
Environmental Engineering)*

Françoise Kayler
Food critic

Jacques Lacoursière
Writer

Josette Le Reun-Gaudicheau
*Teacher (specializing in
seafood)*

Paul Maindiaux
*Development officer,
Ministry of Agriculture*

Laurent Mairet
Oenologist

Jukka Mannerkorpi
Cookery editor

Pascal Orain
Manager, Bertie's Restaurant

Philippe Pilliot
*Secretary-general, Federation
of French Grocers; Editor,
Le Nouvel Épicier
(The New Grocer)*

Jean-Claude Ribaut
*Cookery correspondent,
Le Monde*

Isabelle Richard
Bachelor of Arts

Michel Rigo
*Deputy head, National
Federation of Fruit Brandies*

Françoise Sabban
*Master of ceremonies,
E.H.E.S.S.
(College of Social Sciences)*

Jacques Sallé
Journalist

Jean-Louis Taillebaud
*Chef, Ritz-Escoffier (French
School of Gastronomy); Ritz
Hotel, Place Vendôme, Paris*

Claude Vifian
*Chef and professor, College of
the Hotel Industry, Lausanne*

Leda Vigliardi Paravia
Writer and journalist

Jean-Marc Wolff
*College of the Hotel Industry,
Paris*

Rémy Yverneau
*Secretary-general,
National Federation of
Makers of Cream Cheese*

Contents

Useful information

How to use this book

The recipes are divided into three main chapters: Fish, Seafood and Mixed fish & seafood dishes. Within these chapters entries are grouped by main ingredient in A–Z order. The fourth chapter, Basic recipes & classic additions, has recipes for the sauces, dressings, accompaniments and so on referred to in the first three chapters.

When an entry refers to another recipe, it may be found by first referring to the relevant section and then to the food or dish type. A comprehensive index of entries lists the entire contents.

Weights & measures

Metric, imperial and American measures are used in this book. As a general rule, it is advisable to follow only one set of measures and not to mix metric, imperial and/or cup quantities in any one recipe.

Spoon measures

Spoon measures refer to standard measuring utensils. Serving spoons and table cutlery are not suitable for measuring as they are not standard in capacity.

¼ teaspoon = 1.5 ml
½ teaspoon = 2.5 ml
1 teaspoon = 5 ml
1 tablespoon = 15 ml

Oven temperatures

Below are the standard settings for domestic ovens. However, ovens vary widely and manufacturer's instructions should be consulted. Individual ovens also perform differently and experience of using a particular appliance is invaluable for adjusting temperatures and cooking times to give best results. Those working with commercial cooking appliances will be accustomed to using the higher temperatures attained. Many chefs' recipes refer to glazing or cooking in a hot oven for a short period: as a rule, the hottest setting for a domestic appliance should be used as the equivalent.

Temperatures and timings in the recipes refer to preheated ovens.

If using a fan-assisted oven, follow the manufacturer's instructions for adjusting timing and temperature.

Centigrade	Fahrenheit	Gas mark
110°C	225°F	gas ¼
120°C	250°F	gas ½
140°C	275°F	gas 1
150°C	300°F	gas 2
160°C	325°F	gas 3
180°C	350°F	gas 4
190°C	375°F	gas 5
200°C	400°F	gas 6
220°C	425°F	gas 7
230°C	450°F	gas 8
240°C	475°F	gas 9

Introduction

Larousse Gastronomique is the world's most famous culinary reference book. It was the vision of Prosper Montagné, a French chef who was responsible for the first edition published in Paris in 1938. His aims were to provide an overview of 20th-century gastronomy and its history, as well as a source of reference on the more practical aspects of cookery. Twenty-three years later the first English edition was published and it immediately became the culinary bible of chefs, cooks and food aficionados.

A new English edition of this monumental work was published in 2001. Completely revised and updated, it reflected the social and cultural changes, together with advances in science and technology, that have dramatically influenced our ideas about food, the way we cook and how we eat.

Distilled from the latest edition, in one convenient volume, is this collection of over 500 fish and seafood recipes, together with over 150 recipes for sauces, dressings, pastry, butters, stocks and accompaniments. Whether your interest is in the great traditions of French cuisine or in the wide spectrum of food as the international subject it has become, the recipes reflect the diversity of the world of cooking in the 21st century.

FISH

Anchovies

Anchovy barquettes

A small boat-shaped tart made of shortcrust pastry (basic pie dough) or puff pastry, baked blind and then filled with a variety of sweet or savoury ingredients. In some recipes the pastry boats are filled before they are baked instead of afterwards.

Remove salt from the anchovy fillets by soaking them in a little milk. Dice some mushrooms and onions, fry in butter, and bind with a little béchamel sauce. Dice the anchovy fillets and add to the béchamel mixture. Fill cooked barquette cases with this mixture, sprinkle with fried breadcrumbs, and bake for a few minutes in a preheated oven at 240°C (475°F, gas 9).

Anchovy croustades

Flatten some well-wiped anchovy fillets previously desalted in milk. Spread them with anchovy butter containing chopped tarragon and roll them up into paupiettes. Put a layer of puréed tuna fish with mayonnaise in the base of some very small cooked and cooled puff pastry cases and then place an anchovy paupiette on top of each. Pipe a rosette of anchovy butter on each paupiette and sprinkle with chopped fresh parsley.

Anchovy Dartois

Prepare some puff pastry and a fish, smoked herring, sardine or prawn forcemeat. Roll and cut the pastry into two rectangular strips of equal size and thickness. Add some anchovy butter to the forcemeat and spread one of the strips with it, leaving a border of 1 cm (½ in) all round the edge. Drain the oil from some anchovy fillets and arrange on top. Cover with more fish forcemeat, then place the second pastry strip on top and seal the edges. Cook in a preheated oven at 220°C (425°F, gas 7) for 20–25 minutes.

Anchovy fillets à la portugaise

Cut desalted anchovy fillets into thin strips. Place a layer of tomato sauce cooked in oil in the base of an hors d'oeuvre dish and arrange the anchovy fillets on top in a crisscross pattern. Garnish with capers, chopped parsley and lemon slices with the skin and pith removed. Moisten with a little olive oil before serving.

Anchovy fillets à la silésienne

Poach some fresh soft herring roe in stock and then either rub through a fine sieve or purée in a blender. For 300 g (11 oz) roe, add 2–3 chopped shallots and a few sprigs of parsley (chopped). Place the mixture in an hors d'oeuvre dish and arrange a lattice of pickled anchovy fillets over the top. Make a salad with diced potatoes, dessert (eating) apples and beetroot (beet) moistened with a well-seasoned vinaigrette, and arrange it around the purée. Sprinkle with chopped parsley.

Anchovy fillets à la suédoise

Cut desalted anchovy fillets into thin strips. Arrange them on a layer of diced dessert (eating) apples and beetroot (beet) seasoned with vinaigrette.

Garnish with parsley sprigs and with the yolks and whites of hard-boiled (hard-cooked) eggs, chopped separately. Moisten with more vinaigrette.

Anchovy fillets à la tartare

Thoroughly desalt 12 anchovy fillets. Mix 1 tablespoon finely grated horseradish with the same amount of butter. Mask each fillet with a little of this flavoured butter and roll it into a paupiette. Cut some cooked beetroot (beet) into slices 5 mm (¼ in) thick and trim them with a fluted cutter. Place 1 anchovy paupiette on each slice. Garnish with a little sieved hard-boiled (hard-cooked) egg and chopped parsley, then a few capers. Sprinkle with vinaigrette and serve thoroughly chilled.

Anchovy fillets with hard-boiled eggs

Cut desalted anchovy fillets into thin strips and arrange them in an hors d'oeuvre dish. Garnish with small black Nice olives, hard-boiled (hard-cooked) egg whites and yolks (chopped separately), capers and chopped parsley. Moisten with a little olive oil.

Anchovy fritters

Soak anchovy fillets in milk to remove all the salt. Mix together with a fork (or in a blender) some hard-boiled (hard-cooked) egg yolk, a little butter and some chopped parsley. Spread the mixture on the anchovy fillets and roll up. Dip in batter, deep-fry in hot oil and serve with fried parsley.

Anchovy omelette

Soak 3 anchovy fillets until free of salt and rub them through a sieve. Add the anchovy purée to 8 eggs and beat together. Cook the omelette as usual. Garnish with a criss-cross pattern of fine strips of anchovies in oil.

Anchovy pannequets

Pannequets are sweet or savoury pancakes filled with chopped ingredients, a purée or a cream.

Make a batter with 250 g (9 oz, 2¼ cups) plain (all-purpose) flour, a pinch of salt, 3 beaten eggs, 250 ml (8 fl oz, 1 cup) milk, 250 ml (8 fl oz, 1 cup) water and 1 tablespoon melted butter. Use the butter to make 8 fairly thick pancakes. Prepare 300 ml (½ pint, 1¼ cups) fairly thick béchamel sauce without salt. Soak 8 anchovies in water to remove some of the brine, take out the fillets and reduce them to a purée.

Drain 8 anchovy fillets canned in oil and cut them into small pieces. Mix the béchamel sauce and the anchovy purée and adjust the seasoning. Spread each pannequet with the anchovy béchamel sauce and sprinkle with small pieces of the anchovy fillets. Fold into four and arrange in a buttered ovenproof dish. Sprinkle with fresh breadcrumbs fried in butter and place under the grill (broiler) for 3–4 minutes or in a preheated oven at 230°C (450°F, gas 8) for 10 minutes.

Anchovy-stuffed hard-boiled eggs

Reduce some desalted anchovy fillets to a purée in a mortar or blender. Halve some hard-boiled (hard-cooked) eggs and remove the yolks. Mix the yolks with the anchovy purée and a little mayonnaise; replace in the egg cases. Dip some anchovy fillets in oil and roll each around a stoned (pitted) black olive. Place one on each egg case.

Brioches with anchovies

Using standard brioche dough without sugar, prepare some very small (cocktail size) Parisian brioches. For each brioche take one small ball of dough, put it in a tiny, buttered fluted mould then mould another ball one-quarter of its size into a pear shape. Make a hole in the top of the larger ball and insert the pointed end of the small ball. Press down with the fingertips. Allow to double in volume at room temperature. Bake in a preheated oven at 225°C (425°F, gas 7) for a few minutes. When cooked, allow to cool completely, wrap in foil and place in the refrigerator for 1 hour. Then remove the heads of the brioches and carefully scoop out the insides of the brioche bases, using the bread taken out to make very fine breadcrumbs. Add these to the same volume of softened anchovy butter. Fill the brioches with this mixture and put the heads back on. Put in a cool place until required for serving. The mixture of breadcrumbs and anchovy butter can be lightened by adding a little whipped cream.

Canapés with anchovies

Spread some Montpellier butter on lightly toasted rectangular slices of bread cut to the same length as the anchovies. Garnish each canapé with 2 anchovy fillets separated by cooked egg white and egg yolk (chopped separately) and chopped parsley.

Corsican anchoïade with figs

Soak 5 anchovy fillets in cold water to remove the salt, then wipe them dry. Pound them with 450 g (1 lb) fresh figs and 1 small garlic clove. Spread this paste on slices of bread moistened with olive oil. Sprinkle with chopped onions and serve.

Fried anchovies

Take fresh anchovies, remove the heads and gut (clean) by pressing with the thumb. Wipe, but do not wash the fish as their flesh is very fragile. Dip them in milk, then drain, and roll each one in flour. Plunge them, a few at a time, into very hot fat, then drain, dust with fine salt and arrange them in a pyramid on a napkin. Garnish with fried parsley and quarters of lemon.

Fried eggs with anchovies

Fry some slices of very stale round sandwich bread in butter. Cover each of these croûtons with a fried egg and 2 desalted anchovy fillets arranged in the form of a cross. The fillets may be moistened with noisette butter.

Marinated anchovies

Prepare 500 g (18 oz) fresh anchovies as in the recipe for fried anchovies. Lay them on a plate, dust with salt and leave for 2 hours. Pat the anchovies dry, then fry in very hot oil just long enough to stiffen them. Drain and place them in a dish. Prepare a marinade as follows. Add 5–6 tablespoons fresh oil to the oil in which the anchovies were cooked. Fry a medium onion and a carrot (both finely sliced) with 3 unpeeled garlic cloves and add 100 ml (4 fl oz, ½ cup) vinegar and an equal quantity of water. Season with salt and add a sprig of thyme, half a bay leaf, a few parsley stalks and a few crushed peppercorns. Boil for 10 minutes and pour the hot marinade over the anchovies. Leave to marinate for 24 hours. Serve on an hors d'oeuvre dish, garnished with slices of lemon.

Tapenade

Tapenade is a condiment from Provence, made with capers (from Toulon), desalted anchovies and stoned black (pitted ripe) olives, pounded and seasoned with olive oil, lemon juice, aromatics and possibly marc brandy.

Desalt 100 g (4 oz) canned anchovy fillets, peel 4 garlic cloves and stone (pit) 350 g (12 oz, 3 cups) black (ripe) olives. Blend, using a food processor, 100 g (4 oz) tuna canned in oil, drained, the anchovy fillets, 100 g (4 oz,

1 cup) capers, the juice of 1 lemon, the olives and the garlic. Press the ingredients through a very fine sieve, then pound the purée in a mortar (or use a food processor), gradually adding 250 ml (8 fl oz, 1 cup) olive oil and the juice of 1 large lemon. The finished tapenade should be thick and smooth.

Bass

To prepare

Clean the fish through the gills and through a small incision at the base of the stomach in order to grasp the end of the gut. If the bass is to be braised, fried or grilled (broiled), remove the scales, working from the tail to the head. Do not remove the scales if it is to be poached because the scales help to hold the fragile flesh intact. Wash and dry the fish. When grilling, make a few shallow incisions with a sharp knife in the fleshy part of the back.

Bass à la Dugléré

This dish is named after the famous French chef Adolphe Dugléré, a pupil of Carême and head chef of the kitchens of the Rothschild family.

Butter a shallow flameproof dish thoroughly. Peel and chop 1 large onion, 1–2 shallots, a small bunch of parsley, a garlic clove and, if liked (it is not traditional), 150 g (5 oz, 1⅔ cups) button mushrooms. Skin, seed and chop 4 tomatoes. Spread all these ingredients on the bottom of the dish, then add a sprig of thyme and half a bay leaf. Scale a 1 kg (2¼ lb) bass and cut into sections. Arrange these sections in the dish, dot with knobs of butter, moisten with 200 ml (7 fl oz, ¾ cup) dry white wine and cover with foil. Bring to the boil, then transfer to a preheated oven at 220°C (425°F, gas 7) and cook for 12–15 minutes. Drain the pieces of bass and arrange on a serving dish in the original shape of the fish.

Remove the thyme and bay leaf from the oven dish and add 2 tablespoons velouté made with fish stock. Reduce by one-third, then add 50 g (2 oz, ¼ cup) butter. (The velouté and butter may be replaced by 1 tablespoon beurre manié.) Pour the sauce over the fish and sprinkle with chopped parsley. Sea bream and brill may be prepared and served in the same way.

Bass à la livournaise

Scale and clean 4 bass each weighing 250–300 g (9–11 oz). Season with salt and pepper. Butter or oil an ovenproof dish. Spread 200 ml (7 fl oz, ¾ cup) well-seasoned tomato sauce over the bottom and arrange the bass on top. Sprinkle with breadcrumbs and melted butter or olive oil and bake in a preheated oven at about 230°C (450°F, gas 8) for about 15 minutes. Sprinkle with chopped parsley before serving.

Bass à la portugaise

Scale and clean 2 bass each weighing about 400 g (14 oz). Make incisions in the back and season with salt and pepper. Butter an ovenproof dish, arrange the bass in the dish, and moisten with a mixture of equal proportions of dry white wine and fish stock. Bake in a preheated oven at 230°C (450°F, gas 8) for about 15 minutes, basting the fish two or three times during cooking. Drain the fish. Pour the liquor into a small pan, reduce and add butter. Cover the bottom of the cooking dish with tomato sauce, arrange the bass on top and cover with the remaining sauce. Glaze in a preheated oven at 240°C (475°F, gas 9) and serve sprinkled with chopped parsley.

Bass braised in red Graves wine

Fillet a 1.5 kg (3¼ lb) sea bass. Season with salt and pepper and fry both sides quickly in butter in a frying pan. Drain. In the same butter, fry 100 g (4 oz) thinly sliced mushrooms and 100 g (4 oz) small white onions. Put the fillets back on top of the mushrooms and onions. Add ½ bottle red Graves and a little fish stock. Cover with buttered greaseproof (waxed) paper and simmer for 5 minutes over a low heat. Drain the fillets on paper towels, remove the skin and place them in an ovenproof dish. Drain the garnish and arrange it around the fish. Reduce the cooking juices and thicken with butter; just before serving, stir in a little hollandaise sauce, strain and pour over the fillets. Brown under the grill (broiler) and garnish with croûtons fried in butter.

Bass or brill à la provençale

Prepare a Provençal sauce. Scale some bass or brill, weighing about 400 g (14 oz). Cut off the fins and make an incision in the top of the back, on either side of the backbone. Wash and wipe the fish. Sprinkle them with salt and pepper, dust them with flour and brown them quickly in olive oil in a frying pan. Mask an ovenproof dish with a little Provençal sauce. Arrange the fish in it and just cover with Provençal sauce. Sprinkle with fresh breadcrumbs, moisten with a little olive oil and cook in a preheated oven at 200°C (400°F, gas 6) for about 20 minutes. Sprinkle with chopped parsley and serve piping hot in the cooking dish.

Braised bass

Select a bass weighing 1.25 kg (2¾ lb). Peel and finely chop 2–3 carrots, 2 onions and 1 shallot. Melt 25 g (1 oz, 1 tablespoon) butter in a frying pan, add the chopped vegetables and cook until they begin to change colour. Chop a small bunch of parsley and mix with 1 tablespoon butter, salt and pepper.

Stuff the fish with the parsley butter. Spread the partly cooked vegetables in a large buttered ovenproof dish and gently place the fish on top of the vegetables. Add a bouquet garni and 300 ml (½ pint, 1¼ cups) dry white wine. Melt 25 g (1 oz, 1 tablespoon) butter and pour over the bass, then cover the dish. Bake in a preheated oven at about 220°C (425°F, gas 7) for about 25 minutes. Drain the fish, arrange on a serving dish and keep warm. Discard the bouquet garni, sieve the pan juices and reduce. If desired, beat in butter to thicken the sauce. Skin the bass and cover in sauce. The braised bass may be served on a bed of mushroom duxelles or sorrel fondue, or surrounded by slices of aubergine (eggplant) lightly fried in oil.

Cold poached bass

Clean and wash the bass without removing the scales and place in a fish kettle. Cover with cold salted water and heat gently until simmering. As soon as the liquid is about to boil, reduce the heat and poach the fish in barely simmering water. Allow the fish to cool in the poaching liquor. Drain, arrange on a napkin and remove the skin. Garnish with lemon halves, artichoke hearts and small tomatoes stuffed with chopped vegetables. Serve with mayonnaise, vinaigrette or any other sauce suitable for cold fish.

Cream of ginger bass

Prepare the cream of ginger: soften 4 chopped shallots in butter, add 100 ml (4 fl oz, 7 tablespoons) dry white wine and 200 ml (7 fl oz, ¾ cup) fish fumet, and reduce. Add 325 ml (11 fl oz, 1⅓ cups) double (heavy) cream and a pinch of salt. Reduce by half, until you have the required consistency. Add 1 tablespoon grated fresh root ginger and allow to simmer for 2 minutes. Strain through muslin (cheesecloth) or a fine strainer. Thicken the sauce with 75 g (3 oz, 6 tablespoons) butter (cut into small knobs), beating with a whisk.

Prepare 400 g (14 oz) well-washed spinach without stalks and braise in butter. Take 4 escalopes (scallops) of sea bass, each weighing 175 g (6 oz), and season with ground white pepper and salt. Fry quickly in oil. Drain them on paper towels so as to remove all traces of cooking oil. Make a bed of spinach in the middle of each plate and arrange the sea bass on top. Pour the cream of ginger over them and garnish with sprigs of chervil.

Crowns of bass with red peppers

Fillet and clean a 1 kg (2¼ lb) sea bass. Cut the flesh into strips and plait (braid) 3 strips together. Repeat with the remaining strips. Season with salt. Shape the plaits into crowns and keep chilled.

Grill (broil) 2 red peppers until their skins are blistered and blackened. Cool slightly, then peel, halve and seed them. Cut out 4 strips and 5 small petal shapes. Purée the rest and reduce the purée over a gentle heat. Cook some broccoli in boiling salted water, drain, reserve a little for the crown centres and purée the remainder.

Brown 2 chopped shallots in butter, then add some white wine and reduce by half. Add 500 ml (17 fl oz, 2 cups) single (light) cream and heat through. Divide this mixture in two: stir the pepper purée into one half, and the broccoli purée into the other. Check the seasoning and keep warm.

Fry the crowns of sea bass in butter. Spoon the sauces on to the plates. Arrange the sea bass crowns on top and garnish with the pepper strips and petals. Spoon the reserved broccoli into the centres. Serve the remainder of the sauces separately.

Fillets of bass with lettuce

(from a recipe by Roger Vergé) Clean and scale a 1.4 kg (3 lb) bass. Remove and skin the fillets. Divide each fillet into two pieces, season with salt and pepper, and dust with flour. Melt a knob of butter and a dash of olive oil in a frying pan. Fry the fillets for 1 minute on each side, then put to one side. Plunge the outer leaves of 2 or 3 lettuces into 2 litres (3½ pints, 9 cups) boiling salted water and transfer immediately to a colander. Rinse in cold water and drain. Split the leaves in two vertically and flatten slightly. Then dry them on a towel and wrap the fillets up in them.

Butter a gratin dish, sprinkle with finely chopped shallots and arrange flattened lettuce hearts on top, followed by the fillets wrapped in lettuce leaves. Pour over 3 tablespoons dry white wine and the same amount of vermouth. Bake in a preheated oven at about 180°C (350°F, gas 4) for 12 minutes. Drain the fillets and the lettuce hearts and arrange on a warm serving dish.

Strain the cooking liquor into a pan and reduce to about 175 ml (6 fl oz, ¾ cup) over a fierce heat. In a bowl mix together 3 tablespoons cream and 1 egg yolk and add to the pan. Whisk the mixture. Remove from the heat and beat in 50 g (2 oz, ¼ cup) cubed butter. Season with salt and pepper. Use to coat the fillets and serve. A little diced, peeled and seeded ripe tomato may be added as a garnish, if required.

Fried bass

Clean and scale bass weighing not more than 400 g (14 oz) each. Make incisions along the back, dip in milk and coat in flour. Deep-fry in fat or oil. Drain, pat dry and dust with fine salt. Arrange on a serving dish and garnish with lemon halves. Steaks of a larger bass can be prepared in the same way.

Grilled bass

Scale and clean a bass weighing not more than 1 kg (2¼ lb). Make a few small incisions in the back and brush with seasoned olive oil. Cook gently, preferably using a folding double grill (broiler) grid to enclose the bass so it can be turned during cooking without breaking. In the south of France, small bass are cooked on charcoal, on top of sprigs of dry fennel, which flavour the fish. Serve with anchovy or garlic butter or one of the special sauces for grilled fish, such as béarnaise or rémoulade.

Hot poached bass

Clean and wash the bass without removing the scales and place in a fish kettle. Cover with cold salted water and heat gently until simmering. As soon as the liquid is about to boil, reduce the heat and poach the fish in barely simmering water. Drain the bass, arrange on a dish covered with a napkin (or on a rack) and garnish with fresh parsley. In a separate dish serve melted butter, hollandaise sauce, or any other sauce suitable for poached fish. Serve with boiled or mashed potatoes, spinach, fennel or broccoli.

Bream

Grape harvest bream

Clean a 1 kg (2¼ lb) bream and season the inside with salt and pepper. Butter an ovenproof dish and sprinkle the bottom with chopped shallots; add 2 thyme sprigs and a bay leaf cut into four and lay the bream on top. Moisten with white wine (about 250 ml, 8 fl oz, 1 cup). Cook in a preheated oven at 230°C (450°F, gas 8) for about 20 minutes, basting the fish 3 or 4 times. Meanwhile, peel some large grapes, removing the seeds, and chop some parsley. When the bream is cooked, drain and keep warm. Strain the cooking liquor into a saucepan, add 7 tablespoons double (heavy) cream and reduce by a quarter. Adjust the seasoning. Whisk in 1 teaspoon beurre manié and 1 teaspoon lemon juice (optional). Heat the grapes in the sauce, then pour the sauce over the bream. Sprinkle with chopped parsley.

Brill

To prepare

Clean the fish by making a transverse incision underneath the head, on the dark side. Remove the scales with a sharp knife. Trim all round the fish, slightly shortening the tail, and wash thoroughly. If the brill is to be cooked whole, either braised or poached, make a longitudinal incision along the centre of the dark side. Slightly loosen the fillets and break the backbone in two or three places. If it is prepared in this way, the brill does not lose its shape during cooking.

To fillet the fish, lay the cleaned, scaled and washed brill on the table, dark side down. Make an incision along the centre from top to tail, then slide the knife blade underneath the flesh and, keeping it flat against the bone, gently ease away the fillets and lift them, detaching them at the head (by cutting round the head) and the tail. Turn the fish over and repeat for the other side. Lay the fillets on the table, skin side down. Holding the fillet by the tail end, slide the blade of a filleting knife between the skin and the flesh with one quick movement.

Braised brill

Season the brill and put it in a shallow pan on a bed of sliced carrots and onions lightly fried in butter. Add concentrated fish stock, thyme, parsley and a bay leaf. Bring to a simmer, cover and cook in a preheated oven at 160°C (325°F, gas 3) for 25 minutes for a 1.5 kg (3¼ lb) fish, basting frequently.

Drain the brill and remove the backbone by placing the fish, dark side up, on a well-buttered long plate or dish. Remove the fillets with a very sharp knife, take out the bone and replace the fillets. Reheat briefly.

Choose your garnish and matching sauce from the list below before cooking the fish. Make the sauce using the well-reduced and strained cooking liquor. Braised brill moistened with red wine fish stock reduced to the consistency of a fumet can be served with the following sauces and/or garnishes: bourguignonne, Chambertin or mâconnaise. Brill braised in white wine can be served with one of the garnishes used for fish cooked in white wine, such as button mushrooms and baby (pearl) onions cooked in butter, or croûtons.

Brill à la Bercy

Prepare a brill weighing about 800 g (1¾ lb), making an incision along the middle of the dark side of the fish and gently loosening the fillets. Season with salt and pepper inside and out. Butter a flameproof dish, sprinkle with chopped shallots and parsley and lay the brill on top. Add 7 tablespoons dry white wine and the same quantity of fish stock. Dot with 50 g (2 oz, ¼ cup) butter. Start cooking on top of the stove, then transfer to a preheated oven at 180°C (350°F, gas 4) and cook for 15 minutes, basting frequently. Then place the dish under the grill (broiler) to glaze the fish. Finally sprinkle with a dash of lemon juice and chopped parsley. The fish stock may be replaced by dry white wine diluted with the juice of ½ a lemon and water.

Brill à la Brancas

Clean a brill weighing about 800 g (1¾ lb) and cut it into even-sized pieces. Finely shred 2 large onions, the white part of 2 leeks and half a head of celery. Braise the vegetables for 10 minutes with 25 g (1 oz, 2 tablespoons) butter and a pinch of salt. Then add 125 g (4½ oz, 1½ cups) mushrooms, also finely shredded, and braise for a further 6–7 minutes.

Butter an ovenproof dish and season lightly with salt and pepper. Spread half the shredded vegetables in the dish. Arrange the pieces of brill in the dish so that they form the shape of the original fish, season with salt and pepper, and cover with the remaining vegetables. Add a little lemon juice, 200 ml (7 fl oz, ¾ cup) white wine and a bouquet garni. Dot with butter. Bring to the boil on top of the stove, then cook in a preheated oven at 200°C (400°F, gas 6) for about 15 minutes, basting once or twice, until the fish is tender.

Serve the cooked fish surrounded with tomato fondue, made by gently simmering 4 peeled and chopped tomatoes in butter for 30 minutes with 1 tablespoon chopped onion. Season the tomato fondue with salt, pepper and a little chopped parsley before spooning it around the fish.

This method of cooking, derived from brill *à la Dugléré*, can be used for other flatfish and also for whiting and slices of hake.

Brill à la dieppoise

Prepare 500 ml (17 fl oz, 2 cups) fish fumet. Clean 1 kg (2¼ lb) mussels and cook them *à la marinière*, reserving the cooking stock. Make a white roux with 25 g (1 oz, 2 tablespoons) butter and 25 g (1 oz, ¼ cup) plain (all-purpose) flour and gradually add the fish fumet together with 100 ml (4 fl oz, 7 tablespoons) strained cooking stock from the mussels. Add 1 tablespoon coarsely chopped mushrooms and a bouquet garni. Check the seasoning and boil gently for 20–25 minutes to reduce. Shell the mussels and keep them hot in the remainder of their cooking stock, taking care not to boil them.

Season a brill weighing about 800 g (1¾ lb) with salt and place in a buttered flameproof dish. Pour over 150 ml (¼ pint, ⅔ cup) white wine. Bring to the boil, uncovered, then cook in a preheated oven at 220°C (425°F, gas 7) for 15–18 minutes, basting the fish frequently. Mix 2 egg yolks with a little of the partially cooled mushroom sauce. Add 50 g (2 oz, ⅓ cup) peeled prawns (shelled shrimp) and the cooking liquor from the fish to the remaining mushroom sauce. Mix well, heat, add the hot drained mussels then the egg-yolk mixture and coat the brill with this sauce. This recipe may also be used for fresh cod.

Brill à la fermière

Thinly slice 2 carrots, 2 onions, the white part of 2 leeks and 3 or 4 celery sticks. Cook them slowly in 25 g (1 oz, 2 tablespoons) butter. Place half the vegetables in a greased ovenproof dish. Clean and season a medium-sized brill and place it on top of the vegetables. Cover with the remaining vegetables and add a few tablespoons of dry white wine or, better still, a concentrated fish stock made with white wine. Top with small knobs of butter and cook in a preheated oven at 220°C (425°F, gas 7), basting frequently. When the brill is cooked, place it on a serving dish and keep warm. Add 2–3 tablespoons cream to the cooking liquid from the fish and reduce by half. Pour the sauce over the brill and allow it to caramelize for a few moments in the oven.

Brill à la florentine

Cook some spinach slowly in a little butter. Drain well. Poach some fillets of brill in a little white wine stock. Prepare a Mornay sauce.

Spread out the spinach in a buttered dish and arrange the drained brill fillets on top. Cover with Mornay sauce, sprinkle with grated cheese and a little melted butter, and brown in a preheated oven at 240°C (475°F, gas 9). If a whole brill is used rather than fillets, it should be boned and trimmed before arranging it on the spinach.

Brill bonne femme

Prepare and clean a brill. Butter a dish and sprinkle with chopped shallot and parsley. Add 250 g (9 oz, 3 cups) chopped button mushrooms. Place the brill in the dish and add 7 tablespoons dry white wine and the same quantity of fish stock. Dot with very small knobs of butter. Cook in a preheated oven at 220°C (425°F, gas 7) for 15–20 minutes, basting the brill two or three times. Towards the end of cooking, cover with foil to prevent the fish from drying out. The same method may be used for sole and whiting.

Brill cardinal

Prepare the fish, season with salt and pepper, then stuff with a pike forcemeat, such as godiveau lyonnais or cream forcemeat – a mousseline forcemeat made with pike – which has previously been enriched with lobster butter. Poach the brill in white wine, drain it and then arrange it on the serving dish. Garnish with thin medallions of lobster, cover with cardinal sauce and sprinkle with lobster coral.

Brill chérubin

Prepare and cook as for braised brill. Arrange the fish on a long dish and surround with small mounds of very thick tomato sauce, alternated (if desired) with diced truffles. Fry thin strips of red (bell) pepper in butter. Strain the cooking stock, reduce until syrupy, then add it to a hollandaise sauce with the strips of pepper. Coat the brill with the sauce and glaze rapidly in a preheated oven at 230°C (450°F, gas 8).

Brill stuffed with salmon

Clean a 2 kg (4½ lb) brill and slit it lengthways down the middle on the dark side. Remove the central bone, taking care not to tear the white skin. Season the brill and stuff it with a cream forcemeat made of salmon and truffles. Lay the fish in a buttered flameproof dish, season, moisten with 400 ml (14 fl oz, 1¾ cups) white wine fish fumet, cover and bring gently to simmering point. Poach gently in a preheated oven at 180°C (350°F, gas 4) for 30 minutes. When cooked, drain, blot with paper towels and transfer carefully to a serving dish. Keep warm. Boil down the juices, add to normande sauce and pour over the fish. The following garnishes or sauces are suitable: amiral, cancalaise, cardinal, diplomate, Nantua, Polignac or Victoria. Champagne can be used instead of ordinary white wine in the fumet for a champenoise finish.

Fillets of brill à la créole

Remove the fillets from a brill, clean them and season with salt, pepper and a pinch of cayenne. Coat them in flour and cook them in oil in a frying pan. When they are cooked, sprinkle them with lemon juice and arrange them on a warmed serving dish. In the same pan fry a mixture of chopped garlic and parsley (1 tablespoon for 6 fillets) and pour this over the fillets, together with some oil flavoured with chilli peppers. Brown some halves of tomato in oil and stuff them with rice pilaf. Garnish the fillets with the stuffed tomatoes and with diced sweet peppers that have been slowly cooked in oil.

Fillets of brill Véron

Cut the fillets in half lengthways, season with salt and pepper, dip in melted butter and breadcrumbs, sprinkle with more melted butter and cook gently under the grill (broiler). Arrange the fillets on a hot serving dish and coat with Véron sauce.

Fillets of brill with mushroom duxelles

Prepare about 400 g (14 oz, 3½ cups) mushroom duxelles, bind with tomato sauce and spread in the bottom of a serving dish. Keep warm. Season the fillets, coat with flour and fry in a mixture of butter and oil. Arrange the cooked fish on the mushroom duxelles and coat with the hot butter left in the pan after frying the fish. Garnish with chopped parsley and slices of lemon.

Poached brill

Place the cleaned brill in a fish kettle or large saucepan. Cover with cold fish stock and poach gently for about 10 minutes after reaching simmering point, until just tender. Drain and remove the dark skin. Prepared in this way, it can be served with various sauces – prawn (shrimp), Mornay or Nantua – or garnished with spinach, *à la portugaise, à la provençale, à la russe* or with lobster *à l'américaine*. It can also be served au gratin in the same way as sole.

Capitaine

Capitaine in banana leaves

The capitaine is related to the sea bass, sometimes called *grand pourceau* ('big swine'). It is found living off the coast of West Africa, where it enters the estuaries and swims up the rivers. About 50 cm (20 in) long, it has a pinky-white flesh with a very delicate flavour that it does not lose in cooking.

Wash 4 medium-sized banana leaves, remove the central rib, then scald briefly to soften them. Lay them out flat and place 1 capitaine fillet on each one. Plunge 2 tomatoes in boiling water for a few seconds, then remove the skin and seeds, and roughly chop the flesh. Halve and thinly slice 1 onion, then cook it briefly in a little olive oil until slightly softened but not cooked. Allow long enough to take the raw edge off the flavour of the onion. Season the pieces of fish with salt and pepper. Arrange the tomatoes and onion on top. Fold the banana leaves over and secure with cocktail sticks (toothpicks). Steam for 30 minutes. Sautéed or steamed okra go well with the steamed fish.

Carp

Carp à l'alsacienne

Choose a carp weighing at least 1.5 kg (3¼ lb) and clean and gut it. Fill it with a fish cream forcemeat, place in a buttered ovenproof dish and add a mixture of one-third court-bouillon to two-thirds white wine so that it half-fills the dish. Cook for 30–40 minutes in a preheated oven at 220°C (425°F, gas 7) protecting with buttered greaseproof (wax) paper if necessary. Drain, retaining the liquid. Arrange the fish on a bed of sauerkraut, surround it with small boiled potatoes and keep hot. Reduce the cooking liquid, bind with a little beurre manié and coat the fish with this sauce.

Carp à la chinoise

Clean and gut a carp weighing about 1.5 kg (3¼ lb) and cut it into sections. Finely chop 2 large onions and fry in oil until slightly brown. Add 2 tablespoons vinegar, 1 tablespoon sugar, 1 tablespoon freshly grated root ginger (or 1 teaspoon ground ginger), 1–2 tablespoons rice spirit (or marc brandy), salt, pepper and a glass of water. Stir, cover and leave to cook for about 10 minutes. Fry the carp pieces in oil for 10 minutes, then add the sauce and leave to cook for another 4–5 minutes. Some strips of cucumber may be added to the carp along with the sauce, if desired.

Carp à la juive (1)

(Jewish recipe) Scale and gut (clean) a carp weighing about 1 kg (2¼ lb), taking care to reserve the roe. Cut the fish into slices and rub it with coarse salt. Leave for 20–30 minutes, then drain the pieces, dry them with a cloth and add the roe. Mix 2–3 chopped garlic cloves with some parsley in a small bowl. Heat 3–4 tablespoons oil in a saucepan and sear the fish and the roe. Add enough water to almost cover the fish, then add salt and pepper, the parsley and garlic, and simmer for about 20 minutes. Take out the pieces of fish and the roe and arrange them in a deep dish.

Make a smooth paste with 3 tablespoons cornflour (cornstarch) and a little water, then mix in two-thirds of the liquid from the saucepan. Simmer the sauce until it has reduced it by one-third. Pour it over the fish and leave in the refrigerator to set.

Carp à la juive (2)

(French recipe) Cut a medium-sized carp into regular slices and cook them in 200 ml (7 fl oz, ¾ cup) oil with 100 g (4 oz, ⅔ cup) sliced onion and 50 g (2 oz, ⅓ cup) sliced shallots without browning. Sprinkle with 40 g (1½ oz, ⅓ cup) flour. Pour in enough white wine and fish fumet (or water) to almost cover the fish; add salt, a pinch of cayenne, 2 crushed garlic cloves and a bouquet garni. Moisten with a few tablespoons of oil, bring to the boil, and cook gently for 20 minutes. Drain the carp and arrange on a dish in the shape of the original fish. Boil down the liquor by two-thirds, take off the heat and thicken by beating in 7 tablespoons oil. Pour over the carp and leave to cool.

Carp Chambord

This is a classic method of preparing large fish, such as carp, salmon or sole, which are to be cooked whole. Requiring high-quality produce and meticulous preparation, the fish is stuffed and then braised in red wine. It is served garnished with a mixture of quenelles of fish forcemeat, fillets of sole, sautéed soft roes, mushroom caps, truffles shaped like olives and crayfish cooked in a court-bouillon.

Select a carp weighing 2–3 kg (4½–6½ lb), trim it, stuff it with a cream fish forcemeat and sew it up. Remove a thin strip of skin from the back on either side of the backbone and lard the bare area with small pieces of fat bacon. Butter a baking dish and line it generously with a brunoise of carrot, turnip, leek, celery and onion mixed with mushroom peelings and softened in butter. Add a bouquet garni. Two-thirds cover the carp with a mixture of fish stock and red wine, and cook in a preheated oven at 220°C (425°F, gas 7), basting from time to time. While the carp is cooking, slice some mushroom caps and cook them in a white court-bouillon. Remove the cooked carp, drain and arrange on the serving dish, keeping it hot. Prepare a little brown roux, add it to the pan juices from the carp along with 2 tablespoons tomato purée (paste) and cook for at least 30 minutes. Pass through a conical strainer. Return the carp to the oven until it is glazed, then coat it with the sauce and surround it with a Chambord garnish, including the mushroom caps.

Carp cooked in beer

Prepare a carp weighing about 2 kg (4½ lb) and carefully remove the roe. Season with salt and pepper inside and out. Chop 150 g (5 oz) onions and fry them gently in butter in a covered pan until transparent. Dice 25 g (1 oz) gingerbread and finely chop 50 g (2 oz) celery. Butter an ovenproof dish. Place the onions, gingerbread and celery in the bottom and arrange the carp on top, adding a bouquet garni and sufficient Munich-type German beer to almost cover the fish. Cook in a preheated oven at about 170°C (325°F, gas 3) for 30 minutes. In the meantime, poach the roe in a little stock, then drain and slice thinly. Remove the carp from the oven, arrange on a serving dish with the slices of roe and keep warm. Reduce the cooking stock by one-third, strain and add butter. Serve in a sauceboat with the carp.

Fried carp

Select a small carp, weighing about 400 g (14 oz). Clean, gut, wash and wipe the fish. Immerse it in milk, then in flour, and then deep-fry in hot oil. When cooked, remove, drain and add salt. Garnish with fried parsley and lemon.

Stuffed carp à l'ancienne

(from a recipe by Carême) Take a large carp that is carrying eggs (milt), remove the scales and bones, and lift off the flesh, taking care to leave the backbone intact, complete with head and tail. To the carp flesh, add the meat from a small eel, as well as some desalted anchovies, and make a fairly firm quenelle forcemeat in the usual way, but without adding any sauce to it. Scald the roes, cut into several pieces, sauté in butter with a little lemon juice, add some truffles and mushrooms and bind with a few spoonfuls of thick allemande sauce.

Take a tin tray that is as long as the carp and butter it thickly. Spread a layer of the stuffing on it, about 2.5 cm (1 in) thick, making it into the shape of the carp. On this, place the carp backbone with head and tail still attached. Cover the backbone with a little of the stuffing and cover this with the roe ragoût;

then add another layer of the stuffing, 2.5 cm (1 in) thick, still keeping it in the original shape of the carp. Smooth with a knife dipped in hot water.

Butter a baking sheet large enough to hold the carp and sprinkle breadcrumbs on the butter. Carefully heat the tin tray so that the butter melts and slide the carp on to the baking sheet without damaging the shape. Brush with beaten egg, coat the top with breadcrumbs, press the breadcrumbs down firmly and cover with clarified butter. Then, with the tip of a small spoon, press in a pattern of scales, starting at the head.

Cook the carp in a preheated oven at 200°C (400°F, gas 6) for 45 minutes, basting frequently with clarified butter during cooking so that it turns a golden colour. When it is cooked, transfer it carefully from the baking sheet to the serving dish with a long fish slice. Work some fish essence into a financière sauce and serve in a sauceboat to accompany it.

Cod

Braised cod à la flamande

Season slices of cod with salt and pepper. Butter an ovenproof dish and sprinkle with chopped shallots and parsley. Arrange the cod in the dish and just cover with dry white wine. Place a slice of peeled lemon on each piece of cod. Bring to the boil, then cook in a preheated oven at 220°C (425°F, gas 7) for about 15 minutes. Remove the fish and drain. Arrange on a serving dish and keep warm. Reduce the juices by boiling, then add pieces of butter, stir and pour the sauce over the cod. Sprinkle with roughly chopped parsley.

Cod à la boulangère

Season a piece of cod with salt and pepper and put it in an ovenproof dish. Thinly slice some potatoes and onions and arrange these around the fish, seasoning and adding a pinch of thyme and a pinch of crumbled bay leaf. Sprinkle with melted butter. Cook in a preheated oven at 190°C (375°F, gas 5) for 40 minutes. Cover the dish as soon as the fish turns golden, to prevent it from drying out. Sprinkle with chopped parsley and serve piping hot.

Cod braised in cream

Cut 800 g (1¾ lb) cod fillets into 5 cm (2 in) squares. Season with salt and pepper. Cook 150 g (5 oz, ⅔ cup) chopped onions in melted butter in a pan and then add the cod. Fry the pieces on all sides until firm. Add 200 ml (7 fl oz, ¾ cup) dry white wine and reduce by three-quarters, then add 200 ml (7 fl oz, ¾ cup) double (heavy) cream, cover and simmer slowly until the fish is nearly cooked through. Remove the lid and reduce the cream over a high heat.

Cod in aspic

Prepare a fish aspic. Make a ratatouille with 3 tomatoes, 1 aubergine (eggplant), 2 courgettes (zucchini), 1 onion, 2 garlic cloves, 3 tablespoons olive oil, some thyme, bay leaves and basil. Dissolve 15 g (½ oz, 2 envelopes) gelatine in 4 tablespoons hot water over a pan of simmering water and add to the ratatouille. Lightly oil 4 ramekins and half fill them with the ratatouille. Set aside to cool and then place in the refrigerator. In the meantime, place the cod fillets in an ovenproof dish, add butter and white wine, and cook in a preheated oven at 220°C (425°F, gas 7). Arrange a piece of fillet in each ramekin, and cover with the fish aspic. Refrigerate until it is time to serve, remove from the moulds and serve chilled.

Cod with herbs

Coarsely chop ½ bunch flat-leaf parsley, ½ bunch of fresh coriander (cilantro) and ½ bunch of fresh mint. Finely chop 2 white onions. Mix together. Prepare the sauce with 80 ml (3 fl oz, ⅓ cup) lemon juice, 60 ml (2 fl oz, ¼ cup) groundnut (peanut) oil, 4 teaspoons soy sauce, salt and pepper. Peel the tomatoes, cut into quarters, remove the seeds and cut into diamond shapes. Arrange them round the 4 plates and in the centre of each plate put 25 g (1 oz) spinach shoots. Steam 4 fillets of cod, 200 g (7 oz) each. Pour the sauce over the herb mixture. Place the fish on the spinach and pour the herb sauce over it.

Cold poached cod

Place a piece of cod, either whole or cut up into chunks, in a pan of salted water – allow 1 tablespoon salt per 1 litre (1¾ pints, 4⅓ cups) of water. Bring to the boil, then lower the heat and poach gently until almost cooked, with the lid on, taking care not to boil. Leave to finish cooking as it cools in the salt water. Drain the cooled fish, wipe and arrange on a napkin. Garnish with either fresh parsley or lettuce hearts and quarters of hard-boiled (hard-cooked) eggs. Serve with a suitable cold sauce, such as gribiche, mayonnaise, ravigote, rémoulade, tartare, green sauce, vinaigrette or Vincent.

Fillets of cod with cucumber

Remove both ends of a good firm cucumber and cut it into 3 segments. Peel and cut each segment lengthways into slices, avoiding the seeds. Cut the slices into very thin strips resembling matchsticks and soak in cold water for 10 hours. Chop 2 shallots. Peel and dice a tomato. Prepare about 325 ml (11 fl oz, 1⅓ cups) concentrated stock using bones from white fish. Butter a long ovenproof dish and cover the base with the shallots.

Season 4 cod fillets, each weighing about 175 g (6 oz), with salt and pepper and arrange them in the dish. Add 200 ml (7 fl oz, ¾ cup) dry white wine followed by the warm stock. Cover with buttered greaseproof (wax) paper. Bring to the boil and poach very gently for 6 minutes. Remove the cod fillets and keep warm.

Reduce the cooking liquid by three-quarters in a small pan. Adjust the seasoning and add some lemon juice. Add 500 ml (17 fl oz, 2 cups) double (heavy) cream and reduce by boiling. Drain the cucumber matchsticks and cook them with the diced tomato in a pan of salted water for 1 minute. Drain and add them to the sauce. Coat the fillets with the sauce, with the tomato and cucumber on top, and simmer for 1 minute. Serve with a little roughly chopped parsley.

Grilled cod

Season some prepared cod steaks with salt and pepper. Coat lightly with flour or oil and sprinkle with melted butter. Alternatively, the cod steaks can be marinated in a mixture of olive oil, garlic, chopped parsley and lemon juice for 30 minutes. Cook under a moderate grill (broiler). Garnish the cod with slices of peeled lemon and fresh parsley. Serve with either maître d'hôtel butter or a suitable sauce.

Hot poached cod

Place a piece of cod, either whole or cut up into chunks, in a pan of salted water – allow 1 tablespoon salt per 1 litre (1¾ pints, 4⅓ cups) of water. Bring to the boil, then lower the heat and poach gently with the lid on, taking care not to boil, until the flesh flakes easily. Drain the fish, arrange on a napkin and garnish with fresh parsley. Serve with a sauce suitable for poached fish, such as anchovy, butter, caper, prawn, fines herbes, hollandaise, lobster or ravigote.

Roast cod

Trim a 1.5–1.8 kg (3¼–4 lb) cod. Season with salt and pepper, sprinkle with oil and lemon juice, and leave to steep for 30 minutes. Drain the cod, place it on a spit and brush with melted butter. Then roast before a brisk fire, basting frequently with melted butter or oil, for 30–40 minutes. Place a pan under the cod to catch the juices. Arrange on a serving dish and keep hot. Deglaze the cooking residue in the pan with dry white wine, reduce and spoon the juice over the fish. The fish may also be roasted in the oven, provided that it is placed on a wire rack so that it does not lie in the cooking juices.

Sautéed cod à la crème

Season some cod steaks with salt and pepper, and fry in hot butter until golden. Add enough double (heavy) cream to the pan to reach halfway up the steaks. Finish cooking with the pan covered until the fish flakes easily. Drain the fish, arrange on a serving dish and keep hot. Reduce the cream in the pan and add 2 teaspoons to every 4 slices of fish. Pour the sauce over the cod.

Eel

To prepare

To kill an eel, seize it with a cloth and bang its head violently against a hard surface. To skin it, put a noose around the base of the head and hang it up. Slit the skin in a circle just beneath the noose. Pull away a small portion of the skin, turn it back, take hold of it with a cloth, and pull it down hard. Clean the eel by making a small incision in its belly. Cut off and discard the head and the end of the tail. Wash and wipe dry. Alternatively, when the eel has been killed, it can be cut into sections and grilled (broiled) for a short time. The skin will puff up and can then be removed. This method has the advantage of removing excess fat from the eel, particularly if it is large.

Angevin bouilleture

Also known as *bouilliture*, this is an eel stew thickened with beurre manié and garnished with mushrooms, baby onions, and prunes; it is served with toast and sometimes quartered hard-boiled (hard-cooked) eggs. In Anjou, *bouilleture* is prepared with red wine; white wine is used in Poitou.

For 1 kg (2¼ lb) eel, use 750 ml (1¼ pints, 3¼ cups) red wine, 10 medium shallots, 40 g (1½ oz, 3 tablespoons) butter, 1 glass brandy, 250 g (9 oz) sautéed button or wild mushrooms, 150 g (5 oz) glazed small onions, 250 g (9 oz) prunes, 2 tablespoons flour, a bouquet garni and salt and pepper.

Skin the eel and cut into thick slices. Peel and chop the shallots and soften in butter in a flameproof casserole. Add the slices of eel, brown them and flame with brandy. Season with; add the red wine, bouquet garni and prunes. Cook for 20 minutes, then remove and drain. Prepare some beurre manié, add it to the casserole and boil for 2 minutes, stirring constantly. Pour the prune sauce over the eel. Garnish with the mushrooms and onions.

Ballotine of eel (cold)

A ballotine is a hot or cold dish of meat, poultry, game birds or fish in aspic. The flesh is boned, stuffed, rolled and tied up with string, usually wrapped in muslin (cheesecloth) – sometimes in the skin – then braised or poached.

For this cold ballotine, prepare and cook the ballotine as for the hot ballotine of eel (following recipe). Drain and unwrap, squeeze out the muslin (cheesecloth), and wrap the ballotine up again in the same cloth; tie up with string and cool for 12 hours under a weight. In the meantime, make a fish aspic using the stock in which the ballotine was cooked. Unwrap the eel and place in a dish, coat with aspic and chill until firmly set.

Ballotine of eel (hot)

Skin a large eel weighing at least 900 g (2 lb), cut off the head and tail, open out and remove the backbone. Flatten the eel and season with salt and pepper. Spread with forcemeat for fish and reshape the eel, ensuring that it is the same thickness all the way along. Wrap it in muslin (cheesecloth), tie up with string and place on a grid in a fish kettle. Prepare enough fish court-bouillon to cover the eel in its pan. Allow to cool, then pour over the eel. Cover and poach very gently for about 20 minutes. Drain the ballotine, unwrap it and put it in an ovenproof dish. Strain the stock and reduce by boiling until syrupy. Coat the fish with the stock and put in the oven for a few minutes. Serve very hot.

Ballotine of eel bourguignonne (hot)

Add chopped parsley to godiveau lyonnais or a forcemeat made from whiting. Use to stuff an eel which has been prepared according to the previous recipe for a hot ballotine of eel. Poach in a court-bouillon of red wine; drain and keep warm. Prepare a bourguignonne sauce with the cooking stock and pour over the eel. This dish can be garnished with small fried croûtons.

Canapés with smoked eel

Spread some round slices of bread with mustard butter or horseradish butter. Garnish each slice with 2 or 3 thin slices of smoked eel arranged in a rosette. Surround with a double border of hard-boiled (hard-cooked) egg yolk and chopped chives. Sprinkle with a little lemon juice.

Devilled eel

Cook an eel weighing about 800 g (1¾ lb) in a court-bouillon of white wine and cool it in the liquor. Drain and wipe the eel, smear it with mustard, brush with melted butter, and grill (broil) slowly. Arrange on a round dish and garnish with gherkins (sweet dill pickles) if desired. Serve with devilled sauce.

Eel à la bonne femme

Soften 4 large tablespoons chopped onion in butter and place in a sauté pan. Put slices of a medium-sized eel weighing about 800 g (1¾ lb) on top of the onion layer. Add salt and pepper, a bouquet garni and 300 ml (½ pint, 1¼ cups) white wine. Cover and poach slowly for 25 minutes. Drain the slices of eel and arrange them on croûtons of sandwich bread fried in butter. Garnish with large diced potatoes sautéed in butter. Coat the eel with the liquor from the pan, after reducing it by half and thickening it with 1 tablespoon beurre manié.

Eel à la provençale

Cook 2 tablespoons chopped onion gently in a large pan with a little oil. Cut a medium-sized eel into even-sized slices, add to the pan, and cook until the slices have stiffened. Season with salt and pepper, and add 4 peeled, seeded chopped tomatoes, a bouquet garni and a crushed garlic clove. Moisten with 100 ml (4 fl oz, 7 tablespoons) dry white wine, cover the pan, and cook slowly for 25–30 minutes. About 10 minutes before serving, add 12 black olives. Arrange on a dish and sprinkle with parsley.

Eel au vert

Skin and prepare 1.5 kg (3¼ lb) small eels and cut each one into 4 sections. Cook the sections in a sauté pan in 150 g (5 oz, ⅔ cup) butter until they have stiffened. Add 100 g (4 oz, 1½ cups) each of chopped spinach and sorrel leaves, reduce the heat, and continue cooking until the vegetables are soft. Add 325 ml (11 fl oz, 1⅓ cups) dry white wine, a bouquet garni, 2 table-spoons chopped parsley and 1 tablespoon each of chopped sage and tarragon. Season well and simmer for 10 minutes. Brown 6 slices of stale sandwich bread in butter. When the eels are cooked, add 2 or 3 egg yolks mixed with 2 tablespoons lemon juice to the sauté pan and thicken the mixture without letting it boil. Place the sections of eel on the slices of fried bread and coat with the sauce. Eels *au vert* may also be served cold without the bread.

Eel brochettes

Skin and clean a large eel, cut off the head and the tail. Wash, wipe dry and then cut the body into 8 portions. Prepare a marinade using olive oil, plenty of lemon juice, finely chopped herbs and garlic, fresh crumbled thyme, salt and pepper and marinate the eel portions for 30 minutes with thick strips of streaky bacon. Then, without draining them, thread the pieces of eel on to skewers with the bacon. Grill (broil) under a high heat for about 15 minutes, basting with a little flavoured oil. Serve these brochettes with green sauce, tartare sauce, rémoulade sauce or Bercy sauce (shallot sauce for fish).

Eel brochettes à l'anglaise

Cut a boned eel into even-sized pieces and marinate them for 1 hour in a mixture of oil, lemon juice, pepper, salt and chopped parsley. Drain the eel pieces, roll in flour and coat with fresh breadcrumbs. Thread the eel on to skewers, separating the pieces with slices of fat bacon. Grill (broil) under a low heat until the flesh separates easily from the bone. Arrange on a long dish, garnished with parsley and surrounded with half-slices of lemon. Serve with tartare sauce.

Eel fricassée

Skin and prepare a large eel weighing about 800 g (1¾ lb) or several small eels totalling the same weight. Cut the eels into pieces about 6 cm (2½ in) long. Season with salt and pepper. Peel 12 small onions – if they are spring onions (scallions), trim them first – and blanch them for 3–4 minutes. Place the eel in a buttered frying pan (skillet), together with the onions and a large bouquet garni. Add a mixture of half dry white wine, half water until the ingredients are just covered. Cover the pan, bring to the boil and simmer for 10 minutes. In the meantime, prepare some small croûtons fried in oil or butter. Then add about 12 thinly sliced mushrooms to the frying pan and cook for a further 7–10 minutes. Drain the pieces of eel, the onions and the mushrooms, place in a dish and keep hot. Strain the cooking juices and reduce by two-thirds. Blend 2 egg yolks with 100 ml (4 fl oz, 7 tablespoons) single (light) cream and thicken carefully. Pour the sauce over the eel pieces, garnish with the fried croûtons and serve immediately.

Eel matelote

A matelote is a French fish stew made with red or white wine. The term is generally applied to stews made with freshwater fish: eel in particular, but also carp, small pike, trout, shad and barbel. All matelotes are usually garnished with small onions, mushrooms, rashers of bacon and sometimes with crayfish cooked in court-bouillon and fried croûtons.

Skin 1 kg (2¼ lb) eels and cut them into thick slices. Cook them in 65 g (2½ oz, 5 tablespoons) butter until firm, then flame them in 1 liqueur glass of marc or brandy. Add 2 onions, 1 celery stick and 1 carrot, all thinly sliced. Cover with 1 litre (1¾ pints, 4⅓ cups) red wine and add salt, a bouquet garni, a crushed garlic clove, a clove and 4–5 peppercorns. Bring to the boil and simmer for about 20 minutes.

Meanwhile, glaze 24 pickling (pearl) onions in butter and keep them warm, then sauté 250 g (9 oz, 3 cups) thinly sliced mushrooms. When the eel is cooked, drain and keep warm. Put the cooking liquid through a blender with 1 tablespoon beurre manié. Return the sauce to the pan, replace the eel, add the mushrooms, and simmer for 5 minutes.

Fry 12 small croûtons. Pour the matelote into a deep dish, add the glazed onions, and garnish with the fried croûtons. About 20 small fried pieces of sliced streaky bacon may be added just before serving.

Eel pie

Bone an eel, cut the fillets into 5–6 cm (2–2½ in) slices and blanch them in salted water. Drain and cool the eel slices. Hard-boil (hard-cook) and slice some eggs. Season the fish and eggs with salt, pepper and grated nutmeg, and sprinkle them with chopped parsley. Layer the eel and egg slices in a deep, preferably oval, dish. Add sufficient white wine to just cover the fish and dot with small knobs of butter. Cover with a layer of puff pastry, making a hole for the steam to escape. Brush with beaten egg and score the top. Bake in a preheated oven at 200°C (400°F, gas 6) for 30 minutes, then reduce the temperature to 180°C (350°C, gas 4) and cook for a further 1 hour. Just before serving, pour a few tablespoons of demi-glace sauce (made with fish stock) into the hole at the top of the pie. The pie may also be eaten cold.

Eel pie aux fines herbes (à la ménagère)

Bone an eel and cut the fillets into slices. Flatten each slice and season with salt, pepper and spices to taste. Arrange in a deep dish and moisten with a few tablespoons of dry white wine, a little Cognac and a few drops of oil. Leave to marinate for 2 hours in a cool place. Drain and wipe the slices, and reserve the marinade. Cook the fish briskly until stiff in butter in a sauté pan, then sprinkle generously with chopped parsley and shallots. Take the pan off the heat and pour the marinade over the fish. Leave until completely cold.

Line a shallow oval pie dish with shortcrust pastry (basic pie dough) and spread the base and sides with a layer of pike forcemeat containing chopped parsley – such as forcemeat for fish mousses and mousselines with pike. Fill the pie with alternating layers of the flattened eel slices and the pike forcemeat. Moisten each layer with a little of the marinade. Finish with a 2 cm (¾ in) layer of forcemeat and sprinkle with melted butter. Cover with a layer of pastry (dough) and trim the top with leaves cut from the pastry trimmings. Make a hole in the top for the steam to escape and brush the pastry with beaten egg. Bake in a preheated oven at 180°C (350°F, gas 4) for 1¾–2 hours.

Remove the pie from the dish and place it on a long serving dish. Pour a few tablespoons of demi-glace sauce, made with fish stock, through the hole in the top of the pie. Anchovy fillets may also be included with the eel slices, or some anchovy butter or dry duxelles may be added to the pike forcemeat. If the pie is served cold, pour enough fish jelly into the hole in the top of the pie to fill the gaps left by the cooking process. Leave for 12 hours until completely cold.

Fried eels Orly

Take some eel fillets and slice them. Flatten the slices, season with salt and pepper, and dip them in a thin coating batter. Deep-fry them, garnish with fried parsley and serve with a highly seasoned tomato fondue.

Roulade of eel à l'angevine

Skin a 1.5 kg (3¼ lb) eel, cut off the head and tail, open out and remove the backbone. Flatten the eel and season with sail and pepper. Stuff it with a pike forcemeat, such as godiveau lyonnais, to which a salpicon of finely diced mushrooms and truffles has been added. Reshape the eel and wrap it in thin slices of bacon. Tie it up in the form of a ring. Slice a large onion and a carrot and soften in butter in a sauté pan. Spread the vegetables evenly in the pan and place the eel on top, with a large bouquet garni, a leek and a sprig of savory in the centre. Add just enough medium dry white wine, such as Anjou, to cover the eel. Bring to the boil, skim, then cover and simmer slowly for 35 minutes. Prepare 24 small mushroom caps, keeping the stalks, and toss in butter. Drain the eel (reserving the liquor), remove the bacon slices, and put into another sauté pan with the mushrooms. Keep hot.

To prepare the sauce, strain the cooking liquor and make a white roux with 50 g (2 oz, ¼ cup) butter and 50 g (2 oz, ½ cup) plain (all-purpose) flour. Moisten with the strained juices and add the mushroom stalks. Reduce the sauce over a high heat and add 350 ml (12 fl oz, 1½ cups) single (light) cream. When the sauce has reached the correct consistency, take it off the boil and add 100 g (4 oz, ½ cup) crayfish butter. Coat the rolled-up eel with the sauce.

Grouper

Ceviche of grouper

Also known as *cebiche*, ceviche is a dish, characteristic of Peruvian cookery, that is based on raw fish marinated in lemon juice and is served with sweet limes, raw onion rings, tomatoes and boiled sweetcorn.

Clean and trim 4 grouper steaks of 200 g (7 oz) each. Cut into 1 cm (½ in) cubes. Squeeze the juice from 4 limes. Place the diced fish in a large salad bowl sitting on a bed of ice cubes. Sprinkle the lime juice on the fish and allow to marinate for 2–3 hours, stirring several times to cook the grouper, which must remain pink in the middle. Drain and place in a large bowl. Peel and finely chop diagonally 4 spring onions (scallions) and their stems. Peel, seed and crush 3 cherry tomatoes. Add all these ingredients to the fish. Season with salt and add ½ teaspoon freshly grated ginger, 1 pinch turmeric, chives and chopped flat-leaf parsley. Pour olive oil on top and sprinkle with paprika. Stir well and serve.

Grouper with corcellet sauce

Trim, gut and clean a small grouper, poach it in very concentrated court-bouillon, and allow it to cool in the stock. Take out the fish, remove the skin and garnish with blanched tarragon leaves and thin slices of tomato.

Finely chop 6 large, ripe, peeled and seeded tomatoes and rub through a sieve. Store the resulting fresh tomato purée in the refrigerator. Just before serving, add 2 generous tablespoons aniseed-flavoured Corcellet mustard or other tarragon or aniseed mustard to the tomato purée. Serve chilled.

Gurnard

Baked gurnard

Choose 2 good-quality gurnards, each weighing about 400 g (14 oz). Draw and trim them, remove the fins, then clean and dry them. Score oblique cuts on the back of each fish from the backbone outwards and pour in a few drops of lemon juice. Butter a gratin dish and spread in it a mixture of 2 large onions, 2 shallots and 1 small garlic clove, all very finely chopped. Sprinkle with chopped parsley. Place the fish in the dish and add 200 ml (7 fl oz, ¾ cup) white wine and 50 g (2 oz, 4 tablespoons) melted butter. Season with salt and pepper and sprinkle with a little thyme. Arrange slices of lemon along the backs of the fish and sprinkle with chopped fresh bay leaf. Bake in a preheated oven at 240°C (475°F, gas 9) for about 20 minutes, basting the fish several times during cooking.

Just before serving, flame the gurnards with 4 tablespoons heated pastis.

Haddock

Curried haddock

Soak some smoked haddock in cold milk for 2–3 hours. Prepare a curry sauce. Drain and dry the haddock thoroughly, then bone, skin, and dice the flesh. Cook thinly sliced large onions in butter, allowing 2 onions per 450 g (1 lb) fish. Cool. Add the haddock to the onions, moisten with the curry sauce, then cover and simmer for about 10 minutes. Serve with boiled rice.

Grilled haddock

Place some smoked haddock in a dish, cover it with cold milk, and leave for 2–3 hours. Dry the fish thoroughly, brush with melted butter or oil, and grill (broil) gently. Serve with melted butter seasoned with pepper and lemon juice, but no salt, accompanied by boiled potatoes or buttered spinach.

Haddock gâteau

Boil 1 kg (2¼ lb) potatoes in their skins. Clean and slice the white part of 5 leeks and braise them in a little water and 40 g (1½ oz, 3 tablespoons) butter for 8 minutes. Thinly slice 2 smoked haddock fillets weighing about 350 g (12 oz) each. Clean 150 g (5 oz, 2 cups) mushrooms and slice them thinly. Peel the potatoes and cut them into thick slices. Spread two-thirds of the haddock in the bottom of a buttered ovenproof mould and cover with the mushrooms, potatoes, leeks and the remaining haddock. Top with 6 tablespoons crème fraîche. Sprinkle with pepper. Cover the mould with foil and cook in a bain marie in a preheated oven at 240°C (475°F, gas 9) for 30 minutes. Unmould the gâteau and retain the juices. Cook 1 chopped shallot in 10 g (¼ oz, 1½ teaspoons) butter, add the juices and boil until reduced by one-third. Add 6 tablespoons single (light) cream and pour over the gâteau.

Haddock rillettes

Rillettes is the term for potted meat or poultry and here it describes a similar preparation of fish.

Poach 900 g (2 lb) smoked haddock in a mixture of unsalted water and milk for 3 minutes. Simmer gently, but do not boil. Remove the fish and drain well. In a food processor, mix 5 hard-boiled (hard-cooked) eggs, 40 g (1½ oz, 3 tablespoons) butter, 3 tablespoons parsley and 2 tablespoons chopped chives. Then add the haddock, the juice of ½ a lemon and 6 tablespoons olive oil, and mix together very rapidly. Place the mixture in a bowl.

Peel and seed 2 large tomatoes and place in a food processor or blender. Add the juice of ½ a lemon, 3 finely chopped shallots, 6 tablespoons olive oil, salt and pepper. Blend to a smooth sauce. Cover the bottom of each plate with 3 tablespoons of this sauce. Arrange 3 ovals of the haddock mixture (formed with a spoon) in a star pattern on the sauce. Serve with toast.

Poached haddock

Soak some smoked haddock in cold milk for 2–3 hours, then remove it. Bring the milk to the boil, add the haddock, and poach without boiling (otherwise it will become stringy) for 6–10 minutes, depending on the thickness of the fish. Serve with melted butter strongly flavoured with lemon juice and chopped parsley, accompanied by boiled potatoes.

Hake

Hake à la boulangère

Season a 1 kg (2¼ lb) piece of hake taken from the middle of the fish. Put it into a greased gratin dish and coat with melted butter. Arrange 800 g (1¾ lb) thinly sliced potatoes and 200 g (7 oz, 1¾ cups) sliced onions around the fish. Sprinkle with salt, pepper, thyme and powdered bay leaf. Pour 25 g (1 oz, 2 tablespoons) melted butter over it. Cook in a preheated oven at about 200°C (400°F, gas 6) for 30–35 minutes. Sprinkle the fish with a little water several times during cooking. Serve in the dish garnished with chopped parsley.

Hake cosquera

Cut a 1 kg (2¼ lb) hake into thick slices. Wash 24 clams. Heat 2–3 tablespoons olive oil in an earthenware casserole and cook the fish steaks for 6 minutes. Season with salt and pepper. As soon as the juices from the fish become colourless, add the clams. Sprinkle with chopped garlic and parsley and continue to cook briefly until the shellfish open. Serve immediately.

Hake mère Joseph

Dress a hake weighing about 1 kg (2¼ lb). Remove the head and cut the body into 4 pieces. Dry them and rub each piece thoroughly with the cut surface of a lemon half. Sprinkle with pepper, and brown them in lard in a flameproof casserole. Add 3–4 chopped shallots and allow them to brown slightly. Blend 1 tablespoon tomato purée (paste) with 1 tablespoon brandy and add to the casserole. Season with salt, cover, and simmer gently for 15–20 minutes.

Hake steaks à la duxelles

Clean and chop 500 g (18 oz, 4½ cups) button mushrooms and 2 shallots and mix together with 1 tablespoon lemon juice. Fry the mixture in 20 g (¾ oz, 1½ tablespoons) butter over a high heat for 5 minutes. Line a greased gratin dish with the mushroom duxelles mixture and arrange 4 hake steaks on top. Add 250 ml (8 fl oz, 1 cup) white wine and 250 ml (8 fl oz, 1 cup) fish stock, or 500 ml (17 fl oz, 2 cups) fish fumet. Top with small pieces of butter, season and add a bouquet garni. Place in a preheated oven at 240°C (475°F, gas 9) and cook for 25 minutes. Moisten with small quantities of water during cooking. Drain and keep warm. Reduce the cooking liquid, replace the fish in the dish, pour over some cream and return to the oven for 5–6 minutes.

Hake steaks à la koskera

Flour 4 hake steaks. Heat 2 tablespoons olive oil in a deep, non-stick frying pan. Brown the steaks on both sides, then add 2 chopped garlic cloves. Add 250 ml (8 fl oz, 1 cup) white wine, 250 ml (8 fl oz, 1 cup) of the liquid from a can of asparagus, 100 g (4 oz, 1 cup) petits pois cooked in water, 200 g (7 oz) clams and ½ chopped sun-dried red pepper. Simmer for 15 minutes, or until cooked. Add plenty of parsley and adjust the seasoning. Arrange in a dish, garnish with asparagus tips and quarters of hard-boiled (hard-cooked) eggs.

Herring

To prepare

If fresh, scale the fish, but do not slit them in half. Gut (clean) them through the gills, leaving the hard or soft roes inside. Wash and dry them. If they are to be cooked whole, score the skin lightly on both sides.

The fish is filleted by running a very sharp knife between the backbone and the fillets, starting from the tail end. The fillets can then be eased off the bone, trimmed, washed and dried.

If the herring is smoked, take out the fillets, then skin and trim them. Before cooking, soak them for a while in milk to remove some of the salt.

If the fish is salted, wash the fillets and soak them in milk, or a mixture of milk and water, to remove the salt. Drain, trim and dry them.

Carolines à la hollandaise

Prepare an unsweetened choux paste. Using a piping bag, pipe out some small éclairs, about 4 cm (1½ in) long, on to a baking sheet. Brush with beaten egg, bake in a preheated oven at 220°C (425°F, gas 7) for 10 minutes. Reduce the temperature to 180°C (350°F, gas 4) and continue to cook for 10 minutes more. Allow to cool. To make enough filling for 12 carolines, desalt 4 herring fillets, if necessary, trim and wipe them. Pound or blend the fillets together with 2 hard-boiled (hard-cooked) egg yolks and 75 g (3 oz, 6 tablespoons) butter. Add 1 teaspoon chives and 1 teaspoon chopped parsley. Gently split the éclairs along the side and put the filling into this opening with a piping bag. Brush the carolines with melted butter and immediately sprinkle with a little hard-boiled egg yolk and chopped parsley. Cool before serving.

Devilled herrings

Scale, wash and dry some herrings, then slit them along the back and sides. Season and coat with mustard, sprinkle with fresh white breadcrumbs and oil, and cook slowly under the grill (broiler). Serve with mustard sauce, ravigote sauce or devilled sauce.

Fillets of herring à la russe

Boil some potatoes in their skins, then peel and slice them. Take some large herring fillets in oil and slice them very thinly. Reshape them, placing a slice of potato between each slice of herring. Arrange on a long serving dish and dress with a herb vinaigrette (made with parsley, chervil, tarragon and chives) to which some finely chopped fennel and shallots have been added.

Fried herring

Choose small herrings weighing about 125 g (4½ oz). Clean, trim, score and soak them in milk for about 30 minutes. Drain. Coat with flour and deep-fry in oil at 175°C (347°F) for 3–4 minutes. Drain well on paper towels. Sprinkle with salt and serve them with lemon quarters.

Grilled herring

Clean and trim medium-sized herrings. Brush them with oil or melted butter, season with pepper and cook under a moderate grill (broiler). Sprinkle with salt and serve with maître d'hôtel butter or a mustard sauce.

Herring à la boulangère

Clean 6 good herrings, preferably some with soft roes, and season with salt. Butter an ovenproof dish and place the herrings in it. Slice 400–500 g (14–18 oz) potatoes and 150 g (5 oz) onions, blanch in boiling water to parcook and arrange around the herrings. Add salt, pepper, a pinch of thyme and a crumbled bay leaf. Sprinkle with about 40 g (1½ oz, 3 tablespoons) melted butter and cook in a preheated oven at 200°C (400°F, gas 6) for 30 minutes, basting from time to time. Cover the dish with foil if the potatoes begin to dry out in the final stages of cooking.

Herring canapés à la hollandaise

Spread some slices of bread with a purée of herring soft roe. Garnish each canapé with strips of smoked herring fillet, arranged to form a lattice, sprinkle with a little lemon juice and fill the lattice spaces with chopped hard-boiled (hard-cooked) egg yolk.

Herring fillets à la livonienne

Remove the fillets from large smoked herrings, trim them and cut into dice. Boil potatoes in salted water. peel and slice them into rounds. Peel and halve sweet crisp apples, core them, cut into slices and dip in lemon juice. Arrange the herring, potato rounds and apple slices in concentric circles. Sprinkle with vinaigrette and chopped parsley, chervil and fennel. Refrigerate.

Herring fillets marinated in oil

Put lightly smoked herring fillets into an earthenware dish. Soak them in milk and leave in a cool place for 24 hours. Drain the fillets and wipe them dry. Wash the dish. Slice 2 onions for every 450 g (1 lb) fillets and spread half over the bottom of the dish. Arrange the fillets on top and cover with the rest of the onion, some sliced carrot, coriander seeds and half a bay leaf cut into pieces. Sprinkle a little thyme over the top, pour on some groundnut (peanut) oil, cover the dish with foil and leave to marinate for several days at the bottom of the refrigerator.

Marinated herrings

Clean and trim 12 small herrings, sprinkle them with fine salt and leave for 6 hours. Chop 3 large onions and 3 carrots. Choose a flameproof dish just big enough to hold the herrings and half-fill it with the chopped vegetables. Add a pinch of chopped parsley, a pinch of pepper, 2 cloves, a bay leaf cut into small pieces, and a little thyme. Arrange the fish in the dish and pour in enough of a mixture of half white wine and half vinegar to just cover the fish. Top with the remaining vegetables, cover the dish with foil and bring to the boil on the top of the cooker (stove). Then cook in a preheated oven at 220°C (425°F, gas 7) for about 20 minutes. Leave the herring to cool in the cooking liquid and refrigerate until ready to serve.

Sautéed herring à la lyonnaise

Clean and trim 6 herrings. Chop 2 medium-sized onions. Season the fish with salt and pepper, coat with flour and fry in butter until golden brown on both sides. Fry the onions until golden brown in a separate pan. Turn the herrings over, add the onions and continue cooking for about 10 minutes. Arrange the fish on a serving dish, cover with the onions and sprinkle with chopped parsley. Deglaze the frying pan in which the fish were cooked with a generous tablespoon of vinegar and pour the sauce over the fish.

Swedish herring balls

Fillet 3 herrings. Boil 3 large floury (baking) potatoes in salted water, peel and mash. Cook 3 finely chopped onions slowly in a covered pan for about 10 minutes. Chop the herring fillets finely, add the potato, onions, salt, pepper and, if desired, a little grated nutmeg. Mix everything together thoroughly and form into small balls. Fry them in butter or oil and serve with hot cranberry sauce.

John Dory

Fillets of John Dory palais-royal

Poach some John Dory fillets in a mixture of white wine, fish fumet and the juice of a lemon. Boil some potatoes in their skins, peel them, mash them and put in a greased ovenproof dish. Place the fillets on top. Using part of the reduced court-bouillon, make some Mornay sauce, pour it over the fish and brown in a preheated oven at 220°C (425°F, gas 7).

Grilled John Dory with deep-fried butter pats

Cut 8 rounds of very cold, slightly salted butter, each weighing 25 g (1 oz). Thickly coat them in breadcrumbs and chill them in the refrigerator. Fillet a John Dory, then grill (broil) it. Just before serving, carefully place the rounds of butter into hot deep fat. As soon as they are golden, drain on paper towels and quickly arrange on top of the portions of fish. Garnish the dish with fried parsley and serve straight away.

John Dory fillets in a soufflé

Steam 4 John Dory fillets, each weighing 150 g (5 oz), for 4 minutes. Sprinkle with salt and pepper. Whisk 8 egg whites until stiff and fold in 3 tablespoons mustard. Arrange the fillets in an ovenproof dish, pile up the egg whites on top, and cook in a preheated oven at 230°C (450°F, gas 8) for about 4 minutes.

John Dory fillets with lemon

Fillet a John Dory weighing about 1.25 kg (2¾ lb); this should provide 600 g (1 lb 6 oz) flesh. Remove the skin and cut the flesh into 1 cm (½ in) dice.

Finely shred the zest of 2 lemons, blanch and refresh it, then cook it in a little water and 50 ml (2 fl oz, ¼ cup) olive oil. Remove the white pith from the lemons, break up the lemon segments and dice them. Cut 350 g (12 oz) courgettes (zucchini) into small pieces, trim them to the shape of olives and blanch them.

Lightly grease 4 pieces of foil large enough to wrap round a piece of fish and some vegetables. On each one place a quarter of the fish, courgettes, lemon dice and rind, 20 g (¾ oz, 1½ tablespoons) butter, and some salt and pepper. Seal the foil and bake in a preheated oven at 230°C (450°F, gas 8) for about 8 minutes. Open the envelopes and sprinkle with chopped chives.

John Dory fillets with melon

Fillet a John Dory weighing about 1.5 kg (3¼ lb) and quickly sauté the fillets in a nonstick frying pan without fat, allowing 2 minutes for each side. Keep the fillets warm. Blanch a julienne of 2 carrots and 1 leek for 1 minute in boiling water. Pat them dry and sauté briskly in 20 g (¾ oz, 1½ tablespoons) butter for 2 minutes. Sprinkle with salt and pepper and keep warm.

In another pan, fry slices of a 400 g (14 oz) melon in 25 g (1 oz, 2 table-spoons) butter, sprinkle with salt and pepper and caramelize slightly. Arrange ¼ of the melon slices and a John Dory fillet in a ring on each plate, place a spoonful of vegetables in the centre, and sprinkle with fresh chopped mint.

John Dory fillets with red peppers

Fillet a John Dory. Braise the fillets in fish fumet: they should be just cooked. Arrange them on a dish and keep warm. Reduce the braising liquid, add 200 ml (7 fl oz, ¾ cup) double (heavy) cream, and reduce once again. Remove from the heat, add 3 tablespoons hollandaise sauce, and adjust the seasoning. Bake 4 whole red (bell) peppers in a preheated oven at 240°C (475°F, gas 9) or put under the grill (broiler) until the skin blackens and blisters. Peel and seed them and purée the flesh in a blender. Season with salt and pepper and heat the purée. Coat the fish with the sauce and with 4 tablespoons pepper purée. Garnish with sprigs of chervil. Serve with French (green) beans.

John Dory steaks in whisky velouté sauce with vegetable julienne

Fillet 2 John Dorys, each weighing 1.25 kg (2¾ lb). Grease an ovenproof dish and sprinkle it with 2 finely chopped shallots. Season the fillets with salt and pepper and lay them in the dish. Moisten with 7 tablespoons dry white wine and 7 tablespoons whisky. Cover with buttered greaseproof (wax) paper and bake in a preheated oven at 180°C (350°F, gas 4) for 10–12 minutes.

Drain the fillets and reduce the cooking liquid by one third. Remove from the heat, whisk in 50 g (2 oz, ¼ cup) butter in small pieces, then add 500 ml (17 fl oz, 2 cups) whipped double (heavy) cream. Mix well, still off the heat. Put the fish back in the oven or under the grill (broiler) for 2 minutes, then coat with the sauce.

Serve the fish with steamed potatoes and a vegetable julienne made with 2 carrots, 1 celery heart, the white parts of 2 leeks, a bulb of fresh fennel and 4 large mushroom caps.

John Dory with rhubarb

Fillet a John Dory weighing 1.5 kg (3¼ lb) and cook the fillets in a little butter over a gentle heat, allowing 1 minute for each side. Keep warm. Add 150 g (5 oz) rhubarb, peeled and thinly sliced, to the butter in which the fish was cooked, and cook for 30 seconds. Add 200 ml (7 fl oz, ¾ cup) double (heavy) cream and reduce by half. Season with salt and pepper and add a pinch of sugar and a pinch of chopped basil. Mix well and pour the sauce over the fish.

Stuffed John Dory with sea-urchin cream

Bone a John Dory, keeping it intact. Stuff it with 300 ml (½ pint, 1¼ cups) leeks stewed in butter mixed with a duxelles of grey chanterelles. Place the fish in an ovenproof dish with chopped onion, thyme, bay leaf, 250 ml (8 fl oz, 1 cup) white Cassis wine and 7 tablespoons cream. Bake in a preheated oven at 180°C (350°F, gas 4) for 20 minutes. Meanwhile, open up 4 sea urchins, discard the digestive system and put the coral into a small sauté pan. Clean the shells and heat them in the oven. Beat together 2 egg yolks and 7 tablespoons double (heavy) cream in a bain marie. When this mixture is really frothy, add it to the sea-urchin coral, whisking vigorously, and season with salt and cayenne. Pour some of the cream sauce over the fish and put the rest into the heated sea-urchin shells. Arrange these shells around the fish.

Lamprey

Lamprey à la bordelaise

Bleed a medium lamprey, reserving the blood to flavour the sauce. Scald the fish and scrape off the skin. To remove the dorsal nerve, cut off the lamprey's tail, make an incision around the neck just below the gills, then take hold of the nerve through this opening and pull it out. Cut the fish into slices 6 cm (2½ in) thick and put them into a buttered pan lined with sliced onions and carrots. Add a bouquet garni and a crushed garlic clove, season with salt and pepper, and add enough red wine to cover the fish. Boil briskly for about 10 minutes, then drain the slices, reserving the cooking stock and vegetables.

Clean 4 leeks, cut each into 3 slices, then cook in a little butter with 4 tablespoons finely diced ham. Add the lamprey. Make a roux with 2 tablespoons butter and an equal quantity of flour. Add the reserved cooking stock and vegetables from the lamprey and cook for 15 minutes. Strain the sauce and pour it over the lamprey in the pan with the vegetables. Simmer very gently until the fish is cooked.

Arrange the lamprey slices on a round dish, gently stir the reserved blood into the sauce and pour this over the fish. Garnish the dish with slices of bread fried in butter.

Mackerel

Fillets of mackerel à la dijonnaise

Fillet 4 large mackerel. Season the fillets with salt and pepper and coat with white mustard seeds.

Soften 2 chopped onions in 2 tablespoons oil in a saucepan. Add 1 tablespoon flour and mix well. Pour a glass of stock or fish fumet into the saucepan, together with a glass of dry white wine. Stir well, add a bouquet garni and cook for 8–10 minutes.

Arrange the fillets in a buttered ovenproof dish and add the sauce. Place the dish in a preheated oven at 200°C (400°F, gas 6) and cook for about 15 minutes. Drain the fish and arrange on a serving dish. Remove the bouquet garni from the sauce, add a little mustard, check the seasoning and pour the sauce over the fillets. Garnish with slices of lemon and sprigs of parsley.

Fillets of mackerel à la lyonnaise

Fillet and season 4 large mackerel. Soften 4 chopped onions in melted butter, then add 1 tablespoon vinegar. Place half the onions in a buttered ovenproof dish, lay the fillets on top and cover with the remaining onions. Moisten with 3 tablespoons dry white wine. Sprinkle with breadcrumbs, dot with knobs of butter and cook in a preheated oven at 220°C (425°F, gas 7) for about 10 minutes. Sprinkle with chopped parsley.

Fillets of mackerel à la piémontaise

Prepare a risotto *à la piémontaise* using 200 g (7 oz, 1 cup) rice. Fillet 4 mackerel; wash and pat them dry with a clean cloth or paper towels, then dip in breadcrumbs and fry in butter on both sides. Butter a long serving dish, cover with the risotto and arrange the fillets on top. Garnish with quarters of lemon. Serve with a slightly thickened tomato sauce.

Fillets of mackerel in white wine

Add 5 tablespoons white wine to 500 ml (17 fl oz, 2 cups) fish stock and boil down to reduce by half. Fillet and season 4 large mackerel with salt and pepper. Arrange the fillets in a buttered ovenproof dish, add the stock and cook in a preheated oven at 220°C (425°F, gas 7) for about 12 minutes. Drain the fish and keep warm on the serving dish. Strain the cooking juices and boil down to reduce by a third. Add 200 ml (7 fl oz, ¾ cup) double (heavy) cream and reduce again by half. Coat the fish with the sauce and sprinkle with chopped parsley.

Mackerel à la boulonnaise

Clean some mussels and cook them in a little vinegar over a brisk heat. Prepare a butter sauce using the strained cooking juices from the mussels. Gut (clean) the mackerel, cut it into thick slices, and poach for about 12 minutes in a court-bouillon with a generous quantity of vinegar. Drain the fish, skin it and then arrange on a long serving dish; keep it warm. Shell the mussels, arrange them around the fish and coat the mackerel and the mussels with the butter sauce.

Mackerel à la nage

To 750 ml (1¼ pints, 3¼ cups) red wine, add 2 garlic cloves, 2 chopped shallots, a clove, a small piece of cinnamon and a bouquet garni. Boil down to reduce, then add 2 chopped carrots, a bulb of fennel cut into 6 pieces, and 3 celery sticks. Cook gently. Finally, add the thickly sliced white parts of 4 leeks and the finely chopped green tops of the leeks. Season with salt and pepper and add a little sugar. Continue simmering until the vegetables are cooked but still firm.

Clean and gut 8 small mackerel. Place in an ovenproof dish, partially cover with the vegetable mixture and cooking stock, then and add a few slices of lemon. Cover the dish with foil and cook in a preheated oven at 180°C (350°F, gas 4) for 5–6 minutes. Serve very hot.

Mackerel in cider Pierre Traiteur

Trim and wash the mackerel and season them thoroughly. Place them on a base of onions and chopped apples in a pan. Cover with cider, add about 3 tablespoons cider vinegar (more if cooking more than 4–6 fish in a very large pan) and bring to the boil. Simmer for 5 minutes. Allow the fish to cool in the pan. Remove the fillets and arrange them on a serving dish surrounded by pieces of apple that have been fried in butter. Boil down the cooking liquid in the pan and pour over the mackerel while still hot. Sprinkle with pepper and chopped chives.

Mackerel with noisette butter

Clean 6 medium mackerel and cut them into thick slices of a similar size. Poach for about 12 minutes in a court-bouillon made with vinegar. Drain, place on a serving dish, and keep warm. Sprinkle with a little vinegar.

Prepare 100 g (4 oz, ½ cup) noisette butter and add 1 tablespoon each of capers and chopped parsley. Pour the noisette butter over the mackerel and serve very hot.

Mackerel with sorrel

Trim 6 mackerel, slit them along the back and dry them. Melt a large knob of butter in a frying pan, place the fish in the hot butter and cook on one side for 5 minutes. Turn and cook the other side. Remove the fish from the pan, season and keep warm.

Pick over 500 g (18 oz) sorrel, wash it thoroughly and add it to the juices in the frying pan. Heat the mixture, stirring constantly, until the sorrel is reduced to a purée (do not allow it to dry out). Check the seasoning, then bind the mixture with butter and 1–2 eggs. Serve the mackerel on a long dish, garnished with the sorrel purée.

Mackerel with two-mustard sauce

Wash and gut (clean) 8 small mackerel (*lisettes* are small mackerel less than 1 year old). Place them in an ovenproof dish, season with salt and pepper, moisten with a glass of dry white wine, and cook in a preheated oven at 240°C (475°F, gas 9) for 8 minutes. Mix 1 tablespoon strong mustard with 1 tablespoon mild mustard in a saucepan. When the mackerel are cooked, add their cooking juices to the mustard mixture. Add 40 g (1½ oz, 3 tablespoons) butter, bring to the boil and cook for 2 minutes. Coat the fish with the sauce and serve with rice *à la créole*.

Marlin

Palm hearts mille-feuille with smoked marlin

Using a blender, make a vinaigrette with 200 ml (7 fl oz, ¾ cup) groundnut (peanut) oil, 100 ml (4 fl oz, 7 tablespoons) wine vinegar, 1 teaspoon prepared mustard and 1 egg. Cut 250 g (9 oz) smoked marlin into 12 slices. Wash 200 g (7 oz) tomatoes and cut into small cubes. Make roses with 4 cherry tomatoes. Cut 4 black olives into fan shapes (3 per olive). Squeeze the juice of 1 lemon. Finely slice 1 palm heart and coat the slices in the vinaigrette and lemon juice to prevent them from going black. Put a ring 7.5 cm (3 in) in diameter and 4 cm (1½ in) high in the centre of each plate. Put a slice of marlin in the bottom and add a thin layer of finely sliced palm heart. Cover with another slice of marlin and a thin layer of palm heart. Finish with a slice of marlin. Place a cherry tomato rose in the centre and arrange 3 of the olive fans. Remove the ring carefully. Place some diced tomatoes round the edge of each plate and garnish with a little parsley.

Monkfish

Blanquette of monkfish

Cut the fish into about 5 cm (2 in) cubes. Seal by frying the cubes in 40 g (1½ oz, 3 tablespoons) butter without browning. Cover with white stock or bouillon, season, quickly bring to the boil and skim. Add 2 onions (one stuck with 2 cloves), 150 g (5 oz, 1 cup) diced carrots and 2 leeks. Simmer gently for 15 minutes. Drain the pieces of fish and place in a sauté pan with 225 g (8 oz) baby onions and 225 g (8 oz) very small button mushrooms that have been cooked *au blanc*, in a thin white sauce. Heat gently and, just before serving, bind the sauce with 2–3 egg yolks, 150 ml (¼ pint, ⅔ cup) double (heavy) cream and the juice of 1 lemon. Place in a deep serving dish, sprinkle with parsley and garnish with heart-shaped croûtons fried in butter.

Blanquette is usually served with rice *à la créole* but may also be served with celeriac (celery root), halved celery hearts, carrots, braised parsnips or leeks, cucumber (cut into chunks and blanched for 3 minutes in boiling salted water), braised lettuce or lettuce hearts.

Escalopes of monkfish with creamed peppers

Cut 500 g (18 oz) thoroughly cleaned monkfish into 8 small escalopes. Season with salt and pepper. Coat them with breadcrumbs, roll in 50 g (2 oz, ½ cup) grated Parmesan cheese, then brown in butter. Cut open 3 green (bell) peppers and remove the seeds. Blanch for about 10 minutes in boiling water, then cut into pieces and purée in a blender or food processor. Enrich the purée with 65–75 g (2½–3 oz, 5–6 tablespoons) butter. Season with salt and pepper and add a dash of Worcestershire sauce. Place 2 escalopes of monkfish on each plate and surround them with a ribbon of the green pepper purée.

Fillets of monkfish braised in white wine

Lightly flatten 2 fillets and season with salt and pepper. Arrange the fillets in a buttered roasting dish just big enough to hold them and half-cover them with reduced fish stock mixed with white wine. Bake in a preheated oven at 220°C (425°F, gas 7) for 7–8 minutes. Turn the fillets over and bake for another

7–8 minutes, then cover with foil and bake for a further 5 minutes. Place them on a serving dish and keep warm. Add cream to the juices in the roasting dish and reduce until the sauce has thickened. Adjust the seasoning if necessary. Pour the sauce over the fish, sprinkle with chopped parsley and serve very hot accompanied by braised spinach or puréed broccoli.

Fillets of monkfish with leeks and cream

Clean 300 g (11 oz) leeks (the white part only), 1 celery stick and 2 turnips. Peel 2 shallots. Shred all these vegetables finely. Melt 25 g (1 oz, 2 tablespoons) butter in a flameproof casserole, add the shredded vegetables and cook until golden, stirring all the time; then cover and cook gently for about 5 minutes, until soft. Take some fillets of monkfish – about 1 kg (2¼ lb) – and place them on top of the vegetable mixture, then turn them over carefully in it. Add 2 more chopped shallots, 1 chopped garlic clove, a small bouquet garni, 1 glass of dry white wine, 1 glass of water, salt and pepper. Cover the casserole. When the mixture begins to boil, turn the heat down and simmer.

Five minutes before cooking is completed, add 250 g (9 oz, 3 cups) mushrooms which have been cleaned, chopped, sprinkled with lemon juice and lightly fried in butter. Adjust the seasoning if necessary and cook until ready (the fish must remain slightly firm). Drain the fillets and keep them warm in a dish. Remove the bouquet garni from the casserole. Leave the juices on the heat and pour in 150 ml (¼ pint, ⅔ cup) double (heavy) cream. Reduce until the sauce is slightly thickened. Mix in another 25–50 g (1–2 oz, 2–4 tablespoons) butter, beating all the time. Pour this sauce over the fish.

Medallions of monkfish with a red-pepper sauce

Prepare a court-bouillon with water and white vinegar, 1 carrot and 1 onion (thinly sliced), a bouquet garni, salt and pepper. Cook for 20 minutes. Halve

69

a red (bell) pepper and remove the seeds. Cook slowly in olive oil, in a covered saucepan, for 6 minutes, then press through a fine sieve.

Cut 675 g (1½ lb) monkfish fillets into medallions 1 cm (½ in) thick. Soften 2 small chopped shallots in white wine and reduce until all the liquid is absorbed. Add 2 tablespoons double (heavy) cream and boil for 2 minutes, whisking all the time then, over a low heat, incorporate 150 g (5 oz, ⅔ cup) butter, whisking all the time. Add the puréed red pepper, season with salt and pepper and add a squeeze of lemon juice.

Arrange the medallions well separated in a gratin dish. Season with salt and pepper. Pour the court-bouillon over the fish and simmer for 4 minutes over a low heat. Remove from the heat and strain. Arrange the medallions on a serving dish and coat with the sauce.

Medallions of monkfish with herbs

Skin 2 large tomatoes and remove the seeds, then dice the flesh and sprinkle with finely chopped chives, salt and pepper. Clean a piece of monkfish weighing 1.4 kg (3 lb), remove the backbone and skin. Cut into medallions 1 cm (½ in) thick. Place these in a heavy-based saucepan with 20 g (¾ oz, 4½ teaspoons) butter, 1 tablespoon Sauvignon white wine, 1 chopped shallot, a squeeze of lemon juice, salt and pepper. Bring to the boil, then simmer for 1 minute. Turn the medallions over and cook for another minute.

Remove the fish from the pan and keep warm and covered. Boil to reduce the cooking juices by half. Add 250 ml (8 fl oz, 1 cup) double (heavy) cream and reduce again by one-third. Add 25 g (1 oz, ½ cup) watercress, 20 g (¾ oz, ¼ cup) sorrel, 20 g (¾ oz, ¼ cup) chervil and 1 lettuce heart, then purée in a blender or food processor. Reheat and check the seasoning. Pour the sauce into a warm dish. Arrange the monkfish medallions on top, cover with the warmed diced tomatoes and chives and serve.

Monkfish à l'américaine

Trim, wash and dry 1.5 kg (3¼ lb) monkfish and cut into even slices. Wash and dry the heads and shells of some langoustines. Chop 4 shallots and crush a large garlic clove. Chop a little parsley and 2 tablespoons tarragon leaves. Skin 500 g (18 oz) very ripe tomatoes, remove the seeds, then chop the flesh finely. Heat 6 tablespoons olive oil in a flameproof casserole or large saucepan and add the langoustine heads and shells and the sliced monkfish. As soon as the monkfish has started to brown, add the chopped shallots and cook until just golden. Pour in 1 liqueur glass of Cognac and set it alight.

Add the crushed garlic, a strip of dried orange zest, the chopped tarragon and parsley, the chopped tomatoes, a small bouquet garni, 1 tablespoon tomato purée (paste) diluted with ½ bottle of very dry white wine, salt, pepper and cayenne (this dish must be strongly seasoned). Cover and leave to cook for about 15 minutes; the fish must remain slightly firm. Drain the fish and keep warm on a serving dish. Remove the bouquet garni, strain the sauce and pour over the fish. Garnish with tarragon sprigs and serve with rice.

Monkfish brochettes

Cut the flesh of a monkfish (taken from the tail, which is less expensive than the middle of the fish) into 2.5 cm (1 in) cubes and marinate with halved slices of aubergine (eggplant) for 30 minutes in a mixture of olive oil, plenty of lemon juice, finely chopped herbs and garlic, fresh crumbled thyme, salt and pepper. Thread the skewers, alternating monkfish and aubergine, and grill (broil) under a medium heat for 16–18 minutes.

Monkfish curry à la créole

Cut about 1 kg (2¼ lb) monkfish into pieces, fry in oil until golden, then drain. In the same oil, fry 100 g (4 oz, ¾ cup) finely chopped onion until golden, then add 2 or 3 peeled crushed tomatoes, a pinch of saffron, 1 table-spoon freshly grated root ginger (or 1 teaspoon ground ginger), 2 finely chopped garlic cloves, a bouquet garni, a piece of orange peel and 2 teaspoons of prepared curry powder. Stir over a medium heat for 5–6 minutes, then add 250 ml (8 fl oz, 1 cup) hot water, cayenne, salt and pepper. Cover and leave to cook very gently for 30 minutes. Remove the bouquet garni and orange peel and serve with rice *à la créole*.

Roast monkfish

Prepare a tomato sauce. While this is cooking, fry some very small button mushrooms and chopped garlic in a little olive oil. Season a well-trimmed piece of monkfish with salt and pepper and bake in an oiled roasting tin (pan) in a preheated oven at 240°C (475°F, gas 9) for 10 minutes, then reduce the heat to 200°C (400°F, gas 6) and leave until cooked, basting from time to time. Serve the fish surrounded with mushrooms and the tomato sauce separately.

Whole monkfish roasted with caramelized shallots

Peel 200 g (7 oz) potatoes and finely slice with a mandoline. Wash and dry thoroughly. Season with salt and pepper. Put them in a bowl and sprinkle with 40 g (1½ oz, 3 tablespoons) melted butter. Arrange in a roasting tin (pan) in a very thin, even layer. Brown in a preheated oven at 240°C (475°F, gas 9). Gently brown a 350 g (12 oz) monkfish tail in 15 g (½ oz, 1 tablespoon) butter. Add 4 shallots in their skins and cook in a preheated oven at 240°C (475°F, gas 9) for 10 minutes. Take the monkfish out of the oven and keep warm. Pour 3½ tablespoons vegetable or fish stock over the shallots. Return them to the oven for 5–10 minutes or until they have become tender. Remove their pulp and put with the cooking juices in a saucepan. Thicken with 25 g (1 oz, 2 tablespoons) butter. Add a few drops of lemon juice, salt and pepper.

Arrange the potatoes in a crown on a hot dish and place the monkfish on top. Strain the sauce through a chinois or fine sieve and pour over the fish.

Mullet

Baked red mullet à la livournaise

Gut (clean) 4 red mullet, make some light incisions on their backs, season with salt and pepper, and lay them head to tail in a buttered or oiled gratin dish. Cover with reduced tomato fondue or sauce, sprinkle with breadcrumbs and 2 tablespoons oil or melted butter, and bake in a preheated oven at 240°C (475°F, gas 9). When the top is brown (after about 15 minutes), add some chopped parsley and a few drops of lemon juice. Serve in the gratin dish.

Baked red mullet with fennel

Soften 25 g (1 oz, ¼ cup) chopped onion in oil, then add 1 tablespoon very finely chopped fresh fennel. Gut (clean) a mullet, make some light incisions on its back, and season with salt and pepper. Butter a small ovenproof dish, spread the base with the onion and lay the fish on top. Sprinkle with breadcrumbs and a little olive oil and bake in a preheated oven at 220°C (425°F, gas 7) for 25 minutes. Sprinkle with parsley and a little lemon juice.

Baked red mullet with shallots

Peel and chop 40 g (1½ oz, ¼ cup) shallots. Boil them in 250 ml (8 fl oz, 1 cup) dry white wine until almost all the liquid has evaporated, then spread the mixture into a buttered gratin dish. Gut (clean) 3 red mullet, dry them, make some incisions on their backs, season with salt and pepper, and lay them in the dish. Pour over 6 tablespoons dry white wine and dot with about 25 g (1 oz, 2 tablespoons) butter. Cook in a preheated oven at 230°C (450°F, gas 8) for 15 minutes, basting several times with the juices; add a little more white wine if necessary. Sprinkle with chopped parsley and a little lemon juice, and serve from the cooking dish.

Escalopes of red mullet with pissalat

Pissalat is an anchovy purée from the Nice region, flavoured with cloves, thyme, bay leaf and pepper and mixed with olive oil. Fillet 3 red mullet, each weighing about 200 g (7 oz). Season with salt and pepper and cook in a frying pan in 2–3 tablespoons olive oil and 25 g (1 oz, 2 tablespoons) butter. When cooked, remove and drain on paper towels. Arrange in a ring on a round serving dish. Prepare some beurre blanc and mix with some *pissalat*. Coat the fillets lightly with this sauce and garnish with small sprigs of chervil or cress.

Fillets of red mullet Girardet

Remove the fillets from 4 mullet weighing 225 g (8 oz) each. Reserve the livers. Heat 25 g (1 oz, 2 tablespoons) butter and brown the bones and the heads with 2 chopped shallots and some rosemary for 2 minutes. Moisten with a glass each of white wine and water and cook for 5 minutes. Strain this stock and reduce it by half. Stir in 250 ml (8 fl oz, 1 cup) double (heavy) cream and reduce again. Blend in the chopped livers, 20 g (¾ oz, 4½ teaspoons) butter, some salt and pepper, and the juice of ½ a lemon.

Heat a little butter in a clean frying pan. Put the fillets in, skin side down, cook for 45 seconds, then turn them and cook the other side for 30 seconds. Pour the sauce into a hot dish and place the fillets on top.

Fried red mullet

Gut (clean) some small mullet, dry them and make a few shallow incisions on their backs. Soak them for 30 minutes in salted boiled milk, then drain them, dip in flour and fry at 175°C (347°F). Drain on paper towels, arrange in a dish and garnish with lemon slices and fried parsley.

Grilled red mullet

Scale 800 g (1¾ lb) red mullet. Cook whole if they are small, but make some light incisions in the skin. Brush them with oil, applied with a small bunch of thyme or rosemary sprigs. Grill (broil) the fish under a moderate heat. Oil them lightly from time to time while cooking, using a herb brush. Turn them as few times as possible so as not to damage them. Sprinkle with salt and serve either as they are or accompanied by a béarnaise or Choron sauce or with melted butter.

A traditional Provençal method is to grill them without any previous preparation, complete with scales and fins, and without salt. They should be eaten, unsalted, when still barely cooked.

Grilled red mullet à l'italienne

Prepare 8 tablespoons Italian sauce and spread half of it over an oiled gratin dish. Clean and gut 4 red mullet, make some light incisions on their backs, season with pepper, grill (broil) them, then season with salt. Arrange them head to tail in the dish. Mask them with the rest of the sauce, sprinkle with breadcrumbs and a little oil, and brown under the grill. Sprinkle with parsley.

Grilled red mullet à la Bercy

Clean and remove the scales from some red mullet, making a shallow slit along the back of each one. Season with salt and pepper, brush with oil and grill (broil) gently. Arrange on a serving dish and top with half-melted Bercy butter. The fish may be marinated in a little olive oil with salt, pepper and chopped parsley before cooking.

Grilled red mullet à la niçoise

Clean, wash and dry the fish, season with salt and pepper, brush with olive oil and marinate for 30 minutes. Make a well-flavoured tomato fondue and boil down until very thick. Grill (broil) the mullet gently for 15 minutes. Cover the bottom of the serving dish with the tomato fondue (capers may be added if desired) and place the grilled fish on top. Garnish with strips of anchovy fillets in oil arranged in a lattice, and small black olives. Place a slice of lemon on the head of each fish.

Red mullet à l'orientale

Clean some very small red mullet, season with salt and pepper, dip them in flour and fry quickly in oil. Arrange them in a flameproof dish. Cover with a fondue of tomato lightly flavoured with saffron, fennel, thyme, a crumbled bay leaf, a few coriander seeds, chopped garlic and parsley. Bring to the boil, cover, then finish cooking in a preheated oven at 220°C (425°F, gas 7), for 6–8 minutes. Leave the fish to get cold in their cooking sauce. Garnish with thin slices of peeled lemon and sprinkle with chopped parsley; serve cold.

Red mullet à la nantaise

Put 150 ml (¼ pint, ⅔ cup) white wine and 2 or 3 finely chopped shallots into a pan and boil down to reduce. Trim and gut (clean) 4 mullet, but do not remove the livers. Wipe the fish, season with salt and pepper, brush with oil and grill (broil). Then remove the livers from the fish, mash them and beat them into the reduced sauce together with a few drops of lemon juice and about 50 g (2 oz, ¼ cup) butter. Pour the sauce into a long serving dish and arrange the grilled mullet on top. Garnish with slices of lemon.

Red mullet charlotte

Wash 1 kg (2¼ lb) aubergines (eggplants), dry them and cut each in half. Make cuts on the flesh, sprinkle with salt and leave for 1 hour so that the juice seeps out. During this time, skin and gut (clean) six 150 g (5 oz) red mullet. Retain the livers and remove the fillets. Drain the aubergines and wipe them. Brush them with olive oil and bake them in a preheated oven at 220°C (425°F, gas 7). When the pulp is completely soft, remove it with a spoon and reduce it to purée. Add the juice of 1 lemon and then stir it over a very gentle heat, adding 150 g (5 oz, ⅔ cup) butter, salt, pepper and 1 crushed garlic clove. Chop the mullet livers and add them gradually. Season the mullet fillets and fry them in olive oil. Drain them and use to line a buttered charlotte mould. Pour the filling into the mould and press down lightly with a plate. Place in the refrigerator for 2 hours. Serve with a tomato sauce.

Red mullet en papillotes

Clean 8 small red mullet, but leave the liver inside. Prepare a forcemeat with 5–6 slices of white bread dipped in milk, some parsley and 4 tablespoons anchovy butter. Season the fish with salt and pepper, stuff with the forcemeat, brush with olive oil and leave to marinate in a cool place for 1 hour. Place each fish on a rectangle of oiled greaseproof (wax) paper and close the papillotes. Cook in a preheated oven at 230°C (450°F, gas 8) for 15–20 minutes.

Red mullet grilled in cases

Grill (broil) some red mullet. Cut pieces of greaseproof (wax) paper large enough to enclose the fish and spread them with mushroom duxelles. Put a fish on each piece of paper and pour over some duxelles sauce; sprinkle with breadcrumbs and melted butter and brown in a preheated oven at 240°C (475°F, gas 9) for a few minutes.

Red mullet in a mille-feuille of cabbage with marrow

Descale and clean 12 red mullet weighing 120–150 g (4¼–5 oz), keeping the livers to one side. Lift the bones with tweezers and remove the gills. Finely chop 1 garlic head, then scald, cool and drain it. Dry it lightly in the oven, then caramelize it with a knob of butter, a little sugar and salt.

Blanch and cool the leaves of 2 green cabbages. Drain and cut 30 rounds, 7.5 cm (3 in) in diameter, avoiding the tough ribs. Cut the red mullet fillets into 2 or 3 thin slices. Cut 150 g (5 oz) blanched bone marrow into very fine slices. On each round of cabbage, arrange the equivalent of a fillet of fish and a slice of marrow. Season with salt and pepper. Allow 4 layers and 5 rounds of cabbage per mille-feuille, making 6 in all. Steam for 8–10 minutes.

Meanwhile, sweat the red mullet livers in 60 ml (2 fl oz, ¼ cup) olive oil and a little marrow. Pour a little fumet on top, correct the seasoning, add 50 g (2 oz, ¼ cup) butter and blend until smooth at the last moment. Place a mille-feuille in the middle of each plate and pour the juice around it. Sprinkle with a pinch of salt, pepper and garlic on top. Garnish with flat-leaf parsley.

Red mullet poached à la nage with basil

Prepare the sauce in advance: finely chop 20 fresh basil leaves, 5 tarragon leaves and 5 sprigs of parsley. Peel and chop a tomato. Marinate these ingredients with a little garlic in 250 ml (8 fl oz, 1 cup) extra-virgin olive oil. Add a few drops of wine vinegar and season with salt and pepper.

On the day of the meal, prepare an aromatic poaching liquid. Finely snip a bunch of chives and dice the flesh of 1 lemon. Squeeze the juice of 1 lemon.

Chop or dice 400 g (14 oz) carrots, 1 medium leek and 300 g (11 oz) celeriac or 2 celery sticks. Bring to the boil 400 ml (14 fl oz, 1¾ cups) fish stock, lightly seasoned with salt and pepper, with 200 ml (7 fl oz, ¾ cup) white wine. Add the vegetables, 4 sprigs lemon thyme and the lemon juice. Bring back to the boil, then reduce the heat. Cook this nage for 30 minutes. Meanwhile, scale 4 red mullet, each weighing 175–200 g (6–7 oz), but do not gut (clean) them. Place a slice of orange, a slice of lemon and a bay leaf on each fish and wrap in foil. Cook the fish gently in the poaching liquid for about 10 minutes; they should still be firm and have retained their shape. Serve with the sauce.

Red mullet with jasmine

Gut, trim and clean the mullet. Remove the backbone. Stuff the fish with a mousse made of whiting flesh bound with cream and flavoured with essence (extract) of jasmine. Wrap in buttered paper and cook in a preheated oven at 180°C (350°F, gas 4) for 25 minutes. Take the fish out of their wrappings and arrange them on a hot dish. Cover with a tomato-flavoured white wine sauce.

Perch

Perch fillets with risotto à la piémontaise

Make a risotto à la piémontaise with 250 g (9 oz, 1¼ cups) rice. Wash the fillets of 4 perches and pat dry with paper towels. Coat in breadcrumbs and fry on both sides in butter. Butter an oval serving dish and put the risotto in it. Arrange the perch fillets on top. Garnish with lemon quarters.

Pike

Consommé à l'amiral

Lightly thicken a fish consommé with arrowroot and garnish with small pike quenelles in crayfish butter, poached oyster halves, julienne of truffles cooked in Madeira and sprigs of chervil.

Pike au beurre blanc (1)

Gut (clean) the pike, clean it carefully and cut off the fins and tail. Prepare a court-bouillon in a fish kettle and boil for about 30 minutes. Add the pike. As soon as the court-bouillon starts to boil again, reduce the temperature to keep it at a barely perceptible simmer. After 12–20 minutes remove the fish kettle from the heat.

Meanwhile, prepare the *beurre blanc*: boil down some vinegar containing 2–3 chopped shallots and freshly ground pepper (one turn of the pepper mill); when it has reduced by half remove from the heat. Soften a large piece of butter – about 225 g (8 oz, 1 cup) to 2 tablespoons reduced vinegar – on a plate using a spatula and incorporate it gradually into the vinegar, beating vigorously with a whisk. It will turn frothy without becoming liquid and will acquire its characteristic whiteness. Drain the pike, arrange on a long dish and coat with the *beurre blanc*, adding fresh sprigs of parsley. Alternatively, serve the *beurre blanc* separately in a sauceboat.

Pike au beurre blanc (2)

Wash the pike in plenty of water, sprinkle with fine salt and leave for about 15 minutes. Wash again and place in the fish kettle, surrounded with parsley,

2 sliced onions, 2 quartered shallots, 2 garlic cloves, 8–20 chives or the green part of a leek, a sprig of fresh thyme, a bay leaf and a few slices of carrot; season with salt and pepper. Cover with sprigs of parsley and add enough dry white wine to cover the whole fish. Leave to marinate for 1 hour. About 35 minutes before serving, place the fish kettle over a high heat; as soon as it begins to bubble, reduce the heat and simmer as gently as possible.

While it is cooking, prepare a *beurre blanc* as in Pike au beurre blanc (1), using 250 g (9 oz, 1 cup) slightly salted butter. Keep the *beurre blanc* warm in a bain marie and do not allow to boil. Trim the pike, drain for a few seconds on a cloth and place on a long, very hot dish. Using the blade of a knife, quickly slit the middle of the side, from the head to the tail, following the lateral line. Detach and remove the main bone, holding the head in the left hand, then reshape the fish. Quickly stir the *beurre blanc* with a spatula to mix the shallots in well, pour over the pike and serve.

Pike au bleu

This method is used mostly for cooking young or very small pike. Cook the fish in a court-bouillon containing a high proportion of vinegar. Drain, place on a napkin and garnish with fresh parsley. Serve with melted butter or with one of the sauces recommended for poached fish. To accompany the fish serve boiled potatoes, various vegetable purées (celery, turnip, onion), leaf spinach or broccoli.

Pike du meunier

Scale, beard, gut (clean), remove the heads from, and wash 3 young pike, each weighing 675–800 g (1½–1¾ lb). Cut into pieces and season; dip in milk and then flour. Cook gently in a sauté pan with 200 g (7 oz, ¾ cup) butter and 1 tablespoon oil. Separately, soften 4 medium chopped onions in butter.

When the pieces of pike are lightly coloured, add the onions and 3 table-spoons very good white wine vinegar. Reduce by half. Season with salt and pepper and serve each portion with 2 croûtons cooked in butter.

Pike in vinegar

Take a pike weighing about 1.5 kg (3 lb). Remove the fillets and season with salt and pepper, then dust with flour. Heat some butter in a frying pan and brown the fish fillets on both sides. Drain them, arrange on a long dish, sprinkle with chopped parsley and lemon juice, and keep them hot. Deglaze the pan with white wine vinegar; reduce, add 3 tablespoons fresh double (heavy) cream, and bind with a little béchamel. Pour the sauce over the fillets. Serve with a sprinkling of chopped parsley.

Pike quenelles

Fillet a pike weighing about 1.25 kg (2¾ lb). Remove the skin and take out the bones, then weigh the flesh – there should be about 400 g (14 oz). Finely mince or pound the flesh, then put it in the refrigerator.

Prepare a panada: bring 300 ml (½ pint, 1¼ cups) water to the boil, adding a generous pinch of salt. Remove from the heat and sift in 150 g (5 oz, 1¼ cups) plain (all-purpose) flour through a sieve; stir vigorously until smooth, then continue to stir over heat until the mixture dries out, taking care that it does not stick to the bottom of the pan. Remove from the heat and beat in 1 whole egg; leave the mixture to get cold, then refrigerate. When the panada is well chilled, process in a blender until it is quite smooth.

Cream 200 g (7 oz, ¾ cup) butter. Put the pike flesh into a bowl placed in another bowl full of crushed ice; season with salt and pepper, then work it with a wooden spoon until it is smooth. Now mix in the panada, 1 whole egg and 4 yolks (one by one), and finally the butter: the mixture should be uniformly blended and smooth. (If all the ingredients are really cold, this last stage can be carried out in a blender, as long as it is powerful enough to work quickly without heating; the blender goblet itself should have been cooled in the refrigerator.) Chill the mixture for 30 minutes. Shape the quenelles, using 2 spoons dipped in hot water, and place on a lightly floured surface. Bring 2 litres (3½ pints, 9 cups) salted water to the boil and poach the quenelles for 15 minutes, without letting the water boil. Drain them and leave to get cold, then finish according to the chosen recipe.

Pike quenelles à la florentine

Prepare some pike quenelles, spinach in cream, and a béchamel sauce enriched with cream: 100 ml (4 fl oz, 7 tablespoons) crème fraîche to 400 ml (14 fl oz, 1¾ cups) béchamel sauce; the sauce should be very thick. Butter a gratin dish and spread the spinach over the bottom of the dish. Arrange the quenelles on top, mask them with the béchamel sauce, sprinkle with grated cheese and dot with pieces of butter. Brown the quenelles in a preheated oven at 230°C (450°F, gas 8).

Pike quenelles à la lyonnaise

Prepare 575 g (1¼ lb) *godiveau lyonnais* and use it to make some quenelles. Make a béchamel sauce with 100 g (4 oz, ½ cup) butter, 1.5 litres (2¾ pints, 6½ cups) milk, 100 g (4 oz, 1 cup) plain (all-purpose) flour, a pinch each of grated nutmeg, salt and pepper, and enrich with 200 ml (7 fl oz, ¾ cup) double (heavy) cream.

Butter a gratin dish and pour in a quarter of the béchamel sauce. Arrange the quenelles on top, cover them with the remaining sauce and dot with small pieces of butter. Cook the quenelles in a preheated oven at 190°C (375°F, gas 5) for 15 minutes (they will swell a great deal). Serve at once.

Pike quenelles mousseline

Work 500 g (18 oz) pike flesh together with 1 teaspoon salt, a pinch of white pepper and a pinch of grated nutmeg in a blender, then add 3 egg whites one by one. When the mixture is smooth, pour into a bowl and chill in the refrigerator. Also refrigerate 600 ml (1 pint, 2½ cups) crème fraîche and the blender goblet. When the fish mixture is cold, pour it back into the blender goblet, add 250 ml (8 fl oz, 1 cup) of the chilled crème fraîche and blend for a few seconds until it is thoroughly incorporated. Add a further 200 ml (7 fl oz, ¾ cup) crème fraîche, blend again, then repeat with the remaining crème fraîche. Shape the mixture into quenelles and poach as for ordinary pike quenelles.

Quenelles Nantua

Make some pike quenelles and poach them. Melt 40 g (1½ oz, 3 tablespoons) butter in a flameproof casserole and add 40 g (1½ oz, ⅓ cup) plain (all-purpose) flour. Cook for 1 minute, stirring with a whisk, without allowing the mixture to colour. Season 500 ml (17 fl oz, 2 cups) milk with salt, pepper and nutmeg and bring to the boil. Add 250 ml (8 fl oz, 1 cup) double (heavy) cream. Add this mixture to the cooled butter-flour mixture. Add 1 medium-sized onion, studded with 2 cloves. Simmer for 30 minutes over a low heat. Strain and add 75 g (3 oz, 6 tablespoons) crayfish or lobster butter and whisk to incorporate.

Wash 250 g (9 oz) mushrooms and cut into quarters. Cook for 4–5 minutes in a little lemon-flavoured, salted water. Pour the sauce into a gratin dish (or individual gratin dishes). Arrange the quenelles and add some shelled crayfish or prawns (shrimps). For a crisp crust, sprinkle with breadcrumbs and pour 50 g (2 oz, ¼ cup) melted butter on top. Bake in a preheated oven at 180°C (350°F, gas 4) for about 15 minutes.

Alternatively, freshly cooked quenelles can be served with crayfish or prawns in the sauce without the gratin topping and mushrooms. Part-shelled crayfish and a little mayonnaise may be added as a garnish.

Terrine of pike with Nantua sauce

Cut the fillets from a pike weighing about 1.5 kg (3¼ lb) and remove the skin. Cut the fillets from the belly into narrow strips, then into dice.

Prepare a frangipane; mix 100 g (4 oz, 1 cup) plain (all-purpose) flour, 40 g (1½ oz, 3 tablespoons) butter and 3 egg yolks with 200 ml (7 fl oz, ¾ cup) hot milk. Work this over the heat, until the dough collects in a ball around the spatula, then spread it on a buttered plate to cool. Clean and finely chop 100 g (4 oz, 1⅓ cups) button mushrooms and chop 4 or 5 shallots.

Brown the diced pike in butter in a frying pan, then add the mushrooms and brown; finally add the shallots, but do not allow them to change colour. Remove all ingredients with a skimming spoon and pour 100 ml (4 fl oz, 7 tablespoons) good dry white wine into the frying pan, stir with a spatula to deglaze, then replace the ingredients and add 25 g (1 oz, ½ cup) chopped parsley. Remove from the heat.

Pound or finely chop the remaining pike flesh – about 500 g (18 oz) – and season liberally with salt and pepper. Add the cooled frangipane in small pieces, then 3 unwhisked egg whites. Mix well, then pass twice through the mincer (or chop finely in a food processor). Beat with 350 ml (12 fl oz, 1½ cups) double (heavy) cream and add the diced fish, mushrooms and shallots.

Generously butter a flameproof pâté dish or terrine and heap the mixture into it. Cover and place in a bain marie. Bring to the boil on top of the stove, then place in a preheated oven at 180°C (350°F, gas 4) and cook gently for about 1½ hours. The top of the terrine should turn pale gold, but not brown. Serve the terrine in the container in which it was cooked, with Nantua sauce.

Pike-perch

Fillets of pike-perch with cabbage

Trim and clean a pike-perch weighing about 1.5 kg (3¼ lb). Remove the 2 fillets, trim and wash them, then cut each in half.

Prepare the flavourings for a court-bouillon: a carrot, a celery stick, 2 small white young onions, a shallot, a garlic clove, a bouquet garni with a sprig of tarragon, a sage leaf and the green part of a leek added, and a muslin (cheesecloth) bag containing 3 lightly crushed peppercorns, a clove, a star anise and 2 coriander seeds. Put all these ingredients in a large saucepan with 1½ teaspoons coarse sea salt and 500 ml (17 fl oz, 2 cups) water, boil for 5 minutes and leave to cool.

Cut away the thick ribs from the leaves of a small green cabbage weighing 675–800 g (1½–1¾ lb), wash the leaves and blanch for 8 minutes in boiling water. Drain, squeeze in a sieve and keep warm.

Prepare the sauce: in a large bowl put ½ teaspoon table salt, a pinch of freshly ground pepper and 4 tablespoons wine vinegar; beat in 150 ml (¼ pint, ⅔ cup) olive oil and keep in a warm place.

Arrange the pike-perch fillets in a fish kettle, on top of the vegetables from the court-bouillon, and just cover with the cooled court-bouillon; add 100 ml (4 fl oz, 7 tablespoons) spirit vinegar and the juice of half a lemon. Bring to the boil, cover, remove from the heat and leave to poach for 5–8 minutes. Arrange the cabbage leaves in the serving dish. Lift out the fillets with a fish slice, removing any vegetables, and arrange on top of the cabbage. Pour the sauce over and sprinkle with 3 small young onions, finely chopped, and 1 tablespoon chopped chives.

Marinated pike-perch with cardoons

Finely chop 5 garlic cloves, a small bunch of parsley and 2 thyme sprigs. Mix with the juice of 2 lemons and 150 ml (¼ pint, ⅔ cup) olive oil in a shallow dish. Lay 4 pike-perch cutlets in the dish, turning once in the marinade to make sure they are well coated. Cover and leave in a cold place for 2–3 hours.

Trim 2 kg (4½ lb) cardoon stalks and cut them into 2.5–5 cm (1–2 in) lengths. Cook the cardoons in boiling salted water, adding a little lemon juice, for 1 hour. Peel 300 g (11 oz) pickling onions and brown them gently in butter, turning occasionally so that they are evenly glazed. Set the onions aside to keep hot. Drain the cardoons and return them to the pan; add a knob of butter and keep them hot.

Remove the fish cutlets from the marinade. Pour the marinade into a saucepan and heat it gently, then cover and leave to infuse over a low heat for about 30 minutes, stirring occasionally. Grill (broil) the fish cutlets until golden on both sides. Arrange the buttered cardoons on a serving platter or individual plates and top with the fish cutlets. Add the glazed onions, then spoon the sauce over the fish and vegetables.

Pike-perch and oyster-mushroom salad

Peel and wash 675 g (1½ lb) oyster mushrooms; slice thinly, sauté briskly in 100 ml (4 fl oz, 7 tablespoons) olive oil with salt and pepper and drain. Gently heat 2 tablespoons vinaigrette with 2 tablespoons cream until warm; add the mushrooms and a vegetable julienne made from 1 carrot, ¼ celeriac, 100 g (4 oz) French (green) beans and 1 turnip, all stewed in butter. Season 4 fillets of pike-perch, each weighing 200 g (7 oz), and cook in a covered dish in a preheated oven at 180°C (350°F, gas 4) for about 20 minutes. Serve with the oyster-mushroom salad, pouring a few drops of vinegar over each fillet just before serving.

Plaice

Plaice à la florentine

Clean a large plaice, put it in a buttered dish, add equal quantities of white wine and concentrated fish stock (or court-bouillon), and bake in a preheated oven at 160°C (325°F, gas 3) for 35 minutes, basting frequently. Drain. Cover the bottom of an ovenproof serving dish with spinach braised in butter and lay the plaice on it, cover with Mornay sauce, sprinkle with grated cheese and clarified butter, and glaze quickly in a preheated oven at 240°C (475°F, gas 9).

Roe & caviar

Barquettes of roe

Bake some small barquettes blind and leave to cool. Mix a skinned smoked cod or grey mullet roe with an equal quantity of butter. Add some finely grated lemon peel, using 1 lemon for 250 g (9 oz, 1 cup) roe mixture. Fill the barquettes and garnish with fluted half-slices of lemon. Chill for 1 hour.

Canapés with caviar

Spread fresh butter on some round slices of bread and garnish with caviar. Sprinkle each with a little lemon juice and a pinch of chopped chives. Very thick soured (sour) cream may be used instead of butter if desired.

Croûtes à la livonienne

Cut some slices of bread and remove the crusts. Lightly fry them in butter. Reduce to a purée some cooked soft herring roes, add to the purée an equal volume of béchamel sauce and coat the croûtes with the mixture. Place on each croûte a spoonful of a salpicon of finely diced kipper fillets and dessert apples, flavoured with lemon. Sprinkle with fine breadcrumbs, which have been fried in butter, and brown in a preheated oven at 220°C (425°F, gas 7).

Grilled roes

Season some fish roes (whiting, cod or salmon) with salt and pepper. Brush with oil, sprinkle with a little lemon juice and leave them for 30 minutes. Then either brush them with clarified butter and grill (broil) gently, or fry in butter over a gentle heat. Serve with rye bread, butter and lemon.

Pannequets with soft roes

Poach some herring soft roes (or other if preferred), drain, cool and cut them into a salpicon. Prepare 8 savoury pannequets, 4 tablespoons mushroom duxelles and 300 ml (½ pint, 1¼ cups) well-reduced béchamel sauce or thin velouté. Mix the duxelles with the béchamel sauce and add the soft roes.

Make 8 fairly thick savoury pancakes, spread with the roe mixture and fold each in four. Place in a buttered ovenproof dish. Sprinkle with fresh breadcrumbs fried in butter with a little grated Parmesan cheese added, and brown under a hot grill (broiler) or in a preheated oven at 230°C (450°F, gas 8) for about 10 minutes.

Poached soft roes in court-bouillon

Soak the roes in cold water for 2 hours, then remove the small blood vessels that run down the sides. Prepare a simple court-bouillon with cold water, a little lemon juice, salt and oil – 2 tablespoons for every 500 ml (17 fl oz, 2 cups) water. Put the roes in this liquid, bring slowly to a very gentle simmer and poach for about 4 minutes. Drain and cool.

Soft roes à la meunière

Soak the roes and blot them dry with paper towels. Coat them with flour, shake off any excess and fry in butter seasoned with salt and pepper. Sprinkle with lemon juice.

Soft roes à l'anglaise

Poach the roes in a court-bouillon and allow to cool. Coat them in flour, then dip them in egg and breadcrumbs. Fry in butter, browning on both sides. Arrange on a serving dish and sprinkle with a mixture of melted butter and lemon juice. Garnish with half slices of lemon.

Soft-roe barquettes

Cook some shortcrust (basic pie dough) or puff pastry barquette cases – small boat-shaped tartlets. Poach some soft roe (carp, herring or mackerel) in court-bouillon. Finely chop and sauté some mushrooms. Prepare a small quantity of béchamel sauce. Fill the bottom of each barquette with mushrooms. Place one piece of roe in each barquette. Coat the barquettes with béchamel sauce, sprinkle with grated Gruyère cheese and brown under the grill (broiler).

Soft roes in noisette butter

Poach the roes in a court-bouillon, dry on paper towels and arrange on a long dish. Sprinkle with capers and chopped parsley, together with a little lemon juice. Top with a few tablespoons of noisette butter.

Alternatively, the lemon juice may be replaced with a few drops of vinegar, and the chopped parsley with 2 tablespoons chervil, which are added to the noisette butter.

Soft roes in scallop shells à la normande

Poach the roes in a court-bouillon and drain them. Put them in scallop shells edged with a border of duchess potatoes, previously browned in the oven. Top the roes in each shell with a poached drained oyster, a cooked mushroom and 1 scant tablespoon shrimps and mussels. Coat with normande, Mornay or butter sauce, and garnish each shell with a generous strip of truffle.

Soft roes of herring with verjuice

Verjuice is the acid juice extracted from large unripened grapes or crab-apples. Soak 800 g (1¾ lb) soft roes of herring for 1 hour in cold water with 100 ml (4 fl oz, 7 tablespoons) white wine vinegar. Drain and wipe. Season with salt and pepper, coat with flour, shaking off any excess, then prick with a needle to prevent them from bursting during cooking. Heat 40 g (1½ oz, 3 tablespoons) butter and 3 tablespoons oil in a frying pan. Carefully place the roes in the hot fat and cook for 3–4 minutes on each side.

Heat 75 g (3 oz, 6 tablespoons) butter in a separate frying pan and brown 75 g (3 oz, 1 cup) diced mushrooms and an equal quantity of diced sour apples for 4 minutes. Then add 75 g (3 oz) diced tomatoes, cook for 1 minute and add 50 g (2 oz) capers, salt and pepper. Arrange the roes on warmed plates, sprinkle with 50 g (2 oz, 1 cup) small sprigs of parsley and garnish with the browned vegetables.

Remove the fat from the pan in which the roes were cooked and add, over a brisk heat, 3 tablespoons cider vinegar and an equal quantity of verjuice. Bring to the boil and pour over the roes.

Salmon

Canapés with smoked salmon

Butter some slices of bread and garnish with slices of smoked salmon cut to the size of the bread. Garnish each canapé with half a slice of fluted lemon.

Chaud-froid of salmon

Poach some slices or steaks of salmon very gently in a plentiful and well-seasoned fish stock: this is later used for making the brown chaud-froid sauce.

When the slices are cooked (they must still be slightly firm), leave them to cool in the stock, then drain them on a rack. Prepare a chaud-froid sauce with the strained stock, keeping it fluid, and coat the slices of salmon with it in three successive applications. After the last, garnish with round slices of truffle or black (ripe) olives and small decorative shapes cut from a green pepper. Glaze with very light aspic.

Cold poached salmon

Poach a whole salmon (or some salmon steaks) in a court-bouillon or a fish fumet and leave to cool in the liquid. Drain the fish, wipe it and arrange on a large dish, garnished with parsley. Alternatively, the skin can be removed and the fish garnished with lettuce hearts, hard-boiled (hard-cooked) eggs or stuffed vegetables, such as cherry tomatoes or slices of cucumber.

The following garnishes are also suitable: small pieces of aspic, prawns (shrimp) or crayfish tails, lobster medallions, a macédoine of vegetables, or small barquettes or cooked artichoke hearts filled with caviar, mousse or a seafood filling.

The cold poached salmon may be served with any one of the following sauces: Andalusian, Chantilly, green, gribiche, mayonnaise, ravigote, rémoulade or Vincent.

Alternatively, the poached salmon can be drained and served hot, with the skin removed, and accompanied by hot melted butter, beurre blanc or a white wine sauce.

Cold salmon cutlets à la parisienne

Poach some thick slices of salmon in court-bouillon and allow them to cool. Cut each slice into two. Cover the serving dish with a macédoine of vegetables in mayonnaise, arrange the half-slices on it and coat them with mayonnaise thickened with gelatine. Between the cutlets arrange some bunches of asparagus tips, some carrots cut into pod shapes and some chopped French (green) beans, all these vegetables being first cooked in salted water and well drained. A thin slice of truffle may be placed on each cutlet.

Colombines of salmon Nantua

Rub the following ingredients through a sieve: 125 g (4½ oz) raw pounded salmon, 125 g (4½ oz) bread soaked in milk and squeezed, 2 whole eggs and 120 ml (4½ fl oz, ½ cup) whipping or double (heavy) cream. Mix them together over ice, season with salt and pepper, and add a little grated nutmeg. Prepare large dumplings with the mixture and poach them in Nantua sauce.

Escalope of salmon with Gigondas

Gently boil 500 ml (17 fl oz, 2 cups) Gigondas wine until reduced by three-quarters. Add 500 ml (17 fl oz, 2 cups) well-reduced fish fumet, 1 chopped tomato, 1 thinly sliced mushroom and 2 thinly sliced shallots. Reduce again until almost dry, then whisk a large piece of crayfish butter into the liquid.

Prepare a fondue with 150 g (5 oz) finely chopped spring onions (scallions) by cooking them gently in butter until they are reduced to a pulp. Poach 1 very large escalope of salmon, weighing about 150 g (5 oz), until just cooked. Drain it and then fry it in butter. Arrange the onion fondue on a plate, lay the salmon escalope on top and pour a ribbon of sauce around it.

Escalopes of raw salmon with pepper

Brush a cold plate lightly with olive oil and lay some thin raw escalopes (scallops) of salmon on it. Brush the escalopes with olive oil. Season with salt and pepper, then sprinkle with crushed green peppercorns. Serve very cold.

Escalopes of salmon

Cut some raw salmon fillets into escalopes (scallops), weighing about 100 g (4 oz) each. Flatten them lightly and trim if necessary. Any of the recipes using salmon cutlets and steaks can be followed for escalopes.

Escalopes of salmon with carrots

Cook 2 sliced carrots in a frying pan with some fish fumet, a little dry vermouth and some paprika. When cooked *al dente*, remove the carrots and set aside. Add 1 tablespoon green peppercorns and 200 ml (7 fl oz, ¾ cup) double (heavy) cream to the frying pan, season with salt and pepper, then boil to reduce. Arrange some raw escalopes (scallops) of salmon with the carrots on hot buttered plates. Coat with the hot sauce and serve at once.

Fried salmon steaks

Season some salmon steaks, 2 cm (¾ in) thick, with salt and pepper. Dust well with flour and deep-fry quickly in oil at 180°C (350°F) until golden brown. Serve with lemon or lime wedges.

Glazed salmon à la parisienne

Place a whole salmon in a fish stock, bring to the boil and simmer for 7–8 minutes. Leave it to cool in the cooking stock, then drain it and remove the skin and bones without breaking the flesh. Pat dry with paper towels. Coat it several times with half-set aspic jelly (prepared from the cooking stock), putting the fish in the refrigerator between applications. Cover the serving dish with a layer of aspic. When the aspic is set, arrange the salmon on top.

Prepare a vegetable macédoine mixed with thick mayonnaise and use it to stuff some small round tomatoes. Halve some hard-boiled (hard-cooked) eggs. Sieve the yolks , mix with some mayonnaise and pipe into the whites. Garnish the border of the dish with the tomatoes, eggs and slices of lemon.

Glazed salmon cutlets with a vegetable macédoine

Prepare, cook and glaze some salmon cutlets as in the recipe for glazed salmon cutlets with Chambertin, but replace the Chambertin with white wine or champagne. Arrange the cutlets in a circle on a round dish and fill the centre with a macédoine of vegetables in thick mayonnaise. Strips of anchovy fillets or small green asparagus tips may be added to this salad.

Glazed salmon cutlets with Chambertin

Cut the salmon into slices about 2.5 cm (1 in) thick and halve each slice. Shape the halves into cutlets and arrange on a buttered dish. Season with salt and pepper and add enough fish aspic stock, made with Chambertin, to cover the cutlets. Poach very gently for 8–10 minutes, then drain and wipe. Allow to cool completely. Clarify the stock, then cool it, but do not allow it to set. Arrange the cutlets on a rack over a dish and coat them with several layers of aspic, placing the dish in the refrigerator between each application. Put a thin layer of aspic to set on the serving dish and lay the cutlets on top.

Glazed salmon en bellevue

Prepare and poach the salmon whole in a concentrated fish stock. Allow to cool completely in the cooking liquor, then drain. Remove the skin from both sides and dry the fish gently with paper towels. Clarify the stock to make an aspic jelly and glaze the salmon with several coats, allowing each coat to set in the refrigerator before applying the next. Coat the bottom of the serving dish with a thin layer of aspic and lay the glazed salmon on top. Garnish with diced or cut shapes of aspic and keep in a cool place until ready to serve. (Salmon steaks and fillets can be prepared in the same way.)

Grilled salmon steaks

Season some salmon steaks, 2.5–5 cm (1–2 in) thick, with salt and pepper. Brush them with olive oil and cook gently under a moderate grill (broiler). Serve with maître d'hôtel butter, béarnaise sauce or gooseberry sauce.

Marinated salmon

Fillet a fresh Scottish salmon and cut the fillets into very thin escalopes (scallops). Prepare a marinade with 1 part olive oil to 2 parts lemon juice and add some salt, pepper and 1 tablespoon chopped herbs (chives, chervil and tarragon). Marinate the escalopes for a maximum of 3 minutes. Make a sauce with a little whipped crème fraîche, some salt and pepper, and 1 teaspoon Meaux mustard. Drain the slices of salmon and arrange them on a serving dish. Serve the sauce separately.

Mille-feuille of salmon au beurre rosé

Cut some thinly rolled puff pastry into 4 rectangles measuring 10 × 7 cm (4 × 2¾ in) and bake them in a preheated oven at 220°C (425°F, gas 7) for 15 minutes. Arrange some thin slices of fresh uncooked salmon on 3 of the pastry rectangles and place them on top of each other, spreading each layer with a mixture of cream and lemon juice seasoned with chopped tarragon, salt and pepper. Cover with the fourth pastry rectangle and bake for 5–10 minutes, then cool. Blend some butter with a little cream and mix in a little cranberry compote or cranberry sauce. Coat the mille-feuille with this butter.

Minute steaks of salmon with aigrelette sauce

Butter some small ovenproof plates and sprinkle with salt and pepper. Place a salmon escalope (scallop) on each plate (the escalopes should be large enough to cover the plates completely). Just before serving, put the plates into a very hot oven for 2–3 minutes. Meanwhile, prepare a mayonnaise with wine vinegar and lemon juice, dilute it with fish fumet and season with salt, pepper, chopped chives and tarragon. Serve the cooked escalopes with this sauce.

Poached salmon steaks

Place some salmon steaks, 4 cm (1½ in) thick, in enough court-bouillon or fish fumet to cover them. Bring to the boil, simmer for 5 minutes, then remove from the heat and drain. Serve the steaks topped with pats of butter flavoured with lemon, parsley, chives or tarragon. Alternatively, dress with melted clarified butter flavoured with lemon zest and juice, maître d'hôtel butter or beurre blanc.

Raw salmon with red new potatoes

Cover a 2 kg (4½ lb) salmon fillet with coarse salt and leave for a few hours. Rinse well and pat dry. Place in a large dish. Mix 500 ml (17 fl oz, 2 cups) groundnut (peanut) oil, 500 ml (17 fl oz, 2 cups) olive oil, 4 chopped red onions, 2 thinly sliced carrots, 15 juniper berries, 10 black peppercorns and 5 small bay leaves. Pour over the salmon. Cover and marinate for 24 hours.

Cook 500 g (18 oz) red new potatoes in boiling water. Slice them and season with coarse salt and thyme leaves. Drain the salmon and cut into slices across the grain. Arrange these on plates with the potato slices. Dress with a little of the marinade and garnish with thyme sprigs.

Rillettes of salmon

Put a bouquet garni, some salt and pepper, a sliced carrot and a sliced onion in a saucepan with a little water. Boil gently for 20 minutes. Add a thick piece of fresh salmon and poach very gently in the stock for 10 minutes. Leave to cool, then drain. Trim the fish and flake it with a fork.

Cut 100 g (4 oz) smoked salmon into dice. Mix both types of salmon thoroughly with 1 egg yolk, 125 g (4½ oz, ½ cup) butter and 1 tablespoon olive oil. Place in an earthenware dish and leave overnight in the refrigerator before serving.

Salmon aiguillettes

Cut some raw salmon fillets into thin strips (*aiguillettes*) and cook them as for salmon cutlets, steaks or escalopes (scallops). The strips can also be dipped in batter and deep-fried.

Salmon brochettes with fresh duck liver

Prepare the brochettes by threading cubes of raw salmon and slightly larger cubes of fresh duck liver alternately on to skewers. Arrange the brochettes, without overlapping, on a julienne of vegetables in an ovenproof dish, and season with salt and pepper.

Boil some dry white wine and some shallots in a saucepan until reduced by half. Add an equal quantity of double (heavy) cream and boil for 5 minutes. Pour the sauce over the brochettes and cook in a preheated oven at

190°C (375°F, gas 5) for 10 minutes. Drain the brochettes and put them on a hot dish. Reduce the sauce, add some truffle juice then whisk with 3 egg yolks in a bain marie until light and fluffy. Pour it over the brochettes.

Salmon cooked in champagne

Prepare a fish fumet with 1 carrot, 1 onion, 25 g (1 oz, 2 tablespoons) butter, 400 g (14 oz) fish bones (preferably without skin), a bouquet garni, 300 ml (½ pint, 1¼ cups) white wine and 200 ml (7 fl oz, ¾ cup) water. Simmer for 30 minutes and then strain.

Prepare a blond roux with 50 g (2 oz, ¼ cup) butter and 40 g (1½ oz, ⅓ cup) plain (all-purpose) flour and then add the fish stock. Bring the sauce to the boil, stirring continuously, and cook for 15 minutes over a low heat.

Gut (clean) a salmon weighing about 2 kg (4½ lb). Butter a large flameproof dish and sprinkle it with salt, pepper and 3 chopped shallots. Place the salmon in the dish and add 500 ml (17 fl oz, 2 cups) champagne. Begin cooking the fish on the hob (stove top) and then transfer to a preheated oven at 220°C (425°F, gas 7) and cook for 20 minutes. Drain the salmon and place it on an ovenproof serving dish.

Boil the cooking juices until reduced by a quarter and add to the sauce. Heat through, remove from the heat and beat in 2 egg yolks mixed with 2 tablespoons double (heavy) cream. Season with salt and pepper and strain. Coat the salmon with some of the sauce and glaze it in a very hot oven for about 5 minutes. Serve at once with the remainder of the sauce in a sauceboat.

Salmon cutlets

Trim some halved salmon steaks into the shape of cutlets and fry them in butter, with or without a coating of breadcrumbs. Serve the cutlets as they are, sprinkled with the cooking butter, or with a sauce and garnish.

Salmon cutlets can also be made with a croquette mixture fashioned into the shape of cutlets. Coat these cutlets with beaten egg and breadcrumbs, fry in butter and serve coated with a sauce and garnished.

Salmon cutlets can also be prepared with a salmon quenelle mixture, put into cutlet-shaped moulds and poached. They are served as a hot appetizer coated with sauce.

Salmon cutlets à l'anglaise

Trim some halved salmon steaks into cutlet shapes and season with salt and pepper. Dust with flour, dip into egg beaten with 1 tablespoon oil and some salt and pepper, and coat them with fresh white breadcrumbs. Brown the cutlets on both sides in clarified butter. Arrange them on a serving dish and coat them with slightly softened maître d'hôtel butter. Place a slice of lemon (with the peel removed) on each cutlet, and surround them with cannelled half-slices of lemon.

Salmon cutlets à la bourguignonne

Poach some salmon cutlets, together with some button mushrooms, in a fish fumet made with red wine. Drain the fish and arrange it on a serving dish with the mushrooms. Garnish with glazed baby (pearl) onions. Reduce the cooking liquid and thicken it with beurre manié. Strain the sauce and pour over the fish.

Salmon cutlets à la florentine

Cook some salmon cutlets in a reduced fish stock (just enough to cover them). Coarsely chop some spinach and cook it gently in butter; season with salt and pepper. Drain thoroughly and place on a flameproof serving dish. Drain the cutlets and arrange them on the bed of spinach. Coat the cutlets with Mornay sauce, sprinkle with some grated cheese and a little melted butter and brown under a hot grill (broiler). Serve immediately.

Salmon cutlets à la russe

Cut fresh salmon steaks in two lengthways to make the cutlets; poach them for 5 minutes in a court-bouillon. Let them cool completely in their juices, then drain, dry and glaze them with aspic.

To serve place a layer of shredded lettuce dressed with vinaigrette on a large serving dish and arrange the salmon cutlets on top. Garnish with very small lettuce hearts, quartered hard-boiled (hard-cooked) eggs, black (ripe) olives, capers and anchovy fillets in oil.

Salmon cutlets Pojarski

Pojarski is the term for a method of preparing veal chops, removing the meat from the bone and chopping then reshaping it on the bones before frying the resulting 'cutlets'. The term has been extended to cover chicken and salmon cutlets.

Chop 300 g (11 oz) fresh salmon flesh, then add 65 g (2½ oz, ⅔ cup) stale breadcrumbs (soaked in milk and strained) and 65 g (2½ oz, 5 tablespoons) fresh butter. Season with salt and pepper and sprinkle with a pinch of grated nutmeg. Divide the mixture into 4 equal portions and shape into cutlets. Coat with breadcrumbs and brown on both sides in clarified butter. Arrange on a serving dish, sprinkle with the cooking butter and garnish with lemon.

Salmon cutlets with mushrooms à la crème

Season 6 cutlets with salt and pepper to taste, dust with flour and cook in 25 g (1 oz, 2 tablespoons) butter for 6–7 minutes. Add 3 mushroom caps (or 3 slices of truffle) per cutlet and continue to cook for a further 6–7 minutes.

Drain the cutlets and keep them hot in a serving dish. Deglaze the pan with 150 ml (¼ pint, ⅔ cup) Madeira, add 200 ml (7 fl oz, ¾ cup) double (heavy) cream and reduce until creamy. Pour over the cutlets and serve immediately.

Salmon cutlets with white wine

Poach some salmon cutlets for 5 minutes in fish fumet made with white wine (just enough to cover them). Drain the cutlets and arrange them in a circle on a round dish. Place some spinach cooked in butter in the centre. Coat with white wine sauce mixed with the reduced cooking liquid. Serve immediately.

Salmon en croûte

Make some puff pastry with 575 g (1¼ lb, 5 cups) plain (all-purpose) flour, 300 ml (½ pint, 1¼ cups) water, 1 tablespoon table salt and 425 g (15 oz, 2 cups) butter.

Trim the salmon and cut off all the fins except the tail fin. Cut off the gills and scale the fish, starting from the tail and working towards the head. Gut (clean) the salmon and remove any clots of blood. Wash the inside of the fish in plenty of water, arching its back slightly. Remove the skin from one side of the fish by making an incision along the back and separating the skin from the flesh on one side of this line, beginning at the tail and working towards the head, lifting it with the thumb. Wipe the salmon.

Divide the pastry into 2 equal portions. Roll out one of them into a long rectangle and place it on a large buttered baking sheet. Lay the salmon on the pastry, skin side down, and season with salt and plenty of pepper. Cut the pastry around the salmon to within 4 cm (1½ in) of the fish, leaving a large piece around the tail. Fold the pastry in towards the tail, tucking in the corners, and brush the edges of the pastry with 1 egg yolk beaten with 1 tablespoon water. Roll out the second portion of pastry like the first and place it over the fish. Seal the edges of the pastry together and trim to within 2 cm (¾ in) of the fish. Fold the projecting top edge of the pastry around the tail over the bottom piece. Using a sharp pointed knife, lightly score the position of the head, draw a line from the head to the tail along the backbone, and trace some oblique lines from this line down the side of the fish to mark it into portions. Glaze the pastry evenly with more beaten egg yolk, paying particular attention to the sealed edges. Bake in a preheated oven at 220°C (425°F, gas 7) for 1 hour. To serve, cut the pastry along the line marking the head, then cut along the median line and finally cut along the oblique lines.

Serve only the top layer of pastry, as the bottom layer will be soft and will have stuck to the salmon.

Salmon fillets Orly with tomato sauce

Trim 14 salmon fillets. Put them into a dish with some salt, coarsely ground pepper, a little grated nutmeg, 2 finely sliced shallots, some sprigs of parsley, the juice of 2 lemons, 100 ml (4 fl oz, 7 tablespoons) olive oil, a little thyme and a bay leaf. Turn the fillets several times in this marinade and drain off the water which they produce. An hour before the meal, drain the fillets on paper towels, sprinkle with flour and turn them in this until they are quite dry. Pat them back into shape with the blade of a knife and dip them into 4 beaten eggs before frying them. When cooked, arrange them in a circle on a plate and serve a light tomato sauce separately.

Salmon fritots

Cut some raw salmon into thin slices or large dice and marinate in a mixture of oil, lemon juice, chopped parsley, salt and pepper. Dip in a light batter and deep-fry until golden brown. Drain on paper towels and serve with fried parsley, quarters of lemon and tomato or hollandaise sauce or sauce verte.

Salmon fritters with apple sauce

Beat 4 egg yolks with 2 tablespoons double (heavy) cream and 2 tablespoons cornflour (cornstarch). Pour the mixture into a saucepan containing 250 ml (8 fl oz, 1 cup) boiling (hard) cider and thicken over a gentle heat. Remove from the heat and add 300 g (11 oz, 1¾ cups) diced salmon and then 2 stiffly whisked egg whites. Put to one side.

Prepare the sauce as follows. Brown 2 sliced shallots and 6 sliced apples in a pan and add 250 ml (8 fl oz, 1 cup) cider. When cooked, purée the mixture in a blender or food processor and keep hot.

Form the salmon mixture into balls using 2 teaspoons and deep-fry them in hot oil, until they have puffed up and are golden brown. Drain well and serve with the apple sauce.

Salmon koulibiac

A Russian pie filled with fish, vegetables, rice and hard-boiled (hard-cooked) eggs. The filling is topped with *vésiga* (dried spinal marrow of the sturgeon), and essential element of an authentic *koulibiac*. European cooks have adapted and varied the recipe in many ways. It can be made with brioche dough or puff pastry, and it may be filled with rice, chicken and mushrooms or with salmon (or even turbot), onions, parsley and shallots. Hard-boiled (hard-cooked) eggs are an essential ingredient, but *vésiga* is now very rarely used.

Make some puff pastry with 350 g (12 oz, 3 cups) plain (all-purpose) flour, 275 g (10 oz, 1¼ cups) butter, 200 ml (7 fl oz, ¾ cup) water and 1 teaspoon salt. While the dough is resting, prepare the filling. Hard boil (hard cook) 3 eggs, shell them and cut into quarters. Cook 100 g (4 oz, ⅔ cup) rice in boiling salted water, then drain. Skin about 400 g (14 oz) boned fresh salmon and poach it in salted water, adding 200 ml (7 fl oz, ¾ cup) white wine, a bouquet garni and 2 teaspoons paprika.

Cook for about 12 minutes, remove from the heat and cool the salmon in its cooking liquid. Chop 3 shallots and 350 g (12 oz, 4 cups) mushrooms, season with salt and pepper, and cook briskly in 15 g (½ oz, 1 tablespoon) butter. Finally, cook 3 tablespoons semolina in boiling salted water.

Roll out two-thirds of the dough into a rectangle 3 mm (⅛ in) thick. Leaving a narrow border free, spread over a layer of rice, then a layer of flaked salmon, the mushrooms and the semolina, then top with the hard-boiled eggs. Roll out the remaining dough and cover the pie. Pinch the edges to seal them, garnish with strips of pastry and brush with beaten egg. Cook in a preheated oven at 230°C (450°F, gas 8) for about 30 minutes. Serve the koulibiac very hot, with melted butter.

Salmon mayonnaise

Cut some cooked salmon into very thin escalopes (scallops) and season with salt, pepper, oil and either vinegar or lemon juice. Finely shred some lettuce leaves and arrange them in individual dishes. Cover the lettuce with the salmon escalopes, coat with mayonnaise and garnish with a mixture of capers, anchovies, black (ripe) olives, together with quarters of hard-boiled (hard-cooked) eggs. Serve well chilled.

Salmon pâté

Prepare 600 g (1¼ lb) pike forcemeat, such as godiveau lyonnais or cream forcemeat made with pike, and add a chopped truffle. Finely slice 575 g (1¼ lb) fresh salmon and marinate it for 1 hour in a little oil with some salt, pepper and chopped herbs. Line a shallow oval pâté mould with butter pastry for pâté en croûte. Cover the bottom with half the pike forcemeat, then add the salmon slices (drained) and the remaining forcemeat. Top with a piece of butter pastry.

Glaze the top with egg and garnish with shapes cut out from leftover pastry (rolled out thinly). Make a hole in the centre and insert a small smooth metal piping nozzle. Glaze the top again. Bake in a preheated oven at 190°C (375°F, gas 5) for 1¼ hours.

Salmon purée

Purée 250 g (9 oz) skinned and boned fresh salmon cooked in a court-bouillon (or well-drained canned salmon with bones and skin removed). Add to this purée 100 ml (4 fl oz, 7 tablespoons) very thick béchamel sauce. Heat, stirring well, then whisk in 50 g (2 oz, ¼ cup) butter. Adjust the seasoning. If desired, add a quarter of its weight of mushroom duxelles.

This purée is used to fill barquettes, pannequets, croustades and hard-boiled (hard-cooked) eggs.

Salmon quenelles

Fillet a salmon weighing about 1.25 kg (2¾ lb). Remove the skin and take out the bones, then weigh the flesh – there should be about 400 g (14 oz). Finely mince or pound the flesh, then put it in the refrigerator.

Prepare a panada: bring 300 ml (½ pint, 1¼ cups) water to the boil, adding a generous pinch of salt. Remove from the heat and sift in 150 g (5 oz, 1¼ cups) plain (all-purpose) flour through a sieve; stir vigorously until smooth, then continue to stir over heat until the mixture dries out, taking care that it does not stick to the bottom of the pan. Remove from the heat and beat in 1 egg; leave the mixture to get cold, then refrigerate. When the panada is well chilled, process in a blender until it is quite smooth.

Cream 200 g (7 oz, ¾ cup) butter. Put the salmon flesh into a bowl placed in another bowl full of crushed ice; season with salt and pepper, then work it with a wooden spoon until it is smooth. Now mix in the panada, 1 egg and

4 yolks (one by one), and finally the butter: the mixture should be uniformly blended and smooth. (If all the ingredients are really cold, this last stage can be carried out in a blender, as long as it is powerful enough to work quickly without heating; the blender goblet itself should have been cooled in the refrigerator.) Chill the mixture for 30 minutes. Shape the quenelles, using 2 spoons dipped in hot water, and place on a lightly floured surface. Bring 2 litres (3½ pints, 9 cups) salted water to the boil and poach the quenelles for 15 minutes, without letting the water boil. Drain them and leave to get cold, arrange on a dish then cover them completely with Nantua sauce, cream sauce, prawn sauce or white wine sauce.

Salmon soufflé

Skin a salmon and remove all the bones with a small pair of tweezers – you need 400 g (14 oz) flesh. Pass this flesh through a blender or food processor very quickly so as not to heat it. Add 4 whole eggs and 250 ml (8 fl oz, 1 cup) crème fraîche. Stir this mixture with a spatula for 15 minutes, keeping the bowl standing in ice. Rub through a sieve and adjust the seasoning. Whisk 4 slightly salted egg whites until stiff and fold gently into the salmon mixture. Pour into a buttered soufflé mould and bake in a preheated oven at 200°C (400°F, gas 6) for about 25 minutes. (This recipe can also be made using salmon trout or brown trout.)

Salmon steaks à l'américaine

Cook a whole langouste as for lobster *à l'américaine*. Split it in half without damaging the shell, then remove the flesh and reserve the entrails.

From the middle of a salmon, cut some steaks, 4–6 cm (1½–2½ in) thick, and season them with salt and pepper. Place the steaks in a buttered flameproof sauté dish with 2 tablespoons raw matignon per steak. Add

2 tablespoons melted butter per steak, fry quickly for 1–2 minutes, then cover the dish and transfer to a preheated oven at 230°C (450°F, gas 8). Baste frequently with the butter, but do not add any liquid. Remove the steaks from the dish and keep hot.

Dice the langouste meat and mix it with an equal volume of braised diced mushrooms. Bind the mixture with 100 ml (4 fl oz, 7 tablespoons) reduced allemande sauce that has been flavoured with chopped tarragon and chervil. Stuff the 2 halves of the langouste shell with this mixture, smooth the surface and sprinkle with grated cheese and clarified butter. Place the shell halves on a lightly oiled baking sheet and brown in a very hot oven, for 10 minutes before serving.

For the sauce, mix the cooked matignon with the langouste cooking liquid and then add 300 ml (½ pint, 1¼ cups) fish fumet and 100 ml (4 fl oz, 7 tablespoons) velouté sauce. Reduce this sauce by one-third over a high heat, stirring all the time. Remove from the heat and bind the sauce with the langouste entrails, rubbed through a sieve and mixed with 100 g (4 oz, ½ cup) butter. Add some chopped parsley, chervil and tarragon and the juice of ½ a lemon; adjust the seasoning.

Arrange the salmon steaks on a serving dish with the stuffed langouste shells at either end. Coat the salmon with the sauce.

Salmon steaks à la meunière

Season some salmon steaks, 2.5 cm (1 in) thick, with salt and pepper and lightly dust with flour. Fry them on both sides in very hot butter. Arrange the steaks on a long serving dish, sprinkled with chopped parsley and add a dash of lemon juice. Just before serving, sprinkle the steaks with the very hot cooking butter (reheated if necessary) and surround them with cannelled half-slices of lemon.

Salmon steaks à la Nantua

Poach some salmon steaks in fish fumet and drain. Coat with Nantua sauce mixed with a little reduced fish fumet and serve with shelled crayfish tails.

Salmon steaks princesse

Ask the fishmonger to cut some steaks of equal thickness from a large fresh salmon. Prepare some fish fumet, leave it to cool and strain. Lay the steaks in a fish kettle with a small amount of fumet and poach them gently for 6 minutes from the time that the fumet starts to simmer. Drain and skin the steaks and arrange on a serving dish; keep warm. Use the cooking liquid to make a normande sauce. Garnish the steaks with slivers of truffle warmed in butter and with green asparagus tips, also cooked in butter (these can be arranged in barquettes made of fine lining pastry). Serve the sauce separately.

Salmon with champagne

Cut some fairly thick salmon steaks. Butter a baking dish and line the bottom with chopped shallots and a few diced vegetables. Arrange the salmon steaks in it and half-cover them with a mixture of equal parts of fish stock and champagne. Cook in a preheated oven at 220°C (425°F, gas 7), then remove the salmon steaks, drain and keep hot. Strain the pan juice and add some double (heavy) cream, using 100 ml (4 fl oz, 7 tablespoons) per 250 ml (8 fl oz, 1 cup) juice, and reduce by half. Adjust the seasoning. Add a generous lump of butter cut into small pieces and beat energetically. Coat the steaks with this sauce. Fillets of sole may be prepared in the same way.

Scallop shells of salmon Victoria

Fill the shells with a mixture of salmon poached in fumet, sliced mushrooms cooked in butter and small diced truffles. Coat with Nantua sauce, dust with grated Parmesan cheese, sprinkle with clarified butter and brown in a very hot oven. Garnish each shell with a slice of truffle heated in butter.

Smoked salmon aspic

Prepare an aspic jelly flavoured with herbs, and use it to coat the mould. Place some Russian salad on slices of smoked salmon and roll them up. Arrange in the mould, alternating a layer of salmon rolls with a layer of fish mousse made using salmon, and finishing with the aspic jelly. Place in the refrigerator to set. Unmould before serving.

Smoked salmon cornets with fish roe

Roll up some small slices of smoked salmon into cornets. Fill them with fish roe (caviar, salmon or lumpfish). Arrange them on a bed of shredded lettuce dressed with vinaigrette. Garnish with fluted lemon halves. The base of the cornet can be filled with a little cream mixed with a few drops of lemon juice and grated horseradish, or else this cream can be served in a sauceboat at the same time as the cornets, with hot blinis.

Smoked salmon frivolities with caviar

Cut six 18 × 7.5 cm (7 × 3 in) rectangles from 6 very fine, large slices of smoked salmon and set aside. Use the leftovers to make a mousse: place in a blender and add 25 g (1 oz, 2 tablespoons) unsalted butter, at room temperature. Purée the contents briefly until smooth. Gently heat 60 ml (2 fl oz, ¼ cup) prawn stock over a low flame. Add 1½ sheets of leaf gelatine or 1¼ teaspoons (½ envelope) powdered gelatine, previously softened or sponged in cold water, to the stock and stir until dissolved. Pour this mixture into the blender, then add 1 drop of Worcestershire sauce and 2 drops of Tabasco. Pulse the blender just 2 or 3 times. Whip 120 ml (4½ fl oz, ½ cup) chilled double (heavy) cream in a cold mixing bowl until it forms stiff peaks on the whisk. Add one-third of the salmon purée and stir carefully until thoroughly combined, then stir in the rest of the purée.

Place pieces of cling film (plastic wrap), slightly larger than the rectangles of salmon, on the work surface. Lay the pieces of salmon on the cling film and spread 2 tablespoons of the mousse lengthways along the centre of each. Using the cling film, roll up the salmon slices from their long sides into cigar shapes. Twist the ends of the cling film to keep the salmon rolls in shape. Chill for at least 2 hours, but not more than 24 hours.

Remove the cling film from the rolls and cut them in half. Arrange in a V-shape on very cold plates and garnish with a ribbon of caviar along the line where the edges meet. Garnish with slices of lemon and serve.

Smoked salmon purée

Using a blender or a food processor purée 200 g (7 oz) smoked salmon together with the juice of ½ a lemon and 4 egg yolks. Add 50 g (2 oz, ¼ cup) butter and work the mixture until smooth.

This purée is used for garnishing canapés, barquettes, cold pancakes or slices of smoked salmon rolled into cornet shapes.

Terrine of salmon

Remove all the flesh from a small well-trimmed salmon and marinate it in dry white wine with salt and pepper. Prepare a forcemeat as follows: blend the flesh from 1 kg (2¼ lb) white fish and 300 g (11 oz) unpeeled shrimps in a blender or food processor. Then add 12 eggs, 175 ml (6 fl oz, ¾ cup) whipped cream, and some salt and pepper. Blend the ingredients thoroughly.

Butter a long terrine dish; spread a layer of forcemeat on the bottom, then add a layer of salmon and repeat the procedure, ending with a layer of forcemeat. Cover the dish and cook in a bain marie in a preheated oven at 180°C (350°F, gas 4) for about 1½ hours. Allow to cool completely and serve with green sauce.

Salt cod & stockfish

To prepare

Wash the dried fish thoroughly under cold running water, then either leave it whole or cut it into sections, which speeds up the desalting process. Place it in a colander, with the skin uppermost, in a bowl of cold water, so that the fish is completely covered. Soak for 18–24 hours (12 hours for fillets), changing the water several times; the fish must be almost or totally free of salt (according to preference) before it is cooked. Drain the cod and place it in a saucepan with plenty of cold water. Add a bouquet garni, bring the water to the boil and keep it simmering for about 10 minutes. Drain well.

Bouchées à la bénédictine

À la bénédictine is the French term applied to several dishes using either a purée of salt cod and potato, or salt cod pounded with garlic, oil and cream. Cod is traditionally eaten during Lent, hence the allusion to the Benedictine monks. Many of these dishes can be enriched with truffles.

Add diced truffle to a purée of salt cod with oil and cream. Use to fill small cooked puff pastry bouchée cases. Garnish each bouchée with a slice of truffle. Heat through in a hot oven.

Chaudrée gaspésienne

This is a variation on a classic fish soup recipe from the Vendée and Saintonge coast. Cut 125 g (4½ oz) salt pork into slices. Fry in a saucepan over a low heat until golden. Arrange 200 g (7 oz) prepared dried cod's tongue, 200 g (7 oz) prepared dried cod's cheek, 250 g (9 oz) diced potatoes and 125 g (4½ oz) chopped onions in successive layers on top of the salt pork. Season with salt and pepper, cover with water and simmer for 45 minutes. Serve very hot.

Estofinado

Soak a stockfish in water for several hours, changing the water frequently to remove the salt. Scrape the skin carefully to remove the scales and cut the flesh into 5 cm (2 in) pieces. Fry 1 or 2 chopped onions lightly in 1 tablespoon oil in a large flameproof earthenware casserole. Then add 3 tomatoes, peeled, seeded and chopped. Cook over a low heat for 4–5 minutes, stirring with a wooden spoon. Add 2–3 garlic cloves, peeled and chopped, a bouquet garni consisting of celery, parsley, basil, bay leaf and thyme, carefully tied together, and a pinch of cayenne pepper. Crushed anchovy or grated nutmeg could also be used to season if wished. Place the pieces of fish in a larger pan and add 100 ml (4 fl oz, 7 tablespoons) white wine, the tomato mixture and enough water to cover the fish. Cook for 30 minutes over a low heat. Cut 4–6 potatoes into thick slices and add to the pan (one potato per person). Add a generous dash of Cognac and 8 olives per person 5 minutes before the end of the cooking time. Remove the bouquet garni and serve.

Fillets of salt cod maître d'hôtel

Desalt the fillets, then drain and cut them into small tongue shapes. Flatten slightly, coat with breadcrumbs and cook in butter. Arrange in a serving dish and coat with half-melted maître d'hôtel butter. Serve with boiled potatoes.

Fried salt cod

Desalt the cod, cut it into small tongue shapes and soak for 1 hour in milk that has been boiled and cooled. Drain the fish pieces, flour them and fry in oil heated to 175°C (347°F). Place on paper towels and sprinkle with fine salt. Serve with lemon quarters.

Nîmes brandade (salt cod)

Desalt 1 kg (2¼ lb) salt cod, changing the water several times. Cut the fish into pieces and poach it very gently in water for 8 minutes. Drain, then remove the bones and skin. Heat 200 ml (7 fl oz, ¾ cup) olive oil in a thick flat-based saucepan until it begins to shimmer. Add the cod, then crush and work the mixture with a wooden spoon, while heating gently. When it forms a fine paste, remove the pan from the heat. Continue to work the brandade and, while stirring continuously, gradually add 400–500 ml (14–17 fl oz, 1¾–2 cups) olive oil, alternating with 250 ml (8 fl oz, 1 cup) boiled milk or double (heavy) cream. Season with salt and white pepper. The result should be a smooth white paste with the consistency of potato purée. Pile the brandade into a dish and garnish with triangles of crustless bread fried in oil. It can also be put in the oven to brown, just before serving.

Pimientos del piquillo stuffed with cod

Soak 300 g (11 oz) salt cod in cold water for 24 hours to remove the salt. Peel 2 onions and slice very finely; peel and cut up 3 garlic cloves. Sweat for 30 minutes in a small saucepan in 4 teaspoons olive oil. Flake the cod, making sure that no bones are left behind. Cook for 1 minute with the onion and garlic. Remove from the heat and add 75 g (3 oz, 1½ cups) breadcrumbs. Check and adjust the seasoning. Put to one side. Stuff 12 *pimientos del piquillo* with this mixture. Finely chop and cook 3 more peppers in 150 ml (¼ pint,

⅔ cup) whipping cream for 5 minutes. Blend and strain this coulis through a conical strainer. Season with salt and add a pinch of sugar.

Beat 1 egg with 3 tablespoons cold milk. Coat the stuffed peppers with flour and dip them in the egg. Fry them on both sides in 5½ tablespoons olive oil over a moderate heat until golden. Coat the serving dish with some of the pepper coulis (serve the rest in a sauceboat). Arrange the stuffed pimientos on the coulis and garnish with a sprig of parsley. Serve piping hot.

Rougail of salt cod

Rougail is a highly spiced seasoning used in the West Indies and Réunion. Made from vegetables, shellfish or fish and pimientos, it is simmered in oil and eaten hot or cold as a condiment with rice-based West Indian dishes.

Soak 300 g (11 oz) salt-cod fillets in cold water for 24 hours, changing the water 2–3 times. Dry, cut into small pieces and dip in flour. Heat 3 tablespoons olive oil – or oil and lard – in a flameproof casserole and cook the fish until golden. Add 3 finely sliced onions, then cover and cook gently until the onions are soft. Then add 4 peeled tomatoes, seeded and coarsely chopped. In a food processor, purée a small piece of fresh root ginger, 1 garlic clove, 1 small red chilli, 1 teaspoon chopped parsley and a few leaves of fresh thyme. Mix this purée into the fish, cover the casserole and cook in a preheated oven at 180°C (350°F, gas 4) for 50 minutes. Serve hot or cold.

Salt cod acras

Place about 500 g (18 oz) salt cod in cold water for 24 hours to remove the salt, changing the water several times. Make a fritter batter with 200 g (7 oz, 1¾ cups) plain (all-purpose) flour, a pinch of salt and enough water to obtain a thick batter, then leave it to stand for 1 hour. Place the desalted cod with a little cold water and a bay leaf in a saucepan; cook gently for 10 minutes.

Drain and flake the fish, then mix it with 4 teaspoons olive oil, salt and cayenne pepper. Finely chop 2 shallots and 4–5 chives, then add these to the cod. Stir the cod mixture into the batter. Stiffly whisk 2–3 egg whites and fold gently into the mixture. Drop spoonfuls of the mixture into hot oil and deep-fry until crisp and golden, turning once. Drain and serve hot.

Salt cod aïoli

Cook 575 g (1¼ lb) small potatoes in their skins in salted water. Keep a little of the cooking water and thicken it with 100 g (4 oz, ½ cup) aïoli (made with egg yolks). Coat the potatoes with the aïoli sauce and sprinkle with chopped parsley. Poach 1 kg (2¼lb) soaked and drained salt cod in a mixture of water and milk. Arrange the cod on plates and put the potatoes on top.

Salt cod à la bénédictine

The French term applied to several dishes using either a purée of salt cod and potato, or salt cod pounded with garlic, oil and cream.

Soak 1 kg (2¼ lb) salt cod in cold water to remove the salt. Poach the fish very gently in water without boiling. Boil 450 g (1 lb) potatoes. Drain the cod, remove the skin and bones, and dry in the oven for a few minutes. Drain the potatoes and pound with the cod in a mortar, then gradually work in 200 ml (7 fl oz, ¾ cup) olive oil and 300 ml (½ pint, 1¼ cups) milk. (A blender or food processor may be used, but for no longer than necessary, or the starch in the potatoes will agglutinate.) Spread the mixture in a buttered gratin dish and smooth the surface. Sprinkle with melted butter and brown in the oven.

Salt cod à la créole

Desalt and poach 800 g (1¾ lb) salt cod, by placing it in a saucepan with plenty of cold water with a bouquet garni, bringing it to the boil and simmering it for 10 minutes. Prepare a fondue with 1 kg (2¼ lb) tomatoes, some olive oil, plenty of garlic and onion, and a dash of cayenne pepper.

Cut 6 tomatoes in half and remove the seeds. Seed 2 green (bell) peppers and cut them into small tongue-shaped pieces. Sauté the tomatoes and peppers in oil. Spread the tomato fondue in an oiled gratin dish, arrange the drained and flaked cod on top, then cover it with the tomato halves and the pieces of pepper. Sprinkle with a little oil and cook in a preheated oven at 230°C (450°F, gas 8) for 10 minutes, moistening with a little lime juice. Serve piping hot with rice *à la créole*.

Salt cod à la florentine

Desalt and poach 800 g (1¾ lb) salt cod; drain and flake it. Blanch 1 kg (2¼ lb) spinach for 5 minutes in salted boiling water, then drain and press it to extract the water. Cook the spinach slowly in 50 g (2 oz, ¼ cup) butter for about 10 minutes then place in a gratin dish. Arrange the cod on top, coat with Mornay sauce, sprinkle with grated Parmesan cheese and moisten with a little melted butter. Brown in a preheated oven at 230°C (450°F, gas 8).

Salt cod à l'anglaise

Desalt and poach some salt cod, arrange it in a dish and garnish with fresh parsley. Serve with boiled vegetables, melted butter and lemon juice with chopped hard-boiled (hard-cooked) egg and coarsely chopped parsley.

The butter may be replaced by bâtarde, caper, cream, curry, fines herbes, hollandaise or mustard sauce, or the cod can be served cold with mayonnaise.

Salt cod à la languedocienne

Completely desalt 1 kg (2¼ lb) salt cod, cut it into square pieces and poach in water, without boiling. Cut some potatoes into even-sized pieces, brown them in oil, sprinkle them with a spoonful of flour and fry for a few seconds, shaking the pan, until the flour has turned brown. Add a crushed garlic clove, the fish, a few spoonfuls of the fish cooking stock, a bouquet garni, pepper and very little salt, as the cod cooking water is already salty. Cook gently in a covered pan for 25 minutes. Take out the bouquet garni and pour the mixture into a deep ovenproof dish, placing the cod in the centre. Sprinkle with chopped parsley, moisten with a little olive oil and finish cooking in a preheated oven at 230°C (475°F, gas 8) for about 5 minutes.

Salt cod à la lyonnaise

A la lyonnaise describes various sautéed dishes including onions glazed in butter until golden. Prepare and cook some salt cod. Drain, separate the individual flakes and put them in a saucepan. Cover the saucepan and place over a low heat to dry out any water the cod might still contain. Dice 3 large white onions and cook them gently over a low heat in 225 g (8 oz, 1 cup) melted butter. As soon as they are golden brown, add the cod and sauté. Season with pepper, grated nutmeg and the juice of 1 lemon before serving.

Salt cod à la parisienne

Desalt 800 g (1¾ lb) fillets of salt cod, cut them into pieces and poach them. Hard boil (hard cook) 3 eggs, shell them and chop them coarsely. Chop a small bunch of parsley. Drain the cod, arrange in a serving dish and sprinkle with the egg and parsley. Keep hot. Fry 4 tablespoons fine fresh breadcrumbs in 100 g (4 oz, ½ cup) butter, sprinkle over the cod and serve immediately.

Salt cod à la provençale

Prepare 500 ml (17 fl oz, 2 cups) tomato fondue with olive oil and season with garlic. Pour this fondue into a shallow frying pan and add 800 g (1¾ lb) desalted cod, cut into pieces, poached and drained. Simmer gently for about 10 minutes, adjust the seasoning, then pour into a serving dish and sprinkle with coarsely chopped parsley.

Salt cod bouillabaisse

Completely desalt 800 g (1¾ lb) fillets of salt cod, changing the water several times, then cut them into square pieces. In some oil, gently fry 100 g (4 oz, 1 cup) chopped onions and 50 g (2 oz, ½ cup) chopped leeks, without allowing them to change colour. When these vegetables are soft, add 2 peeled, seeded, and finely chopped tomatoes and 1 crushed garlic clove. Cook rapidly for 5 minutes, then add 6 tablespoons white wine, 500 ml (17 fl oz, 2 cups) water or fish stock and a generous pinch of saffron. Bring to the boil and place the drained cod in the cooking liquor; cover and continue to boil rapidly for about 25 minutes. Just before serving add 1 tablespoon chopped parsley. Serve the bouillabaisse in a deep dish with slices of dried bread. Alternatively, the stock may be served separately from the fish, garnished with slices of French bread.

Salt cod croquettes

Soak some salt cod in water to desalt it. Poach in water, then crumble it very finely. Add one-third of its volume of duchess potatoes and just enough béchamel sauce to bind the mixture well. Stir the mixture well, over the heat, then spread evenly on a buttered baking sheet and dab the surface with butter to prevent it from forming a crust. Leave to cool completely before making the croquettes.

Divide the cold mixture into portions of 50–75 g (2–3 oz). Roll these out on a floured flat surface and shape them into balls. Dip them in a mixture of egg and oil beaten together and then cover them with fine breadcrumbs.

Place the croquettes in a frying basket, plunge into oil heated to 175–180°C (347–350°F), and deep-fry until they are crisp and golden. Drain on paper towels and arrange on a napkin in a pyramid or turban shape. Serve with a well-seasoned or garlic-flavoured tomato sauce.

Salt cod en bamboche

Bamboche is a French term for a preparation of fried cod, sometimes served with fried eggs. The word is derived from the Italian *bamboccio*, meaning 'jumping jack', perhaps referring to the way the cod jumps in the hot fat.

Soak the fish to remove the salt and cut into thick slices the size of fillets of sole. Moisten with milk, dust with flour and plunge into boiling fat. Drain, pat dry and arrange on a bed of assorted vegetables mixed with butter or cream.

Salt cod with flageolet beans

Desalt 1 kg (2¼ lb) quartered dried salt cod. Soak 400 g (14 oz, 2½ cups) dried green flageolet beans in plenty of cold water for 24 hours. Cook the beans in water for 30 minutes with an onion stuck with cloves, 1 thinly sliced carrot, 1 bouquet garni and 3 crushed garlic cloves. Drain and season with pepper. Heat some groundnut (peanut) oil in a frying pan and lightly brown the cod on both sides. Arrange in a buttered ovenproof dish, sprinkle with 3 finely chopped garlic cloves, then cover with the drained flageolets. Coat with 250 ml (8 fl oz, 1 cup) crème fraîche and cook in a preheated oven at 200°C (400°F, gas 6) for 20 minutes. Sprinkle with coarsely chopped chervil.

Soft-boiled or poached eggs à la bénédictine

Add white or black truffles to salt cod à *la bénédictine*. Prepare soft-boiled (soft-cooked) or poached eggs. Shape the purée in a dome, arrange a circle of eggs around the dome and cover with a cream sauce.

Stockfish à la niçoise

Soak 1 kg (2¼ lb) stockfish in water for 48 hours, then chop it into pieces. Prepare 750 ml (1¼ pints, 3¼ cups) rich tomato fondue flavoured with garlic. Put the stockfish and the tomato fondue in a saucepan, cover and let it poach gently for 50 minutes. Then add 400 g (14 oz) thickly sliced potatoes and 250 g (9 oz, generous 2 cups) pitted black (ripe) olives. Cook for a further 25 minutes, adding 1 tablespoon chopped fresh basil 5 minutes before the end of the cooking time.

Stockfish and turnip soufflé

Poach 300 g (11 oz) well-soaked stockfish in champagne without boiling, then rub it through a sieve or purée in a blender or food processor. Make a béchamel sauce using 40 g (1½ oz, 3 tablespoons) butter, 40 g (1½ oz, ⅓ cup) plain (all-purpose) flour, 400 ml (14 fl oz, 1¾ cups) milk and salt and pepper. Add to this 50 g (2 oz, ½ cup) grated Gruyère cheese and the stockfish purée. Thinly slice some young turnips and cook gently in butter over a low heat. Add 4 egg yolks to the béchamel sauce and then fold in 5 very stiffly whisked egg whites. Pour the mixture into some buttered ramekins, arranging layers of turnip slices between layers of soufflé mixture. Cook in a preheated oven at 200°C (400°F, gas 6) for 20 minutes.

Tongues of salt cod in pistou

Thoroughly desalt 800 g (1¾ lb) salt cod tongues. Poach them for 6 minutes in a mixture of equal quantities of water and milk. Drain and lightly flour them, then fry quickly in olive oil. Crush 2 blanched garlic cloves and some basil in a mortar. Mix with olive oil, add some freshly puréed tomato and sprinkle with pepper. Sauté this pistou and the tongues in a non-stick frying pan and serve very hot.

Sard

Sard with chive butter

Sard is related to the sea bream, found off the coast of Provence. Known as *lou sar* in Provençal cookery, it may be grilled (broiled), boiled or deep-fried.

Sprinkle a sard weighing about 800 g (1¾ lb) with salt and pepper. Grill very rapidly over charcoal or on a preheated serrated griddle until the marks of the grill begin to show, then turn the fish through 90° and repeat to form a criss-cross pattern. Carefully fillet the fish and place the fillets in a roasting tin (pan) with 2 tablespoons olive oil and 1 head of garlic previously cooked in its skin, split into cloves and peeled. Bake in a preheated oven at 230°C (450°F, gas 8) for 5 minutes, then dry on paper towels. Alternatively, fillet the fish raw and prepare in the same way, but increase the cooking time to compensate for not grilling. Arrange on a dish and pour over beurre blanc mixed with chopped chives. Top with a walnut-sized piece of crushed tomato. Surround with garlic cloves and heart-shaped croûtons spread with tapenade.

Sardines

To prepare

Before cooking, the scales should be removed, the sardine gutted (cleaned) and wiped, and the head cut off, unless the fish is to be grilled (it is less likely to break up when turned if whole). Very fresh small sardines do not need to be gutted, but simply wiped. Their freshness can be judged by their rigidity, the brilliance of their eyes and the absence of bloodstains at the gills.

Baked sardines

Wash and gut (clean) 12 sardines. Sprinkle 2–3 chopped shallots in a greased ovenproof dish. Lay the sardines over them and pour over a little lemon juice and 60 ml (2 fl oz, ¼ cup) white wine; dot with 25 g (1 oz, 2 tablespoons) butter, cut into small pieces. Bake in a preheated oven at 220°C (425°F, gas 7) for 10–12 minutes until just cooked. Sprinkle with chopped parsley.

Fried sardines

Scale, wash and gut (clean) the sardines; open out and remove the backbones. Sprinkle with lemon juice and marinate in a cool place for 30 minutes. Wipe dry, coat in breadcrumbs and oil and deep-fry in hot oil at 180°C (350°F) for about 3 minutes. Drain, sprinkle with lemon juice and serve very hot.

Gratin of sardine fillets with lemon juice

Wash 800 g (1¾ lb) sardines and wipe them dry with paper towels. Remove the fillets with a kitchen knife and place the fish in a buttered roasting tin (pan), skin side down. Put the grated zest of 1 lemon and 100 g (4 oz, ½ cup) crème fraîche in a bowl. Season with salt and pepper and add the juice of 2 lemons. Stir and pour over the sardines. Cook in a preheated oven at 240°C (475°F, gas 9) for 7–10 minutes. Serve with toasted bread.

Raw sardine terrine

Remove the scales from the sardines, fillet them and wipe dry. Pour a layer of olive oil into a terrine, add the grated zest of 1 orange, 1 clove, 1 small piece of bay leaf, 1 thinly sliced white onion, pepper and a few drops of brandy. Cover with a layer of fish fillets, another layer of spices and chopped onion, and a second layer of fish. Leave to marinate. Serve with farmhouse bread, toasted and buttered, and freshly ground sea salt.

Raw sardines

Lay the sardines on a wicker tray, without removing the scales or gutting (cleaning) them. Put a generous pinch of mixed salt and pepper on each head. Refrigerate for 2 days. Remove the heads and gut the sardines, then skin and serve with toast and slightly salted butter.

Sardine bouillabaisse

Fry 1 chopped onion and 2 chopped leeks (white part only) in olive oil. Add 1 large peeled, seeded and chopped tomato, 2 large crushed garlic cloves, a bay leaf, a fennel stick, and a small piece of dried orange peel. Add 750 ml (1¼ pints, 3¼ cups) water. Season with salt, pepper and a generous pinch of powdered saffron. Add 6 potatoes, sliced fairly thickly. Cover and simmer for 25 minutes. Meanwhile, clean some fresh sardines and remove the scales under the cold tap; wash them and wipe dry. When the potatoes are almost cooked, lay the sardines on top and cook for 7–8 minutes. Pour the liquid on to slices of stale French bread arranged in a soup tureen; place the sardines and potatoes in another dish. Sprinkle both with chopped parsley.

Sardine escabèche

Scale, wash and gut (clean) the sardines; remove the heads and wipe thoroughly. Heat in a frying pan enough olive oil to half-cover the sardines. Fry the fish, turning them when golden; drain and place in a deep dish. Add to the cooking oil an equal quantity of fresh oil and heat. Add to this mixture a quarter of its volume of vinegar and an eighth of its volume of water, some peeled garlic cloves, thyme, rosemary, bay leaves, parsley, Spanish chilli peppers, salt and pepper. Boil for 15 minutes, remove from the heat and leave to cool. Marinate the sardines in this mixture for 24 hours before serving.

Sardine fritters

Remove the scales from the sardines, fillet them and dry thoroughly. Dip in batter and fry for a few seconds in grapeseed oil.

Sardines gratinées

Slice 1.5 kg (3¼ lb) aubergines (eggplants); place in a colander and sprinkle with a little salt. Peel and remove the seeds from 1 kg (2¼ lb) tomatoes. Fillet 14 large fresh sardines and clean thoroughly. Wash and dry the aubergines and brown them in a frying pan with a little very hot olive oil. Drain on paper towels. Purée the tomatoes in a blender with 2 garlic cloves, 3 basil leaves, salt, pepper and ½ teaspoon olive oil. Lay the aubergines and the sardine fillets in an ovenproof dish, in alternate layers, with grated Parmesan cheese between the layers. Cover with the puréed tomatoes. Bake in a preheated oven at 220°C (425°F, gas 7) for about 20 minutes.

Souffléed sardines with sorrel

Scale, wash and gut (clean) 6 good sardines and remove the backbones. Shred a large bunch of sorrel and cook in butter with salt and pepper until soft; leave to cool and add a little raspberry vinegar. Make 6 very thin savoury crêpes. Whisk 2 egg whites until very stiff and spread over the crêpes. Stuff the sardines with the sorrel purée and lay a sardine on each crêpe. Roll up loosely, arrange in a wide dish, dot with a few small pieces of butter and bake in a preheated oven at 230°C (450°F, gas 8) for about 10 minutes.

Stuffed sardines with white wine

Scale, wash and gut (clean) 12 large sardines. Remove the heads, then open out and remove the backbones. Stuff with a little fish quenelle forcemeat, such as pike forcemeat or godiveau lyonnais. Close them up again and place in a greased roasting tin (pan). Sprinkle with salt and pepper and moisten with 100 ml (4 fl oz, 7 tablespoons) white wine. Start cooking on the hob (stove top) and continue in a preheated oven at 220°C (425°F, gas 7) for 8–10 minutes until just cooked through. Drain the sardines, arrange on a long dish and pour over a few tablespoons of white wine sauce mixed with the strained cooking liquid.

Scorpion fish

Fillets of scorpion fish à l'antillaise

Cut 800 g (1¾ lb) brown scorpion fish fillets into strips 2 cm (¾ in) wide. Peel and seed 1 kg (2¼ lb) very ripe tomatoes and rub the pulp through a sieve. Peel and slice 800 g (1¾ lb) potatoes and cook until golden in 4 tablespoons oil. Take the potatoes out of the pan and cook the fish until golden. Remove from the pan and set aside. Put 2 large sliced onions into the pan, then the tomato pulp, some salt and pepper and 1 small red (bell) pepper. Bring to the boil, then add the potatoes and 1 bay leaf. When the potatoes are almost cooked (but still firm when they are pierced with a knife), add the fish and continue to cook for a further 7–8 minutes. Serve very hot with rice *à la créole*.

Sea bream

Braised gilthead bream with apples

Remove the scales from a gilthead bream weighing about 800 g (1¾ lb), clean it through the gills and wipe it. Retain the liver. Peel and chop 3 shallots, 1 small fennel bulb and 1 onion. Peel and crush 2 garlic cloves. Remove the zest from 1 lime and blanch, cool and dry it. Arrange a bed of fresh fennel sprigs in a long flameproof casserole. Add the shallots, fennel, onion, garlic, lime rind and some parsley stalks; moisten with 250 ml (8 fl oz, 1 cup) fish fumet, 1 tablespoon olive oil and 2 tablespoons white rum. Bring to the boil.

Place the bream on this bed, make 3 slits in the uppermost surface and insert lemon or orange slices and diced streaky (slab) salted bacon. Coat with olive oil and sprinkle with pepper and salt. Around it arrange the liver, cut into quarters, and 2 apples, also cut into quarters. Cover with foil and cook in a preheated oven at 180°C (350°F, gas 4) for 20–30 minutes. Arrange on a serving dish. Strain the reduced cooking juices, adjust the seasoning and serve separately in a sauceboat.

Fillets of sea bream with vegetable julienne

Fillet a sea bream weighing about 1.7 kg (3¾ lb). Prepare a julienne of vegetables comprising the white parts of 2 leeks, 4 sliced celery sticks, ½ fennel bulb and 2 young turnips. Arrange it in a buttered gratin dish. Season the fillets with salt and pepper, fold them in half and place them in the dish. Add some crème fraîche and a little lemon juice and cook in a preheated oven at about 220°C (425°F, gas 7) for about 30 minutes, covering the dish with a sheet of foil.

Gilthead bream with lemon in oil

Remove the scales from 1 large gilthead bream; clean it and make small parallel cuts in its back. Oil a gratin dish and line it with 8 slices of lemon preserved in oil. Place the sea bream on top and season with salt and pepper. Add 1 small handful of coriander seeds. Garnish with 6 slices of lemon preserved in oil. Pour over 2 tablespoons lemon juice and a few spoonfuls of olive oil. Cook in a preheated oven at 230°C (450°F, gas 8) for 30 minutes, basting several times.

Sea bream à la meunière

Scale and gut (clean) the fish, each weighing less than 575 g (1¼ lb) and make a few incisions along the back. Season with salt and pepper and coat with flour (shake the fish lightly to get rid of the excess flour). Heat some butter in a frying pan and brown the fish on both sides. Drain them, arrange on a long dish, sprinkle with chopped parsley and lemon juice, and keep hot. Add some butter to the frying pan and cook until golden then pour the bubbling butter over the fish.

Sea bream stuffed with fennel

Remove the scales from a sea bream weighing about 1.5 kg (3¼ lb) with a sharp knife. Clean it through the gills, wash, wipe and season it with salt and pepper. Cut along both sides of the backbone, then cut through the backbone at the head and tail and remove it. Moisten 250 g (9 oz, 2½ cups) dry breadcrumbs with milk.

Clean and thinly slice 1 fennel bulb. Squeeze the breadcrumbs and mix with the fennel plus 2 tablespoons pastis, 1 tablespoon lemon juice, and a little crumbled bay leaf and thyme. Fill the bream with this stuffing and tie it up like a ballotine.

Butter a gratin dish, sprinkle with chopped shallots and place the bream on top. Pour in white wine (or a mixture of wine and fumet) to a third of the depth of the fish, sprinkle with olive oil and cook in a preheated oven at about 240°C (475°F, gas 9) for about 30 minutes, basting from time to time. If necessary, protect the fish with a piece of foil towards the end of the cooking.

Shad

To prepare

A migratory fish belonging to the herring family, which lives in the sea and travels upriver to spawn. The allis shad, which can measure up to 60 cm (2 ft) in length, and the smaller twaite shad are the main species found in Europe. The American shad is found in both Pacific and Atlantic waters. Shad flesh is tasty and quite rich, but quickly deteriorates and is full of small fine bones. Traditionally served with sorrel, shad is often stuffed and may be grilled (broiled) or baked.

Carefully scale and gut (clean) the shad, keeping the roe. Using plenty of cold water, wash the fish well on the outside to remove the remains of the scales, and on the inside to wash away the blood. Dry it with paper towels.

Fried shad

Cut the fish into slices and soak in milk. Coat them with flour and plunge into hot fat. Fry the fish until golden, then drain and arrange on a napkin with fried parsley and lemon quarters.

Grilled shad with sorrel

Gut (clean), scale, wash and dry a shad, weighing about 1 kg (2¼ lb). Make regular slits in the fleshy part of the back and both sides. Season with salt and pepper and marinate for 1 hour in oil, with a little lemon juice, chopped parsley, thyme and a bay leaf. Drain the fish, grill (broil) under a medium heat for 30 minutes or until tender, then arrange the fish on a long dish, surrounded by lemon quarters or slices. Serve with maître d'hôtel butter and a garnish of lightly braised sorrel.

Shad à la bonne femme

Butter a dish and sprinkle with chopped shallot and parsley. Add 250 g (9 oz, 3 cups) chopped button mushrooms. Place a 675–800 g (1½–1¾ lb) shad in the dish and add 7 tablespoons each of dry white wine and fish stock. Dot with very small knobs of butter. Cook in a preheated oven at 220°C (425°F, gas 7) for 15–20 minutes, basting the shad two or three times. Towards the end of cooking, cover with foil to prevent the fish from drying out.

Shad à la portugaise

Lightly butter a ovenproof dish and cover with a thick tomato sauce flavoured with garlic. Trim, prepare and season a 675 g (1½ lb) shad and lay it in the dish. Moisten with 1 tablespoon lemon juice and 2 tablespoons each olive oil and fish stock. Cook in a preheated oven at 230°C (450°F, gas 8) for about 10 minutes, basting with its cooking juices. Sprinkle with breadcrumbs, brown under the grill (broiler), then sprinkle with chopped parsley.

Shad à la provençale

Choose a shad weighing 675–800 g (1½–1¾ lb). Heat 2 tablespoons olive oil in a heavy-based saucepan. Soften in it without browning 3 tablespoons peeled and chopped onions, then add 800 g (1½ lb, 3 cups) peeled, seeded and crushed tomatoes and cook gently for about 15 minutes. Add 1 crushed garlic clove and a bouquet garni together with 200 ml (7 fl oz, ¾ cup) dry white wine and 200 ml (7 fl oz, ¾ cup) meat stock. Cover and leave to cook for about 15 minutes, then adjust the seasoning. Continue to cook uncovered until the sauce is reduced by half. Add some freshly chopped parsley or basil. Mask an ovenproof dish with a little of this Provençal sauce. Arrange the fish in it and just cover with Provençal sauce. Sprinkle with fresh breadcrumbs, moisten with a little olive oil and cook in a preheated oven at 200°C (400°F, gas 6) for about 20 minutes. Sprinkle with chopped parsley and serve piping hot in the cooking dish.

Shad au plat

Choose a shad weighing 675–800 g (1½–1¾ lb). Gut (clean) the fish and fill the cavity with a mixture of 50 g (2 oz, ¼ cup) butter kneaded together with 1 tablespoon finely chopped parsley, 1½ teaspoons finely chopped shallot and salt and pepper. Place the shad on a long buttered ovenproof dish. Season with more salt and pepper, sprinkle over 100 ml (4 fl oz, 7 tablespoons) dry white wine, dot with small pieces of butter and cook in a preheated oven at about 200°C (400°F, gas 6) for 15–20 minutes. Baste frequently with the liquor during cooking. If the liquid reduces too quickly, add a little water. Serve on the cooking dish.

Stuffed shad à la mode de Cocherel

For a 2 kg (4½ lb) fish, prepare a stuffing by crushing in a mortar or processing in a blender 300 g (11 oz) whiting flesh. Add 1 egg white, salt, pepper and grated nutmeg, then 350 ml (12 fl oz, 1½ cups) double (heavy) cream. Mix together well with a wooden spatula, preferably standing the bowl in a large container of ice to prevent the cream from turning. Finally, add 4 teaspoons blanched, drained and snipped chives and 2 teaspoons finely chopped parsley.

Stuff the shad with this mixture and wrap very thin strips of bacon around it. Then tie it up to hold its shape and cook in a preheated oven at 180°C (350°F, gas 4) or on a spit over a high heat for 30–45 minutes. Remove the bacon strips and cook for another 5 minutes to brown the fish. Deglaze the dripping pan with 175 ml (6 fl oz, ¾ cup) dry white wine, add 400 ml (14 fl oz, 1¾ cups) double (heavy) cream, and reduce, finally adding salt and pepper. Arrange the shad on a long dish and surround with small new potatoes cooked in butter, quarters of small artichokes blanched and gently cooked in butter, and some small glazed onions.

Shark

Shark à la créole

Slice the flesh of a small shark and marinate it for several hours in the juice of 2 limes that has been diluted with water, together with garlic, salt, pepper and 1 chilli pepper. Slice 2 onions and 4–5 shallots and wash and roughly chop 3 tomatoes; brown all these in a saucepan along with 2 chilli peppers, 3 garlic cloves and 1 bouquet garni. Drain the fish pieces, place them on top of the vegetables and cook with the pan covered. To serve, sprinkle with lime juice, chopped parsley and a little grated garlic. Serve with rice *à la créole* and red kidney beans.

Skate

Fried skate

Select some very small skinned skate (or the wings from a small or medium fish). Pour some cold milk over them and soak for 1 hour, then drain, coat with flour and deep-fry at 180°C (350°F). When cooked, drain on paper towels, sprinkle with salt and arrange on a serving dish. Garnish with fluted lemon halves.

Skate au gratin

Butter a flameproof casserole and sprinkle the bottom with 2 tablespoons chopped shallots and the same amount of chopped parsley. Add 150 g (5 oz, 1⅔ cups) finely sliced mushrooms. Season 2 skate wings with salt and pepper and arrange them in the dish. Moisten with 5 tablespoons white wine, dot with 25 g (1 oz, 2 tablespoons) butter cut into small pieces, and cook in a preheated oven at 230°C (450°F, gas 8) for 10 minutes. Remove the skate and drain it. Add 1 tablespoon crème fraîche to the cooking liquid and reduce it by half. Return the skate to the dish, pour over the cooking juices, sprinkle with breadcrumbs, dot with butter and brown under the grill (broiler).

Skate liver fritters

Poach some skate liver for 6 minutes in court-bouillon, then drain it and leave it to cool. Make some fritter batter. Slice the liver and marinate it in salt, pepper, oil and a little lemon juice for 30–60 minutes. Drain the slices of liver, dip them into the batter and deep-fry them at 180°C (350°F). Drain on paper towels, sprinkle with salt and serve with fluted lemon halves.

Skate liver with cider vinegar

Poach 400 g (14 oz) skate liver very gently in court-bouillon for 5 minutes. Leave it to cool in its own stock.

Peel and core 4 firm apples (preferably Cox's Orange Pippins or Granny Smiths), then slice them and cook them over a low heat in 15–20 g (½–¾ oz, 1–1½ tablespoons) butter. Season with salt and pepper. Slice the liver and brown in a little butter. Drain and arrange the slices on a hot dish. Pour the butter from the pan in which the livers were cooked, then add 2 tablespoons cider vinegar to the pan, boil for 1–2 minutes and pour over the liver. Surround with the cooked apple and sprinkle with chopped chives.

Skate with lemon

Poach a skate wing, about 150 g (5 oz), in a little salted water with 1 chopped shallot. Peel 1 lemon, taking care to remove all the pith, and divide it into segments. Peel and grate 1 apple, then mix the apple and the lemon segments and add them to the fish halfway through the cooking time. Just before serving the fish, add 1 tablespoon crème fraîche, a little pepper and a pinch of grated nutmeg.

Skate with noisette butter

Cut the skate flesh into chunks, leaving the wings whole. Poach in court-bouillon or in water to which have been added 200 ml (7 fl oz, ¾ cup) vinegar and 1 teaspoon salt per 1 litre (1¾ pints, 4⅓ cups) water. Bring to the boil, skim the liquor and simmer for 5–7 minutes, according to the thickness of the fish. Make some noisette butter. Drain the fish and arrange it on a hot dish. Sprinkle with lemon juice and, just before serving, pour the noisette butter over it. Sprinkle with capers and garnish with a little parsley; serve at once with plain-boiled potatoes.

Smelt

To prepare

The smelt is a small marine fish of the salmon family, with fine delicate flesh. It grows up to 20 cm (8 in) long, is silvery in colour and has a second dorsal fin, which distinguishes it from similar, but poorer quality, fish, such as bleak and *athérine*, which are often used as substitutes. It spawns in estuaries but seldom travels up river beyond the tideline.

The fish are gutted (cleaned), washed and dried. The classic method of preparation is frying, but they can also be marinated, grilled (broiled), cooked in white wine, coated with flour and fried, or cooked *au gratin*. In Scandinavian countries, smelt are used to make fish oil and meal.

Brochettes of fried smelt

Dip prepared smelt in salted milk, then roll them in flour. Impale them on metal skewers (6–8 fish per skewer) and deep-fry in very hot oil.

Cold marinade of smelt

Prepare the smelt, roll them in flour and shake off any excess. Brown them in oil in a frying pan. Drain, season with salt and pepper, then arrange in a dish. Peel and slice some onions and scald them for 1 minute in boiling water. Cool, then wipe dry and arrange over the fish. Add some peppercorns, cloves (2–3 for every 30 smelt), thyme and bay leaves. Add vinegar and soak for at least 24 hours before serving as a cold hors d'oeuvre.

The vinegar in the marinade can be replaced by white wine boiled with 2 chopped shallots, 1 bouquet garni and some salt and pepper.

135

Fried smelt

Dip the smelt in salted milk, then roll them in flour and shake off any excess. Deep-fry in very hot oil at 175–180°C (347–350°F), then drain the fish on paper towels and sprinkle with fine salt. If desired, arrange in a cluster and garnish with fried parsley. Serve with lemon quarters.

Grilled smelt à l'anglaise

Split the smelt lengthways along the back and remove the backbone. Gently open them out and season with salt, pepper and a little cayenne pepper. Dip them one by one in melted butter and in fresh breadcrumbs, then grill (broil) them quickly. Sprinkle with fine salt and serve with maître d'hôtel butter.

Smelt velouté soup à la dieppoise

Make a velouté: with 75 g (3 oz, ⅓ cup) white roux, 750 ml (1¼ pints, 3¼ cups) fish stock and 100 ml (4 fl oz, 7 tablespoons) mussel-cooking liquid. Cook 250 g (9 oz) smelt and 1 tablespoon chopped onion in butter. Fillet and purée the fish, add to the velouté, then sieve. Thicken with 1 or 2 egg yolks. Garnish with 12 poached mussels and 12 peeled prawns (shelled shrimp).

Sole

To prepare

To skin a sole, take hold of the tail fin with a cloth and cut the black skin at a slight angle just above the fin. Gently detach the skin with your thumb, then take hold of it with the cloth and remove it with one sharp pull towards the head. Remove the head and, for the white side, pull the skin from the head towards the tail. Cut the side fins close to the flesh with scissors. The head can also be cut in half at an angle. To remove the fillets, cut the flesh down to the bones on each side of the backbone with a filleting knife. Detach the flesh with the knife, from the backbone to the sides, to make 4 fillets. Remove any debris attached to the flesh and flatten slightly. Wash gently but thoroughly under running water.

Fillets of sole à l'anglaise

Coat 8 fillets of sole with egg and breadcrumbs and cook them in clarified butter. Arrange on a long plate and cover with maître d'hôtel butter. Serve with potatoes or a boiled or steamed green vegetable such as leeks or spinach.

Fillets of sole poached in salted water and milk are also known by this name. They are served with boiled potatoes and melted butter. Whole sole can be cooked in the same way.

Fillets of sole à la bordelaise

Prepare some button mushrooms and baby (pearl) onions and cook in butter. Butter a small fish kettle or flameproof casserole and sprinkle the bottom with finely chopped onions and carrots. Season the fillets of sole with salt and pepper and arrange in the fish kettle. Add a bouquet garni and 175–350 ml (6–12 fl oz, ¾–1½ cups) white Bordeaux wine, according to the size of the container. Poach the fillets for 6–7 minutes, then drain, retaining the liquor. Arrange the fillets on the serving dish surrounded by the mushrooms and baby onions; cover and keep warm. Add 2 tablespoons demi-glace or fish stock to the cooking liquor and reduce by half. Add a knob of butter, sieve and pour over the fillets.

Fillets of sole à la cancalaise

Fillet the soles and poach some oysters, allowing 2 per fillet. Fold the fillets and poach them in a full-bodied fish fumet to which the poaching water from the oysters has been added. Drain the fillets, retaining the juices, and arrange them on a dish in the form of a turban. Garnish the centre of the dish with peeled prawns (shelled shrimp) and arrange 2 oysters on each fillet. Coat with a white wine sauce to which the reduced cooking juices have been added.

Fillets of sole à la cantonnaise

Trim 2 good fillets for each guest. Sprinkle each one with a very small pinch of ground coriander, cinnamon, mixed spice, nutmeg and chopped onion. Add 2 slices of fresh root ginger and fold the fillets in half. Sprinkle with oil and a little more seasoning, then steam for 10–12 minutes. Arrange on a warm plate and season with salt and pepper.

Prepare the sauce separately. Heat 4 tablespoons oil in a pan and add 2 large chopped green (bell) peppers, 50 g (2 oz, ⅔ cup) sliced mushrooms, 8 thin strips of smoked pork, a slice of ham cut into strips, 100 g (4 oz, ¾ cup) chopped shrimps and a drained 225 g (8 oz) can of crabmeat. Cook for 5 minutes, stirring continuously. Beat 2 eggs with 1 tablespoon soy sauce; stir into the pan and dilute with a little stock blended with 2 tablespoons tomato purée (paste). Reheat and pour over the fillets of sole.

Fillets of sole à la panetière

Cut the top off a large, round loaf and remove three-quarters of the crumb. Butter the inside and lightly brown in a preheated oven at 200°C (400°F, gas 6). Season some fillets of sole with salt and pepper, fold them in two, coat with flour and cook in butter. Prepare a ragoût of mushrooms in cream: either sliced or small button mushrooms reduced in butter until their juices have evaporated and moistened with either single (light) or double (heavy) cream. Drain the fillets of sole and arrange them in a crown shape in the bread. Pour the mushroom ragoût into the centre and heat through in the oven for about 5 minutes.

Fillets of sole à la Riche

Make a Riche sauce: prepare 250 ml (8 fl oz, 1 cup) normande sauce and add to it 2 tablespoons lobster butter, 1 tablespoon chopped truffle skins, a pinch of cayenne pepper and 2 tablespoons Cognac. Keep warm.

Cook a small lobster in a well-seasoned court-bouillon, drain and shell it, then cut the meat into a salpicon. Fold 8 sole fillets in half and poach them for 5 minutes in fish fumet. Drain and arrange them in a ring on a hot serving dish. Fill the centre with the lobster salpicon and mask everything with the hot Riche sauce.

Fillets of sole à la vénitienne

Fold the fillets of sole in half and poach them in a fish fumet made with white wine. Drain and wipe them and arrange them in a ring on a serving dish, alternating with heart-shaped croûtons fried in butter. Coat them with vénitienne sauce mixed with the reduced cooking liquid from the sole.

Fillets of sole à la Walewska

Poach some sole fillets in a fish fumet for 5 minutes, using very little liquid. Arrange on a long ovenproof dish and on each fillet place a slice of lobster or langouste flesh (cooked in court-bouillon) and a slice of raw truffle. Coat with Mornay sauce containing 1 tablespoon lobster or langouste butter (made as for either lobster butter or crayfish butter) for every 150 ml (¼ pint, ⅔ cup) sauce. Glaze quickly in a very hot oven.

Fillets of sole au gratin

Butter a gratin dish and coat the base with 4 tablespoons dry mushroom duxelles. Arrange 8 seasoned fillets of sole on top. Garnish with sliced mushrooms around the dish and place 2 mushroom caps cooked in butter on each fillet. Coat with a little duxelles sauce to which some concentrated fish fumet has been added, sprinkle with breadcrumbs and clarified butter, and cook in a preheated oven at 230°C (450°F, gas 8) until brown. Sprinkle with the juice of ½ a lemon and serve in the cooking dish.

Fillets of sole Crécy

Wash, clean and fold up the fillets of sole. Poach them in a fish fumet for 5 minutes, drain them and arrange on a long dish. Strain the stock, reduce, and add 2 tablespoons béchamel sauce and the same amount of carrot purée. Mix well and heat. Coat the fillets with this sauce and garnish them with very small glazed new carrots.

Fillets of sole Cubat

This dish is named after Pierre Cubat, chef at the court of Russia in 1903. Poach fillets of sole in mushroom stock and butter. Place on a long ovenproof dish and cover with a thick mushroom duxelles. Place 2 slices of truffle on each fillet. Coat with Mornay sauce and brown in the oven.

Fillets of sole Drouant

Arrange trimmed fillets of sole in a buttered dish. Season with salt and pepper, sprinkle with 1 finely chopped shallot and moisten to the level of the fish with white wine and mussel stock. Cover and cook in a preheated oven at 220°C (425°F, gas 7) for 7 minutes. Drain the fillets and reduce the cooking juices by half. Add an equal amount of crème fraîche. Remove from the heat and add 100 g (4 oz, ½ cup) butter and the same amount of américaine sauce (prepared as in the recipe for lobster *à l'américaine*). Strain and pour over the fillets. Glaze quickly in a preheated oven. Serve the fillets surrounded with shelled mussels and peeled prawns (shelled shrimp).

Fillets of sole homardine

Fillet 3 × 800 g (1¾ lb) sole, reserving the trimmings for the fumet or stock. Prepare a fish fumet with 500 g (18 oz) lean fish trimmings, 200 ml (7 fl oz, ¾ cup) Chablis, 200 ml (7 fl oz, ¾ cup) water, 1 onion, 1 shallot, 1 lemon, 1 bouquet garni, a bunch of parsley, salt and pepper.

Prepare a lobster *à l'américaine*: peel, seed and chop 5 tomatoes; make a mirepoix of 1 onion, 2 shallots, 2 garlic cloves, 1 carrot and ¼ celery stick. Remove the leaves from a tarragon sprig and chop them. Remove the lobster's tail. Split the shell in half and reserve the juices (greenish parts) and the coral. Cook the lobster halves and tail with 100 ml (4 fl oz, 7 tablespoons) olive oil until red; add the mirepoix, mix and pour over 100 ml (4 fl oz, 7 tablespoons) brandy. Flame, then add the chopped tomatoes, ½ teaspoon concentrated tomato purée (paste), 300 ml (½ pint, 1¼ cups) Chablis, some tarragon and 1 bouquet garni. Add just enough water to cover the lobster. Season with salt, pepper and a pinch of cayenne pepper. Cover and cook for 20 minutes.

Prepare some beurre manié by mixing the reserved coral and juices of the lobster with 75 g (3 oz, 6 tablespoons) butter and 1 tablespoon flour. Drain the cooked lobster and reduce the cooking juices by half.

Strain the fish fumet and poach the fillets of sole in it for about 10 minutes. Drain the fillets, reduce the fumet and strain.

Cover the bottom of an ovenproof dish with 300 g (11 oz, 3½ cups) sliced mushroom caps; put the fillets and shelled sliced lobster tail on top. Cover the dish with foil and keep warm in a preheated oven at 140°C (275°F, gas 1).

Make a hollandaise sauce with 100 g (4 oz, ½ cup) butter, 3 eggs, the juice of ½ a lemon, and salt and pepper. Mix the beurre manié into the reduced cooking juices, stir for about 3 minutes, then add the fish fumet and the hollandaise sauce. Mix thoroughly and then stir in 2 tablespoons crème fraîche. The sauce should be rich and smooth. Coat the fillets with the sauce, garnish with little puff-pastry flowers and then glaze in a very hot oven. This dish should be served immediately.

Fillets of sole Joinville

Clean 250 g (9 oz) mushrooms; dice them, sprinkle with lemon juice, and cook slowly in butter over a low heat. Fillet 2 sole. Make a fumet from the sole trimmings and poach the fillets in this for 6 minutes. Drain thoroughly. Cook 8 giant prawns (shrimp) in boiling salted water for 4 minutes. Prepare 300 ml (½ pint, 1¼ cups) normande sauce using the fish fumet and the cooking juices from the mushrooms; add 15 g (½ oz, 1 tablespoon) prawn butter to the sauce.

Mix 100 g (4 oz, ⅔ cup) peeled prawns with a finely diced truffle and the mushrooms; bind with a little sauce. Arrange the sole fillets in a circle on a round dish; stick a prawn into each fillet. Put the mushroom garnish in the centre of the dish and cover with the sauce.

Formerly, the fillets were arranged on a border of fish forcemeat and truffle slices, with the garnish in the middle.

Fillets of sole Marco Polo

Roughly chop some tarragon, fennel and 1 celery stick. Crush some lobster or langouste shells and put them in a frying pan. Flame with brandy and add the trimmings from 4 sole. Moisten with 300 ml (½ pint, 1¼ cups) white wine and simmer, allowing the liquid to reduce slightly.

Place 50 g (2 oz, ¼ cup) butter, ½ chopped shallot, and half a peeled, seeded and crushed tomato in a saucepan and moisten with 200 ml (7 fl oz, ¾ cup) champagne. Season with salt and pepper. Poach the fillets of sole in this mixture for 5–6 minutes.

Sieve the cooking juices of the shells, crushing the latter firmly, then strain through muslin (cheesecloth). Add 100 g (4 oz, ½ cup) butter and whisk in 2 egg yolks and 100 ml (4 fl oz, 7 tablespoons) crème fraîche.

Serve the sole fillets in their cooking juices, well reduced, and offer the lobster sauce separately.

Fillets of sole Marguery

Fillet 2 sole. Using the bones and trimmings, make a white wine fumet, adding a little chopped onion, a sprig of thyme, a quarter of a bay leaf and a sprig of parsley. Season with salt and pepper and boil for 15 minutes. Add to the fumet the cooking liquid from 1 litre (1 quart) mussels cooked in white wine. Season the sole fillets with salt and pepper and lay them in a greased dish. Pour over a few spoonfuls of the fumet and cover with a sheet of buttered greaseproof (wax) paper. Poach gently, then drain the fillets and arrange them in an oval dish; surround with a double row of cooked shelled mussels and peeled prawns (shelled shrimp). Cover and keep warm while the sauce is being made.

Strain the fumet and the cooking liquid from the sole, reduce by two-thirds, remove from the heat and, when slightly cooled, mix in 6 egg yolks. Whisk the sauce over a gentle heat, like a hollandaise sauce, incorporating 350 g (12 oz, 1½ cups) softened butter. Season the sauce with salt and pepper and strain it; pour over the fillets and their mussel and prawn garnish. Glaze quickly in a preheated oven at 230°C (450°F, gas 8) and garnish with pastry motifs pointing outwards.

Fillets of sole Mornay

Season some fillets of sole with salt and pepper, place them in a buttered gratin dish, spoon over a little fish stock, and poach gently in a preheated oven at 200°C (400°F, gas 6) for about 7–8 minutes, until cooked. Drain them and cover with Mornay sauce, sprinkle with grated Parmesan cheese and clarified butter, and brown in a preheated oven at 240°C (475°F, gas 9).

Fillets of sole Nantua

Poach some fillets of sole in a little court-bouillon made with either white wine or a concentrated fish stock. Arrange the fillets in a circle on a round serving dish and garnish the centre of the circle with a ragoût of crayfish tails *à la Nantua*. Coat the fish with Nantua sauce and garnish the dish with thin slices of mushroom.

Fillets of sole princesse

These are prepared in the same way as salmon steaks princesse, but they are poached folded in half. The asparagus tips are sometimes cut very short and arranged in barquettes made from fine lining pastry. Both the barquettes and the fillets are garnished with slivers of truffle cooked in butter.

Fillets of sole Robert Courtine

Fillet 2 × 675 g (1½ lb) sole. Sprinkle with lemon juice and keep cool. Sweat 2 chopped shallots in a knob of butter over a gentle heat, moisten with 100 ml (4 fl oz, 7 tablespoons) white wine and add a pinch of salt and pepper. Reduce slightly and add 250 ml (8 fl oz, 1 cup) soured (sour) cream. Reduce by a third, remove from the heat and whisk in 150 g (5 oz, ⅔ cup) butter cut into small pieces. Strain into a sauceboat and keep warm in a bain marie. Reserve the shallots for the forcemeat.

144

Flake 200 g (7 oz) white fish in a bowl, mix with the reserved shallots and season with salt and pepper. Place the bowl over crushed ice and work in 150 ml (¼ pint, ⅔ cup) double (heavy) cream. Lay the fillets of sole skin-side up and season lightly. Spread the forcemeat along the fish and fold into three. Steam (on seaweed, if possible) for 7–8 minutes. Arrange on a dish and sprinkle with a little sevruga caviar. Add about 75 g (3 oz) caviar – to the sauce, mix gently and pour over the fillets.

Garnish with chunks of peeled, blanched, steamed cucumber bound with soured (sour) cream or, better still, make a garnish of small potato pancakes: rub 250 g (9 oz) boiled potatoes through a fine sieve into a basin. Add 3 tablespoons plain (all-purpose) flour and 2 tablespoons double cream, mix with a fork and beat in 5 eggs, one at a time. Heat a heavy pan over a gentle heat, lightly cover the bottom with oil and pour in the mixture to make small pancakes, which require about 3 minutes cooking on each side. The potato pancakes can be made in advance and kept warm.

Fillets of sole Saint-Germain

Fillet 2 soles. Flatten them out and sprinkle with salt and pepper. Brush with melted butter, dip in fine fresh breadcrumbs, spoon over 50 g (2 oz, ¼ cup) melted butter and grill (broil) gently on both sides. Arrange on a long dish, surround with 575 g (1¼ lb) small noisette potatoes, and serve with béarnaise sauce in a sauceboat.

Fillets of sole with apples

Boil 2 teaspoons green peppercorns with 2 tablespoons fish fumet in a pan. Add 3 tablespoons crème fraîche, pepper and a pinch of salt. Reduce, add 2 sliced tart apples and cook for a few seconds. Gently poach 4 fillets of sole in a little fish fumet for 2 minutes. Drain, arrange on a plate and surround with the apples. Add the cooking juices of the fish to the peppercorn mixture and bring to the boil. Pour over the fish and serve.

Fillets of sole with basil

Cover the bottom of an ovenproof dish with a mixture of 4 finely chopped shallots, 1 tablespoon basil and 1 tablespoon olive oil. Arrange the seasoned fillets of 2 × 800 g (1¾ lb) sole on top. Moisten with 5 tablespoons fish stock and an equal amount of white wine. Cover with foil and bring to the boil over a brisk heat, then place in a preheated oven at 230°C (450°F, gas 8) for 5 minutes. Drain the fish and keep warm on 2 plates. Reduce the cooking juices by two-thirds. Whisk in 125 g (4½ oz, ½ cup) butter chopped into small pieces, adjust the seasoning and add the juice of ½ a lemon. Plunge a tomato into boiling water for 30 seconds, peel, seed and dice, then top the fillets with the diced tomato and coat with the sauce. Sprinkle with freshly chopped basil.

Fillets of sole with Chambertin

Season some fillets of sole with salt and pepper and fold them in two. Butter an ovenproof casserole and line the bottom with finely diced carrots, chopped onions, fresh crumbled thyme and a crushed bay leaf. Add some chopped mushroom stalks (the caps will serve for the garnish). Arrange the fillets in the dish, dab them with knobs of butter and barely cover them with Chambertin. Cover with the lid and bake in a preheated oven at 240°C (475°F, gas 9). Remove and drain the fillets, then arrange them in the serving dish; keep hot. Reduce the cooking liquid by one-third, pass through a conical strainer and bind the strained liquor with 1 tablespoon beurre manié. Coat the fillets with this sauce and garnish with sautéed mushroom caps and small glazed onions.

Fillets of sole with mushrooms

Fold each fillet of sole over 2 large mushroom caps and cook over a gentle heat in a fish fumet prepared with white wine. Carefully invert the drained fish on to a long dish so that the mushrooms face upwards. Add an equal quantity of crème fraîche to the cooking juices and reduce by half. Whisk in 25 g (1 oz, 2 tablespoons) butter, strain and pour over the fish.

Fillets of sole with noodles

Lay 8 fillets of sole in a buttered dish. Sprinkle them with chopped shallots and season. Moisten with white wine and fish fumet (made with the skin and bones of the sole). Add a crushed tomato and cook in the oven for 8 minutes.

Meanwhile, make a hollandaise sauce. Cook some fresh noodles *al dente*; refresh them, turn into a buttered gratin dish and bind with 100 ml (4 fl oz, 7 tablespoons) crème fraîche, then place the drained fillets on top of the noodles; reduce the cooking juices and add them to the hollandaise sauce with a little crème fraîche. Adjust the seasoning, coat the fillets and glaze in a very hot oven.

Fillets of sole with vermouth

Place the fillets of sole in a buttered pan. Moisten with 100 ml (4 fl oz, 7 tablespoons) fish fumet and 100 ml (4 fl oz, 7 tablespoons) dry vermouth. Poach gently for 10 minutes. Remove the fish and keep warm. Cook 125 g (4½ oz, 1⅓ cups) sliced mushroom caps in butter over a brisk heat for 4 minutes, with salt, pepper and lemon juice. Strain both cooking juices into a pan and reduce to 4 tablespoons; add 400 ml (14 fl oz, 1¾ cups) double (heavy) cream and boil. Remove from the heat and bind with 3 egg yolks. Reheat, stirring, without allowing the mixture to boil. Garnish the fillets with the mushrooms and coat with the sauce.

Fried fillets of sole en goujons

Cut 2 large sole fillets diagonally across in slices about 2 cm (¾ in) wide. Dip in salted milk, drain, coat with flour and fry in hot fat or oil at 180°C (350°F). Drain on paper towels, sprinkle with fine salt and heap on a napkin. Garnish with fried parsley and lemon wedges. The fillets, also known as *goujonnettes*, can be used as a garnish for large braised fish and for sole *à la normande*.

Grilled fillets of sole

Season the fillets of sole, baste with oil or clarified butter and grill (broil) each side for 4 minutes. Arrange on a long dish surrounded by lemon slices and fried parsley. Serve with melted butter flavoured with lemon juice.

Grilled sole

Skin a sole of at least 400 g (14 oz). Lightly season, soak in oil and drain well. Grill (broil) on both sides. Serve with half slices of canelled lemon, fried parsley and any sauce suitable for grilled fish.

Grilled sole à la niçoise

Arrange a grilled sole on a warmed dish. Surround with tomato fondue seasoned with tarragon and mixed with anchovy butter (allow ½ teaspoon butter to 3–4 tablespoons fondue). Finish with capers and stoned (pitted) black (ripe) olives.

Paupiettes of sole

Prepare a forcemeat from 500 g (18 oz) puréed whiting, salt, pepper and 200 ml (7 fl oz, ¾ cup) crème fraîche, working in a bowl over crushed ice.

Remove and prepare the fillets from 2 × 800 g (1¾ lb) sole. Lightly flatten them on a damp worktop and season both sides. Spread the forcemeat over the 8 fillets, roll them up and tie loosely, so that the forcemeat does not escape. Butter a flameproof dish large enough to hold the fillets upright, side by side, then sprinkle it with 2 or 3 chopped shallots and arrange the fillets in it. Season. Moisten with 175 ml (6 fl oz, ¾ cup) each of white wine and fish fumet. Cover with foil, bring to the boil, then place in a preheated oven at 230°C (450°F, gas 8) and cook for 10–15 minutes. Drain the paupiettes and arrange on a serving dish. Keep warm.

Strain the cooking juices into a small saucepan and whisk in 1 tablespoon butter. Pour this on to 2 egg yolks beaten with the juice of half a lemon, then return it to the saucepan and whisk until thick, without allowing it to boil. Pour over the paupiettes and serve very hot.

Paupiettes of sole à l'ancienne

Cover 8 fillets of sole with a thin layer 250 g (9 oz) whiting forcemeat (prepared using the same proportions as those for paupiettes of sole) mixed with 75 g (3 oz) dry mushroom duxelles. Roll up the fillets, coat with egg and breadcrumbs and cook in 40 g (1½ oz, 3 tablespoons) clarified butter. Shape some small cutlets of whiting forcemeat and cook separately. Arrange the paupiettes and cutlets alternately in a ring. Garnish with a ragoût of shrimp tails, mushrooms and truffles, flavoured with Madeira.

Paupiettes of sole paillard

Flatten some fillets of sole, season them with salt and pepper, and cover with a thin layer of fish forcemeat finished with mushroom purée. Roll them into paupiettes and place in a sauté dish lined with thinly sliced onions and mushrooms; add a bouquet garni and moisten with fish stock or dry white wine. Cook the sole, covered, in a preheated oven at 220°C (425°F, gas 7) for 12 minutes.

Drain the paupiettes, arrange them on artichoke hearts in a deep buttered dish, cover and keep them hot. Strain the cooking liquid through muslin (cheesecloth) or a fine sieve. Add an equal volume of mushroom purée, 2 egg yolks, and 200 ml (7 fl oz, ¾ cup) crème fraîche. Bring to the boil, whisking all the time, and adjust the seasoning. Coat the paupiettes with this sauce, glaze in a preheated oven at 230°C (450°F, gas 8) and serve immediately.

Ring of sole à la normande

Generously butter a ring or savarin mould and fill with a cream forcemeat made with fish. Poach in a bain marie in a preheated oven at 180°C (350°F, gas 4) for about 25 minutes. Stand for 30 minutes in the oven with the door open then turn out on to a serving dish. Fill the centre with a shellfish ragoût mixed with normande sauce, then add some fried smelts. Poach some folded fillets of sole in white wine and arrange on top of the ring. Also poach some oysters and place one on each fillet. Garnish with sliced truffle. Warm the dish through and garnish round the edges with shrimps cooked in court-bouillon.

Sole à l'arlésienne

Poach 2 sole for 5–6 minutes in a fish fumet. Arrange on a serving dish and garnish with 4 small peeled tomatoes, cooked in butter, and 4 steamed sliced artichoke hearts to which 100 ml (4 fl oz, 7 tablespoons) reduced double (heavy) cream has been added. Then reduce the fish cooking juices and add 1 tablespoon tomato purée (paste). Add a little crushed garlic and 50–75 g (2–3 oz, 4–6 tablespoons) butter to the sauce. Pour over the sole.

Sole à la dieppoise

Poach 4 soles, each weighing 350 g (12 oz), in 100 ml (4 fl oz, 7 tablespoons) white wine and 100 ml (4 fl oz, 7 tablespoons) fish stock, seasoned with salt and pepper. Keep warm. Cook 100 g (4 oz) button mushrooms in white stock. Cook 100 g (4 oz) prawns (shrimp) in salted water. Remove their shells and keep them warm. Cook 500 g (17 oz) mussels with a bouquet garni over a high heat. Remove them from their shells and keep warm.

Prepare a roux with 40 g (1½ oz, 3 tablespoons) butter and 40 g (1½ oz, 6 tablespoons) plain (all-purpose) flour; add some of the reduced cooking liquid from the soles and the strained liquid from the mussels and that of the mushrooms. Bind with 100 ml (4 fl oz, 7 tablespoons) double (heavy) cream and 25 g (1 oz, 2 tablespoons) butter. Arrange the soles on a dish, surround with the prawns, mussels and mushrooms and pour the hot sauce on top.

Sole à la Dugléré

Skin and clean a sole weighing about 500 g (18 oz) and cut it into sections. Butter a shallow flameproof dish. Peel and chop 1 medium onion, 1 shallot, a small bunch of parsley, a garlic clove and, if liked, 75 g (2½ oz, ¾ cup) button mushrooms. Skin, seed and chop 2 tomatoes. Spread these ingredients on the bottom of the dish, then add a sprig of thyme and half a bay leaf. Arrange the fish in the dish, dot with knobs of butter, moisten with 100 ml (3½ fl oz, scant ½ cup) dry white wine and cover with foil. Bring to the boil, then cook in a preheated oven at 220°C (425°F, gas 7) for 7 minutes. Drain the pieces of sole, arrange on a dish in the original shape of the fish and keep hot. Remove the thyme and bay leaf from the oven dish and add 1 tablespoon velouté made with fish stock. Reduce by one-third, then add 25 g (1 oz, ⅛ cup) butter. Pour the sauce over the fish and sprinkle with chopped parsley.

Sole à la ménagère

Skin and prepare a sole weighing about 1 kg (2¼ lb). Break the backbone at the head and at the tail. Sauté 200 g (7 oz, 1¾ cups) chopped carrots, 150 g

(5 oz, 1 cup) chopped onions, and 2 chopped celery sticks in butter until soft. Season with salt and pepper and sprinkle with a pinch of thyme, a little ground bay leaf and 1 tablespoon chopped parsley.

Place the vegetables in an ovenproof dish and arrange the sole on top. Add 150 ml (¼ pint, ⅔ cup) red wine, cover the dish and cook in a preheated oven at 240°C (475°F, gas 9) for about 10 minutes. Pour the wine from the cooking dish into a saucepan, thicken with 1 tablespoon beurre manié, then pour it back into the dish over the sole. Glaze in a hot oven.

Sole à la meunière

Skin, gut (clean), wash and trim 4 sole, each weighing 250–300 g (9–11 oz); lightly flour and season with pepper. Heat 75–100 g (3–4 oz, 6–8 table-spoons) clarified butter and 1 tablespoon oil in a frying pan. Brown the sole for 6–7 minutes on each side. Drain and arrange on a heated serving dish. Pour over 75 g (3 oz, 6 tablespoons) butter melted in a saucepan with the juice of 1 lemon. Sprinkle with chopped parsley. Serve with sliced vegetables fried in oil or butter.

Suitable vegetables include aubergines (eggplants) and courgettes (zucchini) fried in oil, chunks of cucumber sweated in butter, sliced artichoke hearts fried in butter, mushrooms (especially ceps) fried in butter or oil and red or green (bell) peppers that have been cut into thick julienne strips and sweated in oil.

Sole à la normande

For a sole weighing about 400 g (14 oz), prepare a garnish of 4 debearded and poached oysters, 12 mussels cooked in dry white wine, 25 g (1 oz) peeled prawns (shelled shrimp), 4 fluted mushrooms cooked in dry white wine, 6 slices of truffle, 4 gudgeon (or smelt) coated with breadcrumbs and fried,

4 trussed crayfish cooked in court-bouillon, and 4 heart- or lozenge-shaped croûtons of bread fried in butter (or puff-pastry crescents).

Trim the sole, split it, skin one side only, and carefully raise the fillets a little. Break the backbone in 2 or 3 places to facilitate its removal after cooking. Poach the fish in a little fish fumet made with white wine, to which the cooking liquids from the oysters, mushrooms and mussels have been added. Drain the fish on paper towels and remove the backbone.

Arrange the fish on a long buttered serving dish together with the various garnishes and cover with normande sauce made from the fish cooking stock. The fish can be garnished with a ribbon of light fish aspic or meat glaze.

Sole à la paysanne

Thinly slice a carrot, an onion, a celery stick and the white part of a small leek. Braise in butter, seasoning with salt and a pinch of sugar. When cooked, add enough warm water to just cover. Then add 1 tablespoon diced French (green) beans and an equal quantity of fresh peas. Finish cooking all the vegetables together, then boil the liquid to reduce it by one-third.

Place a trimmed sole weighing about 300 g (11 oz) in a buttered, oval, earthenware dish, season with salt and pepper and cover with the vegetables and their cooking liquor. Poach the fish in a preheated oven at 180°C (350°F, gas 4). When cooked, remove most of the cooking liquor from the dish, boil to reduce and then whisk in 2 tablespoons butter. Coat the sole with the sauce and glaze in a very hot oven. Serve immediately.

Sole à la portugaise

Lightly butter a long ovenproof dish and cover with a thick tomato sauce flavoured with garlic. Trim, prepare and season a 675 g (1½ lb) sole and lay it in the dish. Moisten with 2 tablespoons olive oil, 1 tablespoon lemon juice and 2 tablespoons fish stock. Cook in a preheated oven at 230°C (450°F, gas 8) for about 10 minutes, basting the sole from time to time with its cooking juices. Sprinkle with breadcrumbs, brown under the grill (broiler), then sprinkle with chopped parsley.

Sole and mushroom brochettes

Cut the fish into square pieces of equal size. Sandwich them together two by two with a stuffing made from hard-boiled (hard-cooked) egg yolks, fresh breadcrumbs and parsley. Thread them on skewers, alternating them with mushrooms tossed in melted butter. Season with salt and pepper and baste with clarified butter. Cover with white dried breadcrumbs and grill (broil).

Sole armenonville

Prepare a pancake of pommes Anna. Skin and prepare 2 good sole and poach them in a very shallow dish in fish stock. Make a white wine sauce and stir in the cooking juices from the sole. Cut some cep mushrooms into thin strips, cook them gently in butter in a covered pan and add them to the sauce. Arrange the pommes Anna on the serving dish, place the sole on top, coat with sauce and serve immediately. In the traditional recipe, the sole is served surrounded by a border of duchesse potatoes enriched with truffles.

Sole bagatelle

Prepare a salpicon from a lobster *à l'américaine*, mushrooms and truffles. Bind with very thick américaine sauce with a little added cream – 100 ml (4 fl oz, 7 tablespoons) double (heavy) cream to 300 ml (½ pint, 1¼ cups) sauce. Lay out the fillets of sole and spread with the salpicon; fold the fillets over the stuffing and coat with egg and breadcrumbs. Lightly brown them in a frying pan and arrange on a dish, garnished with sliced truffles. Keep warm.

Cook 1 tablespoon grated shallot in butter without allowing it to colour. Moisten with 175 ml (6 fl oz, ¾ cup) dry white wine and reduce by half. Then double the volume with fish fumet and season. Add chopped parsley and the juice of 1 lemon. Thicken with 50 g (2 oz, ¼ cup) beurre manié. Cook for 10 minutes; finish with 25 g (1 oz, 2 tablespoons) butter and some finely chopped chives. Pour over the sole.

Sole Bercy

Butter an ovenproof dish and sprinkle with chopped shallots and parsley. Place the prepared sole in the dish, add 2 tablespoons dry white wine and a dash of lemon juice and dot with 15 g (½ oz, 1 tablespoon) butter. Cook in a preheated oven at 220°C (425°F, gas 7) for 15 minutes basting the fish several times in order to glaze it.

Sole Colbert

Remove the dark skin from the sole and slit the flesh on either side of the backbone. Raise the fillets and break the backbone in 2 or 3 places so that it may be easily removed after cooking. Dip in milk and coat in egg and breadcrumbs. Fry the sole, drain it and remove the backbone. Fill the cavity with Colbert butter. Serve on a long dish and garnish with fried parsley.

Sole diplomat

Remove the skin from a good-sized sole, slit its flesh along the backbone and free the top fillets, working outwards from the centre. Cut the backbone at the head and tail and remove it completely. Prepare 125 g (4½ oz, ½ cup) cream forcemeat made with whiting, adding 1 tablespoon diced truffles. Insert the forcemeat underneath the top fillets. Gently poach the sole in a fish fumet but do not cover. Drain, remove the small lateral bones, arrange on the serving dish and surround with diced lobster flesh. Keep hot. Use the cooking liquid to make some diplomat sauce and coat the fish with it.

Sole fillets à la Daumont

Prepare about 150 ml (¼ pint, ⅔ cup) salpicon of crayfish tails *à la Nantua*. Fillet 2 large sole. Prepare 400 g (14 oz, 2 cups) fine whiting forcemeat and add 50 g (2 oz, ¼ cup) crayfish butter. Spread the sole fillets with the forcemeat and fold them over. Place them in a buttered gratin dish, add sufficient fish fumet just to cover them and poach gently. Gently cook 8 large mushroom caps in butter, drain and top each with some of the crayfish salpicon. Drain the sole fillets and place one on each mushroom. Coat with normande sauce and serve very hot.

Sole fritots

Cut some sole fillets in two (or four if large fillets), then dip them in a light batter and deep-fry until they are golden brown. Drain on paper towels and serve with fried parsley and quarters of lemon. Serve with a flavoured mayonnaise sauce, for example, with grated lemon zest and chopped capers.

Sole meunière Mont-Bry

Prepare in advance 200 g (7 oz) thin noodles. Scald, peel and seed 6 tomatoes, then crush them to remove any liquid. Chop a medium onion and brown in butter. Add the crushed tomatoes, a pinch of salt, a pinch of caster (superfine) sugar and a little crushed garlic; cover and cook slowly.

Then prepare 3 sole weighing about 300 g (11 oz) each. Remove the brown skin and carefully detach the fillets from the backbone. Season the fillets with salt and pepper, roll them in flour and cook in clarified butter in a frying pan until golden brown on both sides.

Using another frying pan, sauté the noodles in 5–6 tablespoons clarified butter until they are lightly browned and slightly crisp. Place the sole fillets in a hot long serving dish, sprinkle with lemon juice and chopped parsley, and arrange the tomato mixture around them. Pile mounds of noodles at each end of the dish. Baste the fish copiously with noisette butter, which should be bubbling and frothy.

Sole sur le plat

Remove the black skin from 2 × 800 g (1¾ lb) sole and cut off the heads at an angle. Cut along the backbone and open out. Remove the bone, taking care that the fillets remain attached. Moisten with fish fumet with added lemon juice to the level of the fish and dot with knobs of butter. Cook in a preheated oven at 230°C (450°F, gas 8) for about 15 minutes, basting frequently (the cooking juices should become syrupy and glaze the surface of the fish). Serve in the cooking dish.

Sole with orange

Brown a trimmed floured sole in a knob of butter until cooked through on both sides. Place on a hot serving dish and season with pepper. Garnish with thin slices of peeled orange with the seeds removed. Melt a little butter in a bain marie, season with salt and add a little crème fraîche and Curaçao. Pour over the sole.

Sole with thyme

Cook a small sole in butter in a frying pan for 2 minutes on each side. Season it with salt and pepper and add ¼ teaspoon dried thyme and 2 tablespoons dry white wine. Continue to cook for 30 seconds, then remove the fish. Reduce the juices by half and add 2 tablespoons double (heavy) cream and a peeled slice of lemon, chopped. Boil the sauce until it becomes thick and pour it over the fish. Garnish with small steamed courgettes (zucchini).

Steamed fillets of sole in tomato sauce

Arrange 6–7 sprigs of basil in the basket of a steamer and place on top 4 sole fillets folded in half. Season with salt and pepper. Pour a little water into the lower pan, bring to the boil and cook, covered, for about 8 minutes. Keep the sole fillets hot.

Poach 1 egg for 3 minutes in boiling water with vinegar added; mash well. Cook 1 chopped shallot gently in olive oil in a saucepan. Away from the heat, add the mashed poached egg, a dash of French mustard, the juice of 1 lemon, salt and pepper, as well as some basil leaves, finely chopped. Place over a low heat and whisk the mixture. While whisking, gradually add 100 ml (4 fl oz, 7 tablespoons) olive oil to thicken the sauce to the consistency of a hollandaise. Then add 3 tomatoes, peeled, seeded and diced, and 1 tablespoon chopped chervil. Serve the sole fillets coated with the sauce.

Stuffed sole Auberge de l'Ill

Remove the black skin from 2 × 800 g (1¾ lb) sole and cut off the heads at an angle. Cut along the backbone and open out. Remove the bone, taking care that the fillets remain attached. Put 100 g (4 oz) whiting fillets, 1 egg white, salt, pepper and a pinch of grated nutmeg in a blender or food processor. With the motor running, add 250 ml (8 fl oz, 1 cup) very cold double (heavy) cream, a little at a time. Mix the forcemeat with 150 g (5 oz) diced salmon fillets and 50 g (2 oz, ½ cup) chopped pistachios in a bowl. Stuff the sole with the mixture, season and arrange on a buttered ovenproof dish. Sprinkle with chopped shallots and moisten with 250 ml (8 fl oz, 1 cup) Riesling and 250 ml (8 fl oz, 1 cup) fish fumet. Cover with foil and cook in a preheated oven at

220°C (425°F, gas 7) for 25 minutes. Arrange on a plate and keep warm. Pour the cooking juices into a pan, add 250 ml (8 fl oz, 1 cup) double cream and reduce by half. Whisk in 100 g (4 oz, ½ cup) butter, a little at a time. Add the juice of 1 lemon. Adjust the seasoning and pour over the sole. Garnish with slices of truffle glazed in butter and puff-pastry flowers.

Sprats

Sprats à la vinaigrette

Remove the heads and skin from some fresh sprats. Arrange in a small bowl and sprinkle liberally with chopped shallots and parsley. Coat with oil and shallot-flavoured (or white distilled) vinegar. Marinate in a cool place for 10 hours. Serve with parsley, rye bread and shallot butter.

Sturgeon

Fricandeau of sturgeon à la hongroise

Brown a thick slice of sturgeon in butter with finely diced onions in an ovenproof dish. Season with salt, paprika and a bouquet garni. Moisten with 200 ml (7 fl oz, ¾ cup) white wine then boil down to reduce. Add 300 ml

(½ pint, 1¼ cups) velouté sauce based on fish stock. Finish in a slow oven. Add butter to the sauce and pour it over the fish. Serve with boiled potatoes, cucumber balls or a purée of sweet (bell) peppers.

Sturgeon à la brimont

Fillet a medium-sized sturgeon. Trim the fillets and thread anchovy fillets through them. Place in a baking dish lined with a fondue of carrots, onions and celery, finely sliced and cooked slowly in butter until tender. Cover with 2 peeled, chopped and seeded tomatoes mixed with 4 tablespoons coarsely diced mushrooms and surround with potatoes cut into little balls with a ball-scoop, three-quarters cooked in salted water and drained. Moisten with 100 ml (4 fl oz, 7 tablespoons) dry white wine and dot with 50 g (2 oz, ¼ cup) butter. Bake in a preheated oven at 150°C (300°F, gas 2), basting frequently, for about 40 minutes, depending on the size and thickness of the sturgeon. Gently ease the flakes apart at the thickest part of the fish to see if it is cooked. Five minutes before the end of cooking sprinkle the fish with breadcrumbs and brown lightly.

Trout & salmon trout

Fried trout

Clean, gut and dry some very small trout. Season with salt and pepper and dust with flour. Deep-fry in sizzling oil, then drain and arrange on a napkin. Serve with a green salad and slices of lemon.

Medallions of trout with chive butter

Blanch 100 g (4 oz) spinach for 1 minute. Rinse in plenty of cold water, dry well and chop very finely. In a blender, combine 150 g (5 oz) scallops without their corals, the spinach, 5 tablespoons whipping cream and 3 tablespoons white wine. Season with salt and pepper. Cover 6 good trout fillets with this mixture, then roll them up on themselves. Wrap each trout roll in foil, carefully sealing the ends. Cook in steam for 8–10 minutes. Put to one side. Reduce almost completely 120 ml (4½ fl oz, ½ cup) good white wine with 1 very finely chopped shallot in a saucepan. Add 250 g (9 oz, 1 cup) very cold butter, cut into pieces, and incorporate vigorously. Add 3–4 tablespoons finely chopped chives. Correct the seasoning. Put this chive butter on the plates and place the rolled trout fillets, cut into medallions, on top. Garnish with the vegetables, cooked *al dente*.

Salmon trout Beauharnais

Stuff a salmon trout weighing about 900 g (2 lb) with 250 g (9 oz) forcemeat of whiting and cream mixed with 4 tablespoons vegetable mirepoix lightly cooked in butter. Place on the buttered grid of a fish kettle, half-cover with fish fumet made with white wine and cook in a preheated oven at 230°C (450°F, gas 8), or place the fish kettle on the hob (stove top) across two burners or hotplates, for about 20 minutes. Drain the trout, place in a serving dish and garnish with noisette potatoes cooked in butter and small artichoke hearts cooked in butter and filled with béarnaise sauce. Strain the cooking liquid; reduce, thicken with butter and serve with the trout.

Salmon trout Berchoux

Stuff a 2 kg (4½ lb) salmon trout with a creamy pike forcemeat with chopped truffles. Place the trout in a buttered ovenproof dish on a bed consisting of a chopped carrot, a medium-sized chopped onion (lightly fried in butter), a good handful of mushroom trimmings and a bouquet garni. Add fish stock with white wine until it comes halfway up the trout. Season with salt and pepper, cover, place in a preheated oven at 180°C (350°F, gas 4), and cook for about 40 minutes, basting frequently until the fish is just cooked. Remove the central portion of skin and the dark parts of the flesh. Strain the cooking liquor, pour a few tablespoons of this liquor over the trout and glaze slightly in the oven.

Prepare the garnish: 8 small pastry barquettes filled with soft carp roe and coated with normande sauce; 8 small croquettes made of diced lobster, mushrooms, and truffles bound with a thin velouté sauce; and 8 very small artichoke hearts, partly cooked in white stock, sweated in butter, filled with a salpicon of truffles bound with cream, sprinkled with Parmesan, and browned in the oven.

Add 300 ml (½ pint, 1¼ cups) velouté fish sauce to the remaining cooking liquor and reduce over a high heat, gradually adding 300 ml (½ pint, 1¼ cups) double (heavy) cream to the sauce. Add butter and then strain or sieve. Use to coat the bottom of the serving dish for the fish and serve the rest in a sauceboat. Transfer the salmon trout to the serving dish and add all of the garnishes.

This traditional recipe can be modified by simplifying the garnishes.

Salmon trout with salad

Clean and fillet 4 salmon trout. Slice the fillets into thin strips, lay on a porcelain dish, season with salt and pepper and sprinkle with olive oil. Turn them over and repeat the seasoning. Leave the fillets to marinate overnight in a cool place. On the day of the meal, cook some small artichokes, keeping them crisp, peel 2 very ripe avocados, poach 3 quails' eggs per guest and prepare a very fine julienne of orange zest and peeled ginger root. Cook 3 crayfish per person in a highly flavoured court-bouillon.

Arrange the marinated raw trout fillets in a fan shape on the plates. Place the crayfish, with their tails shelled, at the base of the fan, then complete the fan with avocado slices, artichoke quarters and quails' eggs. Sprinkle with the orange and ginger julienne strips, then season with a dash of lemon juice and a little olive oil.

In autumn, make the garnish with thin strips of Caesar's mushrooms, a boletus cap marinated with the trout fillets, small shaped pieces of beetroot (beet), crisp French (green) beans, artichoke hearts, poached quails' eggs and a julienne of orange zest and fresh ginger.

Trout à la bourguignonne

Clean and dry 4 trout and season with salt and pepper inside and out. Finely slice 250 g (9 oz) cleaned mushrooms, 1 carrot and 1 onion, lightly cook in butter and use to line a buttered ovenproof dish. Place the trout in the dish and add a bouquet garni and just enough red Burgundy to cover the fish. Bring to the boil on the hob (stove top), then cover and cook in a preheated oven at 220°C (425°F, gas 7) for about 10 minutes. Glaze 12 small (pearl) onions. Drain the trout and place in a heated serving dish, with the onions as a garnish. Keep hot. Strain the cooking liquid, thicken with 1 tablespoon beurre manié, and put back on the heat for 2–3 minutes. Add 2 tablespoons unsalted butter, whisk and pour over the trout.

Trout à la nage Jean Giono

Clean and rinse the freshly killed trout. Pour into a dish 1 glass vinegar and season with salt and pepper; put the trout in the dish, turning them over several times, then leave to marinate for 15 minutes.

Heat a little vinegar in a large sauté pan or flameproof casserole (large enough to hold the trout), then pour in 1 glass olive oil beaten with 5 glasses water. Add 1 carrot, 1 leek and 1 onion (all sliced), 1 small chopped celery stick, 3 crushed garlic cloves, 5 crushed juniper berries, a pinch of powdered thyme, salt, pepper and a dozen fennel seeds. Boil rapidly, until the liquid has reduced to about 1 cm (½ in).

Add the trout. Cover, bring to the boil, then cook at maximum heat for 1 minute and over a low heat for a further 4 minutes.

Trout au bleu

For true trout *au bleu*, the fish must be extremely fresh – killed about 10 minutes before cooking and serving. Take the fish out of the water and kill it with a hard blow to the head; gut and clean rapidly, without wiping. Sprinkle with vinegar, then plunge into a boiling court-bouillon containing a high proportion of vinegar. Simmer, allowing 6–7 minutes for fish weighing about 150 g (5 oz). Drain and arrange on a napkin. Garnish with fresh parsley and serve with melted butter or hollandaise sauce.

Trout with almonds

Clean and dry four 250 g (9 oz) trout. Season with salt and pepper and dust with flour, shaking to remove any excess. Melt 50 g (2 oz, ¼ cup) butter in a large oval frying pan and brown the trout on both sides, then lower the heat and cook for 10–12 minutes, turning once. Brown 75 g (3 oz, ¾ cup) shredded (slivered) almonds in a dry frying pan or in the oven and add to the trout. Drain the cooked trout and arrange on a serving dish. Sprinkle with 2 tablespoons lemon juice and some chopped parsley. Keep warm. Add 20 g (¾ oz, 1½ tablespoons) butter and 1 tablespoon vinegar to the pan, heat, then pour over the trout.

Trout with leeks

Remove the backbone from an uncooked trout, season with salt and pepper, and stuff with a fine cream forcemeat made with whiting. Roll up in blanched whole leaves of young leeks. Cook in a buttered dish with a little white wine and shallots. Drain the fish. Reduce the cooking liquid, if necessary, and thicken with cream; adjust the seasoning and pour over the trout.

Tuna

Attereaux à la niçoise

Attereau is the term for a skewer threaded with ingredients, coated in sauce and breadcrumbs and fried.

Assemble the attereaux with large stoned (pitted) olives, mushrooms, pieces of tuna fish marinated in olive oil and lemon, and anchovy fillets. Make a Villeroi sauce and add to it 1 tablespoon reduced tomato sauce and chopped tarragon. Coat the attereaux with sauce, then with breadcrumbs, and fry.

Grilled tuna

Mix some olive oil with lemon juice, salt, pepper, a little cayenne pepper, some finely chopped parsley and, if desired, a crushed garlic clove. Marinate some steaks of white tuna (albacore) 4–5 cm (1½–2 in) thick in this mixture for at least 30 minutes. Grill (broil) the drained steaks under a low heat for 10 minutes on each side. Serve with a flavoured butter, for example made with sweet (bell) pepper or anchovy.

Tuna en daube à la provençale

Stud a slice of bluefin tuna with anchovy fillets. Marinate in olive oil, lemon juice, salt and pepper for 1 hour. Brown the fish in olive oil in a flameproof casserole, remove and set aside. Add 1 chopped onion. Cook for 10 minutes, until soft but not brown. Stir in 2 large peeled, seeded and crushed tomatoes, 1 small crushed garlic clove and a bouquet garni. Replace the tuna, cover and cook for 15 minutes. Pour in 150 ml (¼ pint, ⅔ cup) white wine and finish cooking in the oven, basting often, for 40 minutes. Drain the fish and place on a serving dish. Add the concentrated cooking liquor and serve with a little timbale of ratatouille and a fan of sautéed courgette (zucchini).

Tuna fish in tea

Brown a bluefin tuna steak, weighing about 800 g (1¾ lb), in oil in a frying pan. Meanwhile, prepare an infusion of fairly strong tea (black China tea or lotus tea). Put the tuna into a saucepan together with 100 g (4 oz, ½ cup) diced fresh unsalted belly of pork. Add a piece of fresh root ginger cut into thin strips, pepper, 1–2 teaspoons *nuoc-mâm* (Vietnamese fish sauce), a lump of sugar and the tea (ensure that the liquid just covers the fish). Simmer over a gentle heat for 1 hour.

Tuna omelette

For 6 people, wash 2 soft carp roes and blanch them for 5 minutes in lightly salted boiling water. Chop the roes together with a piece of fresh tuna about the size of a hen's egg so that they are well mixed. Put the chopped fish and roes into a pan with a small, finely chopped shallot and butter and sauté until all the butter is incorporated – this gives the essential flavour to the omelette.

Blend some butter with parsley and chives, and spread it on to the serving dish for the omelette; sprinkle with lemon juice and keep warm.

Beat 12 eggs, add the sautéed roes and tuna, and mix well together. Cook the omelette in the usual way, keeping the shape long rather than circular, and ensure that it is thick and creamy. As soon as it is ready, arrange it on the prepared dish and serve at once.

The roes and the tuna should be sautéed over a very low heat, otherwise they will harden and it will be difficult to mix them properly with the eggs. The serving dish should be fairly deep, and preferably fish-shaped, so that the sauce can be spooned up when serving. The dish should be heated enough to melt the maître d'hôtel butter on which the omelette is placed.

Tuna rouelle with spices and carrots

In this context, rouelle is the term for a neat round of tuna steak. Brown a 1 kg (2¼ lb) tuna rouelle in butter in a flameproof casserole. Add 6 peeled and quartered tomatoes, 10 small, peeled whole onions and 1 kg (2¼ lb) baby carrots, peeled and sliced. Mix with 500 ml (17 fl oz, 2 cups) chicken stock and season with 2 teaspoons fresh root ginger, a pinch of grated nutmeg, ½ teaspoon ground cinnamon, 4 saffron strands, ½ teaspoon ground cumin and salt. Cover, bring to the boil and simmer for 1 hour. Serve very hot.

Turbot

Escalopes of turbot with buttered leeks

Slice some fillets of turbot into escalopes and make a fumet with the trimmings. Seal the escalopes in butter on both sides, then cover with the fumet. Simmer for 5 minutes. Drain the fish. Mix the cooking juices with an equal amount of double (heavy) cream. Arrange the escalopes on a hot dish and pour over the sauce. Serve with an *embeurrée* of leeks: cook 1 kg (2¼ lb) shredded white parts of leeks in a preheated oven at 190°C (375°F, gas 5) with 200 g (7 oz, 1 cup) butter and 175 ml (6 fl oz, ¾ cup) water, covered, for 20 minutes; season with salt and pepper.

Fillets of turbot with leek fondue and beef marrow

Soften some shredded leeks with a knob of butter for 20 minutes over a very low heat. Season with salt and pepper, then add some crème fraîche and cook for a further 5 minutes, then set aside. Steam the turbot for 8 minutes. Reduce for 1 minute half a shallot (finely chopped) in 100 ml (4 fl oz, 7 tablespoons) red wine. Add 2 tablespoons meat glaze. Reduce, then remove from the heat and thicken with 25 g (1 oz, 2 tablespoons) butter cut into small pieces. Line the plates with this sauce, put the fillets of turbot on top, then surround with the leek fondue, alternating it with a *concassée* of tomatoes (this consists of 2 very ripe tomatoes, peeled, seeded, diced and lightly cooked in a little butter with a chopped shallot). Finish off with slices of beef marrow, soaked in cold water for 2–3 hours, then poached for 3 minutes in boiling water. Garnish with parsley.

Steamed turbot steaks

Cut a turbot into steaks; season with salt and pepper and steam for 12 minutes. Chop some shallots and put them in a saucepan with a drop of vinegar and 100 ml (4 fl oz, 7 tablespoons) single (light) cream beaten with 2 mashed bananas. Reduce. Glaze in butter 2 unpeeled garlic cloves per turbot steak. Serve the fish coated with the sauce and surrounded with the garlic cloves and sprigs of parsley.

Turbot en papillote with crispy vegetables and champagne sauce

Fillet a 1.5 kg (3¼ lb) turbot and cut into 12 escalopes of equal thickness. Chill and prepare a fish stock with the bones. Peel and cut 2 medium-sized carrots, 1 celery heart, 1 small turnip and the white part of leek into a coarse julienne. Halve 75 g (3 oz) green beans. Cook the vegetables for 3 minutes in the fish stock with 20 g (¾ oz, 1½ tablespoons) butter. Season when almost cooked. Drain and reserve the liquid. Sweat 2 peeled and chopped shallots in 2 teaspoons butter. Deglaze with 200 ml (7 fl oz, ¾ cup) brut champagne and the reserved cooking liquid. Reduce by half.

Fold 2 sheets of foil 30 × 60 cm (12 × 24 in) in half to make double-thick squares. Cut into semi-circles, leaving the folded edge uncut. Unfold and put 6 escalopes, seasoned with salt, pepper and cayenne pepper, on one half of each. Top with the vegetables and fold the foil over. Seal the edges.

Add 200 ml (7 fl oz, ¾ cup) crème fraîche to the champagne reduction. Bring to the boil and cook for a few seconds. Whisk in 125 g (4½ oz, ½ cup) butter, cut into small pieces. Cook the papillotes in a preheated oven at 220°C (425°F, gas 7) for 7 minutes. Take out of the oven and open the parcels in front of the guests. Pour a little sauce on each plate and place 2 escalopes on top.

Turbot with leeks

Lift the fillets from a young 900 g (2 lb) turbot. Trim and clean in fresh water and cut up into small pieces (*goujonnettes*). Make a fumet from the head and trimmings. Wash, trim and slice 6 small leeks and arrange them in a buttered ovenproof dish. Cover with the fumet, season with salt and pepper, and cook in a preheated oven at 220°C (425°F, gas 7) until they are just cooked but not soft. Drain the leeks, retaining the cooking liquid, and divide them among individual dishes. Keep warm.

Pour 200 ml (7 fl oz, ¾ cup) strained fumet into a pan, add 3 tablespoons crème fraîche, a pinch of sugar, white pepper (2 twists of the pepper mill) and 2 tablespoons dry vermouth. Boil down to reduce. Put the turbot pieces into the sauce. Poach for 5 minutes. Drain the fish and place on top of the leeks. Further reduce the cooking liquid, then pour it over the fish. Serve hot.

Turbot with morels

For 5 or 6 servings, soak 300 g (11 oz) dried morels in plenty of water (use fresh morels in season). Remove the stalks and wash. Cook in salted water, strain, squeeze gently and brown in a saucepan, adding finely chopped shallots at the last moment. Add 200 ml (7 fl oz, ¾ cup) double (heavy) cream and bring to the boil. Adjust the seasoning and simmer for about 10 minutes.

Fillet, skin and trim a 3–4 kg (6½–9 lb) turbot and cut into 100 g (4 oz) escalopes. Season on both sides. Garnish half the escalopes with small piles of morels and cover with the remaining escalopes. Cook in a frying pan with a little butter, then in a preheated oven at 180°C (350°F, gas 4) for about 10 minutes. Arrange in a dish and coat with Américaine sauce, prepared as for lobster *à l'américaine*. Put a medallion of lobster on each escalope.

Weever

Grilled weever

A sea fish that often lies buried in the sand on the sea bed. The poisonous spines and the fins should be cut off before any other preparation and the fish handled with gloves on. Gut and clean the weevers. Make shallow slits on the back of each fish and on each side of the central fin. Marinate them for an hour in a mixture of oil, lemon juice, salt, pepper and chopped parsley, with a little chopped garlic. Then gently grill (broil) them for about 15 minutes, turning once.

Serve with melted butter strongly flavoured with lemon and mixed with chopped herbs or with a mixture of olive oil and raw, crushed tomato pulp.

Whiting

Fried whiting en colère

Soak the whiting for 10 minutes in milk or pale (light) ale. Drain, pat it dry, season with salt and pepper and roll it in flour. Shape the fish into a circle by putting the tail into the mouth and clenching the jaws so that it remains in this position during cooking. Deep-fry in hot (but not smoking) fat, making sure that it is evenly browned on both sides. Drain it on paper towels and serve with fried parsley, slices of lemon and tartare sauce. Whiting can also be fried flat, but in this case a shallow incision should be made along its back.

Fried whiting en lorgnette

Make a deep incision in the fish along each side of the backbone. Do not separate the fillets from the head. Remove the backbone, starting at the tail and breaking it off at the base of the head. Season with salt and pepper and dip in egg and breadcrumbs. Roll up the fillets on either side of the head and secure each of them with a small wooden skewer so that they stay in position. Deep-fry in very hot (but not smoking) fat. Arrange on a napkin and garnish with fried parsley and slices of lemon.

Moscow piroshki

Piroshkis are small filled pasties or turnovers served with soup or as a hot entrée in Russian and Polish cooking.

Prepare some unsweetened brioche dough and cut out small ovals, 6–7 cm (2½ in) wide and 10 cm (4 in) long. Prepare the filling: chop and mix 125 g (4½ oz) cooked white fish fillets (whiting or pike), 75 g (3 oz) cooked *vesiga* (dried spinal marrow of the sturgeon) and 2 hard-boiled (hard-cooked) eggs. Season with salt and pepper. Put a large knob of this mixture on each oval. Moisten the edges of the ovals slightly, fold over to cover the filling and press to seal tightly.

Leave for 30 minutes in a warm place for the dough to rise. Brush with beaten egg and cook in a preheated oven at 220°C (425°F, gas 7) for about 25 minutes. Drizzle with a little melted maître d'hôtel butter.

Paupiettes of whiting

Fillet 3 whiting and remove the skin. Put the bones and heads in a saucepan with 2 grated carrots, 1 shredded onion, 2 chopped shallots, 350 ml (12 fl oz, 1½ cups) dry white wine, a large glass of water, a bouquet garni, salt and pepper. Boil gently for 30 minutes, strain and reduce by half. Leave to cool.

Prepare a fish mousse: reduce 2 whiting fillets to a purée in a blender and put it into a basin. Place the basin in a bowl containing crushed ice. Gradually add 200 ml (7 fl oz, ¾ cup) crème fraîche, working the mixture briskly until it becomes mousse like. Flatten the 4 remaining fillets, season with salt and pepper and coat evenly with the fish mousse. Roll the fillets up tightly and tie them with string. Arrange the paupiettes in a buttered flameproof dish, pour the reduced stock over the top and cover. Bring to the boil on top of the stove, then cook in a preheated oven at 220°C (425°F, gas 7) for 20–25 minutes.

Make some beurre manié by mixing 1 tablespoon butter with an equal quantity of flour. Drain the paupiettes and keep them hot on a serving dish. Thicken the cooking liquid with the beurre manié. Untie the paupiettes, coat them with the sauce and serve piping hot.

Poached whiting with melted butter

Put a large whiting into a cold court-bouillon in a pan. Bring to the boil, cover and poach gently for 10 minutes. Drain the fish and arrange it on a serving dish. Pour a little melted butter over the top and sprinkle with chopped parsley. Serve any remaining butter in a sauceboat. Garnish with steamed potatoes, rice, cucumber slices, spinach or leeks cooked in butter or sautéed courgettes (zucchini) or aubergines (eggplants).

Stuffed whiting with cider

Remove the backbone from 4 × 300 g (11 oz) whiting. Gut (clean) them through the back and season with salt and pepper. Slice 2 carrots, 2 celery sticks and the white parts of 2 leeks finely. Cook very gently for 5 minutes in a covered pan with 25 g (1 oz, 2 tablespoons) butter, and salt and pepper. Leave to cool. Stuff the fish with the vegetables and place them in a large ovenproof dish with 1 tablespoon olive oil. Pour in 350 ml (12 fl oz, 1½ cups) dry (hard) cider and 175 ml (6 fl oz, ¾ cup) fish stock. Cook in a preheated oven at 220°C (425°F, gas 7) for 15–20 minutes or until cooked. Remove the fish, boil down the stock until it is almost evaporated, then add 250 g (9 oz, generous 1 cup) curd cheese and heat gently, stirring, without boiling. Pour this sauce over the whiting, sprinkle with chopped chives and serve very hot.

Turnovers à la Cussy

Fill circles of puff pastry with a cream forcemeat made with whiting or other white fish to which anchovy fillets (cut into small strips) and chopped truffles have been added. Fold the pastry over into turnovers. Place on a buttered baking sheet, brush with beaten egg, and bake in a preheated oven at 230°C (450°F, gas 8) until golden brown.

Whiting à l'anglaise

Open the fish from the back and remove the backbone. Season, roll in flour, dip in egg and breadcrumbs and brown in butter on both sides. Put on a dish, top with slightly soft maître d'hôtel butter and serve with boiled potatoes.

Whiting à l'espagnole

Dip the whiting in egg and breadcrumbs, brown it in oil and place on a bed of tomato fondue seasoned with crushed garlic. Garnish with fried onion rings.

Whiting hermitage

Remove the bone from a large whiting and gut (clean) it through the back. Stuff it with a mixture of breadcrumbs, creamed butter, chopped shallot, egg, chopped herbs, salt and a pinch of cayenne. Put it into a buttered gratin dish with a little cream and some fish stock. Cover with buttered greaseproof (wax) paper and bake in a preheated oven at 220°C (425°F, gas 7) for 15 minutes. Drain the whiting. Boil the cooking liquid to reduce and add some butter, cream, salt and pepper. Bring to the boil and pour over the fish.

Whiting in white wine

Gut (clean) 2 large whiting and season with salt and pepper. Butter a flameproof gratin dish, line it with a layer of chopped onions and shallots and place the fish on top. Add equal quantities of white wine and fish stock so the fish are half-covered. Cover the dish, begin the cooking on the top of the stove, then place in a preheated oven at 220°C (425°F, gas 7) for 20 minutes. Drain the fish and keep them hot in a serving dish. Boil the cooking liquid to reduce by half and add 200 ml (7 fl oz, ¾ cup) single (light) cream. Boil down and pour the sauce over the fish. Glaze for 5 minutes in a very hot oven.

Wrasse

Wrasse with potatoes

The wrasse is a fish of the *Labridae* family, which is fished on coasts from Norway to Senegal and also in the Mediterranean.

Blanch 250 g (9 oz) thick, streaky, lightly salted bacon in water and cut into small strips. Peel and slice 150 g (5 oz, generous 1 cup) shallots. Peel 1 kg (2¼ lb) potatoes, cut into thin slices, wash and wipe dry. Grease an ovenproof dish with lard (shortening) and arrange the strips of bacon and potatoes in it in alternate layers, sprinkled with shallots. Season with salt and pepper. Moisten with 500 ml (17 fl oz, 2 cups) white wine. Place in a preheated oven at 200°C (400°F, gas 6) for 30 minutes.

Meanwhile, scale, clean and wash 4 wrasse, each weighing about 400 g (14 oz), and rub them outside and inside with salt and pepper. Place them on the potatoes, sprinkle with small pieces of lard and return to the oven for 10 minutes. Turn the fish over and continue cooking for a further 5 minutes. Serve very hot in the baking dish.

SEAFOOD

Clams

Clam soup

Clam is the name given to a vast number of related shellfish, including the venus shells (*verenidae*) which cover over 500 types. They are eaten raw or cooked like oysters or *à la commodore*. Small clams are tender and cook quickly, but very large giant clams are cut up and simmered or stewed.

Dice 100 g (4 oz) salted bacon, 1 medium-sized onion, 2 celery sticks, 1 red (bell) pepper and 1 green pepper. Blanch the bacon for 3 minutes in boiling water, then cool it, wipe it and soften it in a pan containing some butter, without colouring it. Then add the vegetables, sprinkle on 1 tablespoon flour and cook for 2 minutes, stirring all the time. Sprinkle with 1.5 litres (2¾ pints, 6½ cups) stock and bring to the boil.

Open 36 clams near a heated oven, retaining the liquid. Prepare the clams; chop up the trimmings and put them in a saucepan with the clam liquor plus 200 ml (7 fl oz, ¾ cup) water. Cook for 15 minutes, strain and add this stock to the soup. Return the soup to the boil, add the clams, bring to the boil again, cover, then turn off the heat. Boil 300 ml (½ pint, 1¼ cups) double (heavy) cream and add it to the soup along with 1 tablespoon chopped parsley and 100 g (4 oz, ½ cup) butter. Heat and serve with crushed or whole crackers.

Crab

To prepare

To kill a live crab, stab it several times with a sharp metal skewer into the underside directly behind the eyes or centrally under the tail flap. If in doubt about the humane method, consult a fishmonger.

Cook the crab by boiling it in salted water for 20–30 minutes, then drain and rinse under cold water. When cool, remove the claws and legs. Turn the shell over and push the body out by applying pressure behind the tail flap, upwards and outwards. The pale, short finger-like gills (known as dead man's fingers) should be discarded. The stomach sac and related parts attached to the shell should be discarded too, but the soft brown shell meat is edible.

Use a skewer to pick out meat from the body before discarding it. Crack the legs and claws and poke out all the meat.

Canapés with crab

Finely crumble the crab meat (fresh or canned), removing all the cartilage, and flavour with a little lemon juice. Add an equal amount of béchamel sauce seasoned with nutmeg or saffron. Butter some lightly toasted slices of white bread and spread them with the crab mixture. Sprinkle with fresh breadcrumbs and melted butter and brown in a preheated oven at 230°C (450°F, gas 8). Garnish with half a round of fluted lemon.

Crab à la bretonne

Plunge a live crab into boiling lemon or vinegar court-bouillon. Cook for 8–10 minutes, then drain and cool. Remove the legs and claws and take out the contents of the shell. Clean the shell thoroughly. Cut the meat from the shell in two, put it back in the clean shell and arrange the legs and claws around. Garnish with parsley or lettuce leaves and serve with a mayonnaise.

Crab aspic

Prepare a fish fumet with 500 g (18 oz) white fish bones and trimmings, 300 ml (½ pint, 1¼ cups) dry white wine, an onion stuck with 2 cloves, a bouquet garni, a small bunch of herbs and 5 or 6 peppercorns. Do not add salt. Add 1 litre (1¾ pints, 4⅓ cups) water, cover, bring to the boil and cook gently for 30 minutes. Hard boil (hard cook) 2 eggs, cool them under running water, and shell them. Strain the fish fumet through a sieve and allow it to cool. Use a small amount of the fumet to dissolve 45 g (1½ oz, 6 envelopes) powdered gelatine. Whisk 3 egg whites and add the remainder of the fumet, whisking constantly. Add the dissolved gelatine and mix in. Bring the mixture to the boil, still whisking constantly. Check the seasoning, take off the heat and leave to settle for 10 minutes. Strain the fumet through a sieve or fine cloth and set aside to cool.

Slice the hard-boiled eggs and 3 small tomatoes. Wash and dry a few tarragon leaves. Coat the mould with the jelly and arrange the slices of tomato and egg and the tarragon leaves over it. Pour a little more jelly over them and leave to set in the refrigerator.

Shell the claws and feet and take out the flesh from the body. Place the flaked crab in the mould and finish with shrimp mousse, heaping it up a little. Pour in the rest of the jelly and leave in the refrigerator for 5 or 6 hours to set. Unmould and serve on a plate garnished with asparagus tips or lettuce leaves.

• *Lobster or langouste aspic* Cut the tail into sections and remove the shell from the claws and feet.

• *Shrimp aspic* Use the shrimps shelled but whole.

Crab feuilletés

Prepare 500 g (1 lb 2 oz) puff pastry. Wash and scrub 2 crabs; plunge into boiling water for 2 minutes, then drain. Pull off the claws and the legs, crack the shells and halve the bodies. Remove the 'dead man's fingers' and discard. Chop 1 carrot, 1 onion, 1 shallot, the white part of ½ leek and 1 celery stick.

Heat 40 g (1½ oz, 3 tablespoons) butter in a saucepan, add the pieces of crab, then the chopped vegetables and cook, stirring frequently, until the crab shell turns red. Add 3 tablespoons heated Cognac and flame. Then add 1 bottle dry white wine, 1 generous tablespoon tomato purée (paste), a piece of dried orange peel, salt, pepper, a dash of cayenne pepper, 1 crushed garlic clove and a small bunch of parsley. Bring just to the boil, cover the pan and cook for 10 minutes. Remove the crab and cook the sauce, uncovered, for a further 10 minutes. Shell the pieces of crab to remove the meat. Purée the sauce in a blender and rub it through a sieve, then mix half of it with the crab meat. Allow to cool completely.

Roll out the pastry to a thickness of 5 mm (¼ in). Cut it into rectangles measuring about 13 × 8 cm (5 × 3 in), and score their tops in criss-cross patterns with the tip of a knife. Glaze with beaten egg and cook in a preheated oven at 230°C (450°F, gas 8) for about 20 minutes. When the feuilletés are cooked, slice off their tops. Place the bases on serving plates and top with the crab mixture. Replace the pastry tops and serve with the remaining sauce.

Crab soufflé

Prepare a béchamel sauce from 40 g (1½ oz, 3 tablespoons) butter, 40 g (1½ oz, 6 tablespoons) plain (all-purpose) flour, 150 ml (¼ pint, ⅔ cup) milk and 100 ml (4 fl oz, 7 tablespoons) reduced crab cooking liquid. Incorporate 200 g (7 oz, 1 cup) puréed crabmeat and adjust the seasoning. Add 4–5 eggs (the yolks, then the stiffly whisked whites). Preheat the oven for 15 minutes at

220°C (425°F, gas 7). Butter a soufflé mould 20 cm (8 in) in diameter and coat with flour. Pour in the mixture and bake in the preheated oven at 200°C (400°F, gas 6) for 30 minutes, without opening the door during cooking, until well risen and a deep golden-brown on top.

Crabs in broth

Chop a large onion. Peel and roughly chop 4 tomatoes. Peel and crush 2 large garlic cloves. Plunge 2 crabs in salted boiling water, cook for 3 minutes, then remove the claws and legs and take out the contents of the shell. Crush the empty shell and the intact legs and brown them in 25 g (1 oz, 2 tablespoons) fat or 2 tablespoons oil together with the onion. Add the tomatoes, a large pinch of ground ginger, a pinch of saffron, a pinch of cayenne, the garlic and a sprig of thyme. Moisten with plenty of stock (fish, meat or chicken), cover and simmer very gently for about 2 hours.

Strain through a sieve, pressing well to obtain a fairly thick sauce. Adjust the seasoning. Crush the claws and remove the flesh, cut the flesh from the shell in four, then brown all the flesh together in fat or oil in a sauté pan. Pour the sauce over the top, bring back to the boil and cook for 5–6 minutes. Serve in a soup tureen, accompanied with rice *à la créole*.

Stuffed crabs à la martiniquaise

Clean 4 medium sized crabs and cook them in court-bouillon. Add about a cup of milk to a bowl of dry breadcrumbs. Trim and finely chop 3 good slices of ham and, separately, 5–6 shallots. Brown the shallots in oil or butter. Chop together a small bunch of parsley and 3–4 garlic cloves, add them to the shallots and stir. Crumble the crabmeat and add it to the pan together with a good pinch of cayenne, the breadcrumbs (softened but well squeezed) and the chopped ham. Stir thoroughly and reheat.

Adjust the seasoning so that the forcemeat is highly spiced. Mix 2 egg yolks with 2 tablespoons white rum, bind the forcemeat with this mixture and use to fill the shells. Sprinkle with white breadcrumbs, pour on some melted butter and bake in a preheated oven at 180°C (350°F, gas 4).

Stuffed crabs au gratin

Wash and brush some crabs. Plunge them in court-bouillon with lemon. Bring back to the boil, cook for about 10 minutes, then drain and leave to cool. Detach the claws and legs and remove their meat. Take out all the meat and creamy parts from the shells, discarding any gristle. Crumble or dice the meat finely. Wash and dry the shells.

Mix the creamy parts with a few spoonfuls of Mornay sauce (the quantity depends on the size of the crabs) and spread this mixture over the bottom of each shell. Then fill with diced or crumbled crabmeat and top with Mornay sauce. Finally, sprinkle with grated cheese, pour on some melted butter, and bake in a preheated oven at 240°C (475°F, gas 9) until the surface is brown.

Crayfish

To prepare

When preparing live crayfish, add them in small batches to a large pan of vigorously boiling stock or court-bouillon. The liquid must be boiling rapidly and there should be plenty of it in order to kill the crayfish speedily. If the crayfish are to be cooked further in the recipe, boil them for about

3–4 minutes, then use a draining spoon to remove them from the pan. If the crayfish are to be served plain boiled, without further cooking, they should be boiled for 5–6 minutes.

Most of the flesh of a crayfish is in its tail (about one-fifth of its total weight), although the claws, when crushed in a nutcracker, also yield a little meat. The shell is pounded to make bisques (thick soups) and savoury butters. Before the preparation of any crayfish dish, the bitter-tasting gut must be removed. The 17th-century writer Nicolas de Bonnefons described the task: 'They have to be cleaned by removing the gut, which is attached to the media lamina at the end of the tail. After giving it half a turn, pull it, and the gut comes out at the end.' This task is not necessary if the crayfish are kept without food for two days and hung up in a net in a cool place.

Buisson of crayfish

Clean and gut the crayfish, then boil them in plenty of water for 5–6 minutes, then drain them. Roll a napkin into a cone shape, tucking in the bottom to make it flat and thus keep it stable, and place it on a round serving plate. Truss the crayfish by tucking the ends of the 2 claws over the top of the tail. Arrange the crayfish along the napkin, tails in the air, wedging them against each other. The top of the dish can be garnished with a sprig of parsley.

Crayfish à la bordelaise

Prepare a finely diced mirepoix of vegetables. Toss 24 prepared crayfish in melted butter and season them with salt, pepper and a little cayenne. Pour brandy over the crayfish and set alight, then just cover with dry white wine. Add the vegetable mirepoix and cook together with the crayfish for a maximum of 10 minutes. Drain the crayfish and arrange in a deep dish. Keep them hot. Bind the cooking stock with 2 egg yolks, then beat in 40 g (1½ oz,

3 tablespoons) butter. Adjust the seasoning to give the sauce a good strong flavour. Cover the crayfish with this sauce and serve at once, piping hot.

Crayfish à la nage

Prepare an aromatic nage. Finely snip a bunch of chives and dice the flesh of 1 lemon. Squeeze the juice of 1 lemon. Chop or dice 400 g (14 oz) carrots, 1 medium leek and 300 g (11 oz) celeriac or 2 celery sticks. Bring to the boil 400 ml (14 fl oz, 1¾ cups) fish stock, lightly seasoned with salt and pepper, with 200 ml (7 fl oz, ¾ cup) white wine. Add the vegetables, 4 sprigs lemon thyme and the lemon juice. Bring back to the boil. Immerse 48 crayfish (cleaned or not) in the liquid and cook for 8 minutes, stirring occasionally. Season with a pinch of cayenne and leave the crayfish in the cooking stock until completely cold. Serve in a large bowl with the cooking stock.

Alternatively, drain the crayfish and prepare a sauce by reducing the cooking stock and stirring in some butter. Pour the sauce over the crayfish and sprinkle with chopped parsley. This method is described as *à la liégeoise*.

Crayfish bisque

Prepare 5–6 tablespoons mirepoix cooked in 40 g (1½ oz, 3 tablespoons) butter until soft. Allow 1.25 litres (2¼ pints, 5½ cups) consommé or fish stock. Cook 75 g (3 oz, ⅓ cup) short-grain rice in 500 ml (17 fl oz, 2 cups) of the consommé until soft.

Dress and wash 18 good-sized crayfish. Add the crayfish to the mirepoix together with salt, freshly ground pepper and a bouquet garni, and sauté the crayfish until the shells turn red. Heat 3 tablespoons Cognac in a small ladle, pour on to the crayfish and set alight, stirring well. Add 7 tablespoons dry white wine and reduce by two-thirds. Add 150 ml (¼ pint, ⅔ cup) consommé and cook gently for 10 minutes.

Shell the crayfish when cold. Finely dice the tail meat and reserve for the garnish. Pound the shells, then process with the cooked rice and the cooking liquor. Press as much as possible through a fine sieve. Place the resulting purée in a saucepan with the remaining consommé and boil for 5–6 minutes. Just before serving, cool the bisque slightly, then add a dash of cayenne pepper and 150 ml (¼ pint, ⅔ cup) crème fraîche, followed by 65 g (2½ oz, 5 tablespoons) butter cut up into very small pieces. Add the diced tail meat and serve piping hot.

Crayfish mousse

Cook 36 crayfish as in the recipe for crayfish *à la bordelaise*. Drain the crayfish and shell the tails. Pound the shells in a mortar with the mirepoix, adding 50 g (2 oz, ¼ cup) cold velouté sauce based on 100 ml (4 fl oz, ½ cup) melted aspic jelly. Press this mixture through a sieve and add 400 ml (14 fl oz, 1¾ cups) partly whipped cream and the crayfish tails, diced. Line a charlotte mould with white paper and fill with the mixture. Leave in the refrigerator for 6 hours, then turn out of the mould and garnish with truffle slices.

Crayfish or langoustines à la marinière

Sauté the shellfish in butter over a high heat. When they are really red, season with salt, pepper, thyme, a little crushed bay leaf and add enough white wine to almost cover them. Cook gently with the lid on for 10 minutes. Drain the shellfish and keep warm in a deep dish. Reduce the cooking liquid and thicken it with butter. Pour the sauce over the shellfish and sprinkle with parsley.

Crayfish tails au gratin à la façon de maître la planche

Make a ragoût of crayfish tails thickened with highly seasoned puréed crayfish, using crayfish cooked in a mirepoix, as for crayfish *à la bordelaise*.

Put this ragoût in a buttered gratin dish, alternating with layers of fresh truffles which have been cut in thick slices, seasoned and quickly tossed in butter. Sprinkle with finely grated cheese and brown in a preheated oven at 190°C (375°F, gas 5) standing the dish in a pan of warm water to prevent the sauce from curdling.

Crayfish timbale à l'ancienne

Prepare a ragoût of crayfish tails *à la Nantua*. Line a shallow pie dish with fine lining pastry. Line with a thin layer of fine pike forcemeat, either godiveau lyonnais or cream forcemeat made with pike. Mix coarsely diced truffles, tossed in butter and left to cool, with the ragoût; fill the pie with this. Cover the ragoût with a layer of pike forcemeat. Cover the pie with pastry and seal. Garnish with pastry motifs. Make a small hole in the pastry lid to allow the steam to escape. Brush with egg. Bake in a preheated oven at 180°C, (350°F, gas 4) for 45–60 minutes. When the pie is ready, pour into it a few tablespoons of thin Nantua sauce.

Crayfish velouté soup

Thicken a generous 750 ml (1¼ pints, 3¼ cups) chicken consommé or fish fumet with a white roux made with 40 g (1½ oz, 3 tablespoons) butter and 40 g (1½ oz, 6 tablespoons) plain (all-purpose) flour. Cook 12 shelled cooked crayfish (reserve the shells for making crayfish butter) with a mirepoix, then rub through a sieve or put through a blender or food processor and add this purée to the thickened consommé. Dilute with a little consommé or fumet to obtain the desired consistency and heat. Remove from the heat and thicken the soup with 100 ml (4 fl oz, 7 tablespoons) double (heavy) cream. Finally, whisk in 65 g (2½ oz, 5 tablespoons) fresh butter. The fresh butter can be replaced by an equal amount of crayfish butter.

Croûtes à la Nantua

Cut some rectangles 2 cm (¾ in) thick from a stale loaf. Score all round a little way in from the edge to mark the lid. Fry in butter or oil. When golden, drain them, remove the lids and hollow them out. Cover with béchamel sauce mixed with crayfish butter. Add some shelled crayfish tails. Coat with cream sauce flavoured with crayfish butter. Sprinkle with grated Parmesan, moisten with melted butter and brown in a preheated oven at 220°C (425°F, gas 7).

Grilled crayfish with garlic butter

Prepare some garlic butter by mixing 100 g (4 oz, ½ cup) softened butter with 1 crushed garlic clove, 1 finely chopped shallot and 2 teaspoons chopped herbs (tarragon, chives and parsley). Gut the crayfish and fry them on their fronts in a little olive oil for a few minutes only (until they turn red). Turn them over, grease with a little garlic butter and finish cooking in a preheated oven at 190°C (375°F, gas 5) for 3 or 4 minutes.

Individual crayfish mousses à la Nantua

Prepare some crayfish *à la bordelaise*. Clean 375 g (12 oz) fillets or steaks of pike, whiting, salmon or sole and pound them in a mortar or put them in a blender with 125–175 g (4–6 oz) of the crayfish *à la bordelaise*. Sprinkle with salt and pepper, then blend in 2–3 egg whites, one by one. Refrigerate for 2 hours. Incorporate a salpicon of crayfish tails *à la bordelaise*. Place the bowl in crushed ice and gradually add 600 ml (1 pint, 2½ cups) double (heavy) cream, stirring the mixture with a wooden spoon. Adjust the seasoning. Butter some dariole moulds. Pour the mixture into them and cook in a bain marie in a preheated oven at 190°C (375°F, gas 5) for about 20 minutes. Turn out the mousses, either directly on to the serving dish or into croûtes of puff or thin shortcrust pastry, baked blind. Serve the mousses with Nantua sauce.

Ragoût of crayfish tails à la Nantua

Cook 150 ml (¼ pint, ⅔ cup) vegetable mirepoix in a pan for about 10 minutes. Add 48 crayfish, season with salt and pepper, and cook until the crayfish turn red. Moisten with 200 ml (7 fl oz, ¾ cup) dry white wine, cover and cook for 8 minutes. Drain the crayfish and shell the tails.

Pound the mirepoix and the shells in a mortar, then add 200 ml (7 fl oz, ¾ cup) béchamel sauce to the resulting purée. Set the sauce aside.

Put the crayfish tails into a small sauté pan with 15 g (½ oz, 1 tablespoon) butter. Heat through without allowing them to brown, add 1 tablespoon flour and mix well. Stir in 2 tablespoons brandy and 6 tablespoons double (heavy) cream and cook over a low heat for 7–8 minutes. Then add either all or part of the prepared sauce. Remove from the heat and incorporate 65 g (2½ oz, 5 tablespoons) butter.

This ragoût may be used to fill vol-au-vent cases, a timbale, or pastry barquettes, small boat-shaped tarts made of shortcrust pastry (basic pie dough) or puff pastry, baked blind and then filled with sweet or savoury ingredients. Add more crayfish if necessary, depending on the recipe.

Langoustes

To prepare

Fresh langoustes should be bought live and undamaged, with all their legs intact and no holes in their shells. Like all shellfish, langoustes should be cooked alive.

Grilled langouste with basil butter

Cut a langouste in two. Place the halves in a roasting dish, carapace side down. Season the cut surface with salt and pepper and moisten with olive oil. Grill (broil) for 10 minutes, turning once. Turn once more, so that the flesh faces upwards, and baste with a mixture of melted butter and coarsely chopped fresh basil. Continue to baste at regular intervals until the langouste is cooked (about 20 minutes). Serve piping hot.

Langouste à la parisienne

Most of the preparation for this dish should be carried out the day before. Prepare a court-bouillon with 4 carrots and 2 medium onions (chopped very finely), a bouquet garni, 175 ml (6 fl oz, ¾ cup) dry white wine, 2 teaspoons salt, some pepper and 3 litres (5 pints, 13 cups) water. Simmer for 20 minutes. Add a langouste weighing 1.8–2 kg (4–4½ lb) and simmer very gently for about another 20 minutes. Drain the langouste by making a small opening below the thorax, then tie it to a board to retain its shape. Leave it to cool completely.

Peel and finely dice 3 carrots and 3–4 turnips. Cut 200 g (7 oz) French (green) beans into small pieces. Cook the carrots, turnips and 100 g (4 oz, ⅔ cup) fresh peas separately in salted water. Cook the French beans in another saucepan of boiling water, uncovered, and do not add salt until they are half-cooked. All these vegetables should be slightly undercooked. Drain and cool.

When the langouste is cold, cut through the membrane underneath the tail and carefully remove the flesh so that the shell is intact. Cut the tail flesh into 6–8 round slices and dice the flesh from the thorax very finely. Make some aspic and glaze the tail slices (several coatings are necessary). Place the shell on a serving dish and glaze it with aspic. Arrange the glazed slices in the shell, overlapping them slightly. Glaze this arrangement once more.

Make a mayonnaise with 2 egg yolks, 1 tablespoon mild mustard, 500 ml (17 fl oz, 2 cups) oil, 3 tablespoons tarragon vinegar, salt and pepper. Toss the cold vegetables and the diced flesh of the langouste in three-quarters of the mayonnaise and set this macédoine aside in a cool place. Hard boil (hard cook) 8 eggs and leave to cool.

The following day, halve the eggs and sieve the yolks. Add some tomato purée (paste) to the remainder of the mayonnaise, blend in the egg yolks and spoon this mixture into the egg-white cases. Cut the tops off 8 small tomatoes at the stalk ends, extract the seeds and juice, sprinkle the insides lightly with salt and turn upside down to drain in a colander.

One hour later, fill the tomato shells with the vegetable macédoine. Slice a truffle and place 1 slice on each slice of langouste. Surround the langouste with the stuffed tomatoes and eggs, and garnish with a lettuce chiffonnade.

Langouste velouté soup

Thicken a generous 750 ml (1¼ pints, 3¼ cups) chicken consommé or fish fumet with a white roux made with 40 g (1½ oz, 3 tablespoons) butter and 40 g (1½ oz, 6 tablespoons) plain (all-purpose) flour. Cook 1 small langouste with a mirepoix. Then rub the meat and crushed shells separately through a sieve or put through a blender or food processor and add the purées to the thickened consommé. Remove from the heat and thicken the soup with a mixture of 3 egg yolks beaten with 100 ml (4 fl oz, 7 tablespoons) double (heavy) cream. Finally whisk in 65 g (2½ oz, 5 tablespoons) butter or langouste butter, made as for crayfish butter.

Langouste with Thai herbs

Roast 4 tablespoons coriander seeds and the same amount of cumin in an ungreased frying pan. Allow to cool, then grind. Mix 4 tablespoons chopped galangal, 8 chopped stems lemon grass and 4 tablespoons chopped fresh coriander (cilantro) with 100 g (4 oz) chopped shallots, 100 g (4 oz) garlic cloves, 2 tablespoons pimento paste, 120 ml (4½ fl oz, ½ cup) roasted, peeled and roughly chopped red (bell) peppers, 65 g (2½ oz) shrimp paste, 1 tablespoon saffron, 3 tablespoons turmeric, 1 tablespoon salt and the zest of 1 makrut lime. Place all these ingredients in a blender and liquidize, then sieve the paste.

Blanch 2 langoustes weighing 800 g (1¾ lb) and cut in two lengthways. Remove the meat from the tail. Cook the meat for 2 minutes in 50 g (2 oz, ¼ cup) butter in a sauté pan without browning it. Take it out and put to one side. Fry the prepared paste with 2 teaspoons grated fresh root ginger. Add 200 ml (7 fl oz, ¾ cup) white port, 20 g (¾ oz) apple julienne, 40 g (1½ oz) carrot julienne and 2 kaffir lime leaves. Reduce until dry, then add 1 teaspoon turmeric and 50 g (2 oz, ¼ cup) butter. Remove from the heat and incorporate 200 ml (7 fl oz, ¾ cup) double (heavy) cream. Finally, pour in 2 tablespoons coconut liqueur and a similar amount of ginger wine. Place the langouste meat in soup bowls. Bring the sauce to the boil and pour over the lobster meat. Sprinkle with chopped parsley.

Langoustines

To prepare

To poach langoustines, add them to a cold court-bouillon, bring to the boil and simmer gently for 6 minutes, or until cooked. Drain and leave to cool.

Black risotto with langoustines and Thai herbs

Wash 175 g (6 oz) black Thai rice and leave to soak for at least 12 hours. Drain, wash again, then steam for 45 minutes in a steamer. Now place the rice in a saucepan, add salt and incorporate 50 g (2 oz, ¼ cup) butter with a fork. Cover and place in a warm place. Cook chopped shallots, 1 teaspoon minutely sliced ginger, 1 stem lemon grass (trimmed and chopped) 2 garlic cloves and 100 ml (4 fl oz, 7 tablespoons) white wine in a small sauté pan. Reduce until all the liquid has been absorbed. Add 200 ml (7 fl oz, ¾ cup) coconut milk and simmer gently to reduce the liquid by half. Add 3 tablespoons single (light) cream, 2 teaspoons grated fresh turmeric root and ½ teaspoon green curry paste. Cook until the sauce begins to coat the spoon. Pour 4 teaspoons olive oil in a non-stick frying pan and fry 24 langoustines, previously salted, for 30 seconds on each side. Remove from the heat and keep in a warm place. Pour the sauce into a small saucepan and bring to the boil. Correct the seasoning, then add 25 g (1 oz, 2 tablespoons) butter, a little lime juice, 2 tablespoons minutely chopped red (bell) pepper, 40 leaves of Thai basil and the cooking juices of the crustaceans. Arrange the rice in a dome in the middle of each plate with the langoustines around and pour the sauce on top.

Langoustine fritters

Choose 12 medium langoustines and shell the tails. Marinate for 30 minutes in a mixture of 3 tablespoons olive oil, 1½ tablespoons lemon juice, 1 generous tablespoon chopped parsley, 1 small chopped garlic clove, 1 small teaspoon herbes de Provence, salt, pepper and a dash of cayenne. Prepare a fairly stiff batter by mixing 250 g (9 oz, 2¼ cups) plain (all-purpose) flour with a little water, then fold in 2 egg whites, stiffly whisked. Drain the langoustine tails, dip them in the batter and deep-fry until golden. Drain on paper towels and serve with lemon halves and tartare sauce.

Langoustines in sea urchin shells

Plunge 4 large tomatoes into boiling water for 1–2 minutes to loosen the skins; peel, halve and seed them, then dice them finely. Heat 25 g (1 oz, 2 tablespoons) butter in a saucepan and gently cook 2 small finely chopped shallots. Add the diced tomato, salt and pepper, cook for 15 minutes, then set the pan aside.

Open 12 sea urchins and extract the edible part; strain the liquid and put it aside. Thoroughly clean the empty shells and set aside. Cut 12 langoustines in half; cook them in a little oil over a very high heat for 2 minutes, then drain and shell them.

Put the sea urchin liquid and 2 tablespoons Cognac into a saucepan with 100 ml (4 fl oz, 7 tablespoons) dry white wine and 2 small chopped shallots; reduce by half. Add the tomatoes and reduce again for 2 minutes. Add 4 tablespoons double (heavy) cream, reduce again for 2–3 minutes, then whisk in 65 g (2½ oz, 5 tablespoons) butter. Heat the langoustines and the sea urchin corals through, without letting them boil.

To serve, heat the reserved sea urchin shells in the oven for a minute or two. Fill each with 1 tablespoon very hot sauce, langoustine and coral. Arrange on hot plates. Sprinkle with chervil leaves.

Langoustines royales with sweet red peppers

Shell 20 large langoustines. Brown 1 sugar lump (dry) in a saucepan, then add 1 tablespoon vinegar and the juice of ½ a Seville (bitter) orange. Reduce to a thick syrup, then add 2 glasses red port wine and 3 strips of orange peel. Reduce by half, leave to cool slightly, then whisk in 60 g (2 oz, ¼ cup) butter.

Cook 2 red (bell) peppers for 10 minutes in a very hot oven or grill (broil) them, turning until the skins blister and blacken. Peel the peppers, remove the seeds and cut the flesh into strips.

195

Steam the langoustine tails for 3 minutes. On each of 4 ovenproof plates pour 1 tablespoon sauce and arrange 5 langoustines in a circle, alternating with strips of pepper. Place in the oven for a few minutes to heat through.

Ninon langoustines

Remove the large, green leaves of 4 leeks. Slice the remaining white part of each leek in two, lengthways. Separate the leaves and wash. Remove the tails of 24 langoustines. Put the heads in a sauté pan with 1 tablespoon olive oil. Crush them slightly. Season with salt and cover with cold water. Bring to the boil, cover and cook for 15 minutes. Strain. Cut the zest of 1 orange into fine strips. Squeeze this orange and another one. Heat 25 g (1 oz, 2 tablespoons) butter in a sauté pan. Add the strips of leeks and cover with water. Cook, uncovered, over a high heat until the liquid has completely evaporated. Pour 350 ml (12 fl oz, 1½ cups) langoustine stock and 175 ml (6 fl oz, ¾ cup) orange juice in a saucepan. Add the orange zest. Bring to the boil and reduce by half. Whisk in 50 g (2 oz, ¼ cup) butter, cut into pieces. Remove from the heat, then season with salt and pepper. Fry the langoustine tails for 2–3 minutes in 50 g (2 oz, ¼ cup) butter. Arrange the langoustine tails and leeks on a heated serving dish. Gently pour the orange sauce on top.

Peking-style langoustines

Soak 6 large diced shiitake mushrooms and 1 tablespoon Chinese lily flowers in hot water until soft. Drain and slice the mushrooms. Shell the tails of 12 langoustines without detaching them from the body. Sauté them in a frying pan in a little oil with 1 bunch of chopped spring onions (scallions) and 1 crushed garlic clove. Take them out and keep hot. Blend 1 tablespoon cornflour (cornstarch), ½ teaspoon sugar and 2 tablespoons soy sauce with a little cold water. Brown some crushed tomatoes in the frying pan in which the langoustines were cooked, reduce, then pour in the cornflour mixture to thicken the sauce. Add the mushrooms and drained lily flowers; bring to the boil, stirring, and simmer for 2–3 minutes. Pour over the hot langoustines.

Scampi fritters

Shell cooked langoustine or scampi tails (discarding the heads) and marinate for 30 minutes in oil, lemon juice and cayenne pepper. Dip in batter, deep-fry in hot oil and serve with fried parsley.

Scampi with walnuts

Soak some walnut kernels in cold water overnight. Dry, peel and fry quickly in hot oil, then drain them and keep hot. Season some shelled langoustine tails or scampi with white wine, fresh root ginger juice, salt and pepper. Roll them in flour and fry in very hot oil. In another pan, quickly fry some spring onions (scallions). Turn all these ingredients out on to a hot dish, mix together and sprinkle with stock to which white wine, soy sauce and ground ginger have been added.

Lobster

To prepare

A live lobster, which can be identified by the reflex actions of the eyes, antennae and claws, should not show any signs of damage from fighting or have any pieces missing when it is bought, especially if it is to be boiled.

Lobsters can be humanely killed by putting them in the freezer, at a temperature at least as low as –10°C (14°F) for 2 hours. The lobster will gradually lose consciousness and die. It can then be plunged into boiling water. If there is no freezer available, make sure that at least 4.5 litres (1 gallon, 5 quarts) water per lobster is boiling fast over a very fierce heat before plunging the lobster in head first, ensuring it is totally immersed. Hold it under the water with wooden spoons for at least 2 minutes. The lobster should die within 15 seconds. If the recipe calls for uncooked lobster, remove it after 2 minutes.

• *Cutting up an uncooked lobster* Wash and scrub the lobster, then lay it on a flat surface with the head towards you. Stun the lobster by inserting the point of a sharp knife between the two antennae. With a sharp movement, separate the head from the abdomen. Remove the claws and set them aside. (The claws may be cracked before cooking but left whole.) Hold the head firmly and use a large knife to cut it in half lengthways. Use a teaspoon to scoop out and discard the gravel pocket. Remove and reserve the coral if there is any.

Bouchées à l'américaine

Prepare some bouchée cases and fill with a salpicon of lobster, crayfish or monkfish *à l'américaine*.

Croûtes cardinal

Cut some round pieces of bread, 4–5 cm (1½–2 in) in diameter and 2 cm (¾ in) thick, from a stale loaf. Use a round cutter with a diameter smaller than that of the croûtes to press lightly on each croûte to mark the lid. Fry the croûtes in butter or oil. When they are golden, drain and remove the central circles for lids, then hollow out. Bind a salpicon of lobster and truffle with a béchamel sauce to which lobster butter has been added. Fill the croûtes with this mixture. Sprinkle with breadcrumbs and brown in a preheated oven at 220°C (425°F, gas 7). Just before serving, garnish each croûte with a small (hot) scallop of lobster and a fine slice of truffle. Instead of frying the croûtes, they can be brushed with butter and browned in a preheated oven at 220°C (425°F, gas 7).

Fish forcemeat ring with medallions of lobster à l'américaine

Prepare a cream forcemeat made with whiting. Butter a ring or savarin mould and press the forcemeat into it. Poach gently in a preheated oven at 180°C (350°F, gas 4) in a bain marie for 25 minutes or until the fish is cooked, then cover and leave for 30 minutes in the oven with the door open (this helps the mould to relax and to set well). Turn the hot fish ring out on to a warm plate and fill the centre with medallions of lobster *à l'américaine.*

Grilled lobster (1)

Plunge 2 lobsters, each weighing about 450 g (1 lb), head first into boiling salted water for about 3 minutes. Drain them, split in half lengthways and crack the claws. Season the meat with salt and pepper, sprinkle with melted butter or oil, and grill (broil) under a medium heat for about 25 minutes. Arrange each half lobster on a napkin. Serve with melted butter flavoured with lemon, maître d'hôtel butter or hollandaise sauce.

Grilled lobster (2)

Plunge 2 lobsters, each weighing 400–500 g (14–18 oz), in boiling water for 1 minute. Take them out and cut in two lengthways. Remove the gravel pouch from the head and the intestine from the tail. Take out the greenish coral and, stirring gently, mix with 2 tablespoons crème fraîche, 1 egg yolk, 1 generous pinch paprika, salt, pepper, 1 teaspoon sherry and a small pinch of herbes de Provence or freshly chopped basil.

Season the lobsters with salt and pepper and place in a grill tin (pan) with the shell down. Spoon some of the coral mixture over the lobsters. Cook the lobsters under a preheated grill (broiler) for 1–2 minutes. Spoon a little more coral mixture over the lobsters, then grill again for about another 1–2 minutes. Repeat twice more, until all the coral mixture is used and the lobsters are cooked. Arrange 2 lobster halves on each plate and serve. Braised fennel with a little saffron and crushed tomato or broccoli are suitable accompaniments.

Lobster à l'américaine

Cut a lobster weighing about 1 kg (2¼ lb) into even-sized pieces; split the body in two lengthways; crack the shell of the claws; reserve the liver and the coral, which will be used to thicken the sauce. Season all the pieces of lobster with salt and pepper. Heat 60 ml (2 fl oz, ¼ cup) olive oil in a pan. Put in the lobster pieces, brown quickly on both sides and remove from the pan. Finely chop a large onion and cook it gently in the oil; when it is nearly done add 2 finely chopped shallots and stir well. Peel, seed and chop 2 tomatoes and put them in the pan; add 1 tablespoon tomato purée (paste), a piece of dried orange peel, a small garlic clove and 1 tablespoon each of chopped parsley and tarragon. Arrange the pieces of lobster on this mixture. Pour over 100 ml (4 fl oz, 7 tablespoons) white wine, 100 ml (4 fl oz, 7 tablespoons) fish fumet and 3 tablespoons brandy. Season with cayenne. Bring to the boil, then cover and cook over a gentle heat for a maximum of 10 minutes. Drain the lobster pieces and remove the flesh from the claws; arrange all the pieces in the split body halves in a long serving dish. Keep warm.

To prepare the sauce, reduce the cooking liquid by half. Chop the coral and liver and work them into 40 g (1½ oz, 3 tablespoons) butter, then add this mixture to the cooking liquid. Take the pan off the heat and blend the mixture well, then whisk in 50 g (2 oz, ¼ cup) butter cut into small pieces. Season the sauce with a pinch of cayenne pepper and a few drops of lemon juice. Pour the boiling sauce over the lobster and sprinkle with chopped parsley.

The chopped onion and tarragon can be replaced by 3–4 tablespoons finely chopped mirepoix, added to the lobster while it is cooking.

Lobster and crayfish with caviar

Gently simmer a lobster weighing about 800 g (1¾ lb) in a well-flavoured court-bouillon for 10 minutes. Remove the lobster, make an incision on the underside of the body between the antennae, then set aside. Boil about 20 crayfish for 2 minutes in the same stock and leave them to cool in the stock. Shell the lobster claws and tail; slice the tail into about 12 even rounds. Drain and shell the crayfish and remove the intestines. Keep hot.

Prepare some *beurre blanc nantais*. Melt a little butter in a sauté pan and stiffen the claws, lobster rounds and crayfish tails. Add a little court-bouillon and 3 tablespoons double (heavy) cream. Heat, but do not let it boil. Place the lobster and crayfish in deep plates. Add a few tablespoons of *beurre blanc nantais* to the sauce and, just before serving, add 4 teaspoons caviar. Cover the shellfish with this sauce and serve immediately.

Lobster bisque

Prepare 5–6 tablespoons mirepoix softened in 40 g (1½ oz, 3 tablespoons) butter. Allow 1.25 litres (2¼ pints, 5½ cups) consommé or fish stock. Cook 75 g (3 oz, ⅓ cup) short-grain rice in 500 ml (17 fl oz, 2 cups) consommé until soft. Cut 2 small lobsters into pieces. Add them to the mirepoix with salt, pepper and a bouquet garni, and sauté until the lobster shells turn red. Heat 3 tablespoons Cognac in a small ladle, pour on to the lobsters and set alight, stirring well. Add 7 tablespoons dry white wine and reduce by two-thirds. Add 150 ml (¼ pint, ⅔ cup) consommé. Cook gently for 10 minutes.

Shell the lobsters when cold. Finely dice the tail meat and reserve for the garnish. Pound the shells, then process with the cooked rice and the cooking liquor. Press as much as possible through a fine sieve. Place the resulting purée in a saucepan with the remaining consommé and boil for 5–6 minutes. Just before serving, cool the bisque slightly, then add a dash of cayenne pepper and 150 ml (¼ pint, ⅔ cup) crème fraîche, followed by 65 g (2½ oz, 5 tablespoons) butter cut up into very small pieces. Add the diced tail meat and serve piping hot. If desired, lobster bisque can be prepared using only the meat from the thorax, legs and claws (the meat should be finely diced). The tails can then be used for medallions.

Lobster cardinal

Cook a lobster in a court-bouillon. Drain, cool a little and split it lengthways. Remove the flesh from the tail and cut it into slices of equal thickness. Cut off the claws, take out the flesh and dice it to make a salpicon. Add an equal quantity of diced truffles. Bind the salpicon with a lobster sauce. Fill the halves of the lobster shell with the salpicon. Place the slices of lobster interspersed with strips of truffles on top. Pour on some lobster sauce. Sprinkle with grated cheese and melted butter. Place the lobster halves on a baking sheet and brown them quickly in the oven. Garnish with curly parsley.

Lobster en chemise

Plunge a lobster head first into boiling water to kill it and drain immediately. Season with salt and pepper and brush with oil or melted butter. Wrap it in a double thickness of oiled greaseproof (wax) paper, tie it securely and put it on a baking sheet. Cook in a preheated oven at 230°C (450°F, gas 8) for 40–45 minutes for a medium-sized lobster. Remove the string and serve the lobster in the paper in which it has been cooked.

It can be accompanied either by half-melted maître d'hôtel butter or by an américaine, béarnaise, bordelaise, Hungarian or curry sauce or bercy butter.

Lobster escalopes à la parisienne

Cook a medium-sized lobster in a court-bouillon and leave to cool. Remove the shell and cut the meat into thick slices. Coat each slice separately with mayonnaise mixed with aspic or dissolved gelatine and garnish with a slice of truffle dipped in the half-set aspic; brush over with more aspic jelly to give a glaze. Finely dice the rest of the lobster flesh and mix it with a salad; finely diced truffles can also be added. Bind with thickened mayonnaise and pack this salad into a dome-shaped mould. Turn the mould out into the centre of a round serving dish and arrange the lobster slices all around it in a border. Garnish with chopped aspic jelly.

Lobster gazpacho

Peel and slice 100 g (4 oz) cucumber. Wash the white part of 4 leeks and 4 sticks of celery and cut them in julienne strips. Blanch all these vegetables in boiling salted water (5 minutes for the cucumber, 10 minutes for the leeks and celery). Drain, cool under cold water and dry thoroughly. Remove the leaves from a bunch of chervil. Peel, seed and slice 1.5 kg (3¼ lb) tomatoes. Seed and slice 350 g (12 oz) red (bell) peppers. Peel and seed a further 250 g (9 oz) cucumber. Peel and crush 5 garlic cloves. Cook 4 lobsters for 5 minutes in court-bouillon. Shell them, put aside the coral and cut the flesh into slices. Arrange the slices on a large dish.

Liquidize the raw vegetables (tomatoes, peppers, garlic and cucumber) with parsley, salt, pepper and 1 tablespoon vinegar. Put the vegetable purée into a saucepan and bring to the boil to make a bouillon. Separately, bring to the boil 500 ml (17 fl oz, 2 cups) single (light) cream. Mix the vegetable bouillon and cream together, adjust the seasoning and boil the mixture for 2–3 minutes. Take off the heat, blend in the reserved coral and strain. Pour this purée over the lobster slices and leave to cool.

Refrigerate until well chilled before serving. Garnish with the slices of cucumber, the blanched julienne of leeks and celery and the chervil leaves.

Lobster Henri Duvernois

Split a lobster in half lengthways or, if it is large, cut it up as for lobster *à l'américaine*. Season with salt and paprika and sauté it in butter. As soon as it is well coloured, take it out of the pan. Add to the butter in the pan 4 tablespoons julienne of leeks and mushrooms that have been tossed in butter. Put the lobster back in the pan and add 150 ml (¼ pint, ⅔ cup) sherry and 2 tablespoons brandy. Reduce the liquid, pour in some single (light) cream, cover and simmer until cooked. Arrange the lobster on a long serving dish and garnish with a rice pilaf. Boil down the sauce, whisk in 40 g (1½ oz, 3 tablespoons) butter and pour over the lobster.

Lobster in court-bouillon

For a really well-flavoured court-bouillon add the following ingredients to 2 litres (3½ pints, 9 cups) water: 2 medium carrots, 1 turnip, the white of a leek and 1 celery stick (all finely diced), a large bouquet garni, an onion stuck with 2 cloves, a small garlic clove, 500 ml (17 fl oz, 2 cups) dry white wine, 200 ml (7 fl oz, ¾ cup) vinegar, salt, pepper and a pinch of cayenne pepper. Bring to the boil and simmer for 30 minutes. Plunge the lobster head first into the boiling court-bouillon and let it simmer gently, allowing 10–15 minutes per 450 g (1 lb). Drain. If it is to be served cold, tie it on to a small board so that it keeps its shape and leave it to get completely cold.

A lobster weighing about 450 g (1 lb) should be split lengthways and served in 2 halves. If the lobster is large, take off the tail, remove the meat and cut it into medallions. Split the body in half lengthways and remove and crack the claws. Arrange the medallions on the tail shell and place the 2 halves of the body together to resemble a whole lobster again. Garnish with the claws. Serve with mayonnaise.

Lobster in cream

Cut up a lobster as described in the recipe for lobster *à l'américaine.* Sauté the pieces of lobster in butter until they are completely red. Season with salt and pepper. Pour off the butter and deglaze the sauté pan with 3 tablespoons brandy. Flame the lobster. Then add 400 ml (14 fl oz, 1¾ cups) double (heavy) cream. Adjust the seasoning, add a pinch of cayenne pepper, cover the pan and cook gently for a maximum of 10 minutes. Drain the lobster pieces and arrange them in a deep serving dish; keep hot. Add the juice of ½ a lemon to the sauté pan and reduce the cream by half. Add 25 g (1 oz, 2 tablespoons) butter, whisk and pour over the lobster.

Lobster Newburg

Wash 2 lobsters weighing about 450 g (1 lb) each and joint them as for lobster *à l'américaine.* Remove the coral and liver and keep for use later. Season the lobsters with salt and paprika and brown them in 75 g (3 oz, 6 tablespoons) butter. Cover the pan and cook with the lid on for 12 minutes. Drain off the butter, add 300 ml (½ pint, 1¼ cups) sherry and boil down over a high heat. Add 300 ml (½ pint, 1¼ cups) fish stock and an equal quantity of velouté sauce. Cover the pan and simmer gently for 15 minutes. Take out the pieces of lobster and arrange them in a deep dish. (The tail pieces may be shelled first if wished.)

Boil down the cooking liquid and add 400 ml (14 fl oz, 1¾ cups) double (heavy) cream. When the sauce is thick enough to coat the back of the spoon, add the coral and liver, rubbed through a fine sieve and blended with 100 g (4 oz, ½ cup) butter. Beat the sauce vigorously and pour it over the lobster.

Lobster ravioli with a glazed coral sauce

Stuff 20 squares of fresh pasta dough with a mixture of diced lobster and a duxelles of mushrooms, bound with 250 ml (8 fl oz, 1 cup) lobster bisque. Reduce 250 ml (8 fl oz, 1 cup) bisque and 500 ml (17 fl oz, 2 cups) white wine sauce, and bind with 200 ml (7 fl oz, ¾ cup) hollandaise sauce and 200 ml (7 fl oz, ¾ cup) whipped cream. Sweat 1 kg (2¼ lb) spinach in butter. Poach the stuffed ravioli for 2 minutes in simmering salted water. Put the spinach in 4 soup bowls or gratin dishes. Arrange the ravioli on top, cover with sauce and brown under a grill (broiler). Garnish each plate with 1 medallion of lobster and 3 claws.

Lobster sautéed à l'orange

Split a lobster in half lengthways, reserving the coral and the liver. Cut off the claws and crack them. Season the meat with salt. Crush and pound the small claws, which should be cut off close to the body. Brown them in a little oil with crushed garlic and a pinch of cayenne pepper. Add enough oil to just cover the contents of the pan and cook over the lowest possible heat so that the oil does not smoke.

Rub the mixture through a sieve and adjust the seasoning. Put 4 table-spoons of this oil into a sauté pan, slice 4 shallots and 1 onion, and brown them in the oil, together with ½ an orange cut into large dice, and some tarragon leaves. Push this mixture to the sides of the pan and put in the lobster, flesh side down. Boil for 3 minutes to reduce the liquid.

Pour the juice of ½ an orange into the pan. Turn the lobster halves over on to the shell sides and add the claws. Purée the coral and the intestines with 2 tablespoons single (light) cream in a blender. Add a little brandy, a pinch of cayenne pepper and some chopped tarragon. Garnish the lobster halves with this mixture. Put under a preheated grill (broiler) for 3 minutes and serve.

Lobster thermidor

Split a live lobster in two, lengthways, Crack the shell of the claws and remove the gills from the carcass. Season both halves of the lobster with salt, sprinkle with oil and roast in a preheated oven at 220°C (425°F, gas 7) for 15–20 minutes. Remove and dice the flesh from the tail and claws.

Prepare a stock using equal proportions of meat juices, fish fumet and white wine, flavoured with chervil, tarragon and chopped shallots. Boil it down to a concentrated consistency, then add a little very thick béchamel sauce and some English mustard. Boil the sauce for a few moments, then whisk in some butter (one-third of the volume of the sauce). Pour a little of this sauce into the two halves of the shell. Fill the shells with the flesh of the lobster, cover with the remainder of the sauce, sprinkle with a little grated Parmesan cheese and melted butter, and brown rapidly in a preheated oven at 240°C (475°F, gas 9).

More simply, the lobster can be split into two and grilled (broiled). The two halves of the shell are then emptied out, lined with a little cream sauce seasoned with mustard, and the sliced lobster flesh is put back, covered with the same sauce and glazed in the oven. Arrange the lobster on a long dish and serve piping hot.

Lobster velouté soup

Thicken a generous 750 ml (1¼ pints, 3¼ cups) chicken consommé or fish fumet with a white roux made with 40 g (1½ oz, 3 tablespoons) butter and 40 g (1½ oz, 6 tablespoons) plain (all-purpose) flour. Cut up and cook 1 small lobster with a mirepoix. Then rub through a sieve or put through a blender or food processor and add this purée to the thickened consommé. Remove from the heat and thicken the soup with a mixture of 3 egg yolks beaten with 100 ml (4 fl oz, 7 tablespoons) double (heavy) cream. Finally whisk in 65 g (2½ oz, 5 tablespoons) fresh butter or lobster butter.

Panaché of lobster and crayfish with caviar

Prepare a well-flavoured court-bouillon. In it cook an 800 g (1¾ lb) lobster for 12 minutes with the liquid gently bubbling. Remove the lobster, cut it under the chest, between the antennae, and set aside. Put about 1 kg (2¼ lb) crayfish (about 20) in the same liquid, boil for 2 minutes and leave to cool in the liquid. Remove the shell of the tail and pincers of the lobster; slice the tail flesh into 12 even rounds. Drain the crayfish and shell them (do not forget to remove the intestines). Make a *beurre blanc nantais*.

Put a little butter in a sauté pan and cook the rounds of lobster tail, the pincer meat and the crayfish tails to make them firm. Add a little court-bouillon and 3 tablespoons double (heavy) cream. Let it heat without coming to the boil. Arrange the lobster and crayfish in shallow plates. Keep the plates warm in the oven. Add a little *beurre blanc nantais* to the sauce (to taste) and, at the last minute, 4 teaspoons caviar. Cover the shellfish with the sauce.

Papillotes of lobster and scallops

Separate the tail from a lobster and set it aside. Open the body and take out the stomach. Crush the carcass and heat the pieces in a heavy-based saucepan with some chopped shallot. Add 250 ml (8 fl oz, 1 cup) vermouth and reduce by half, then add 150 ml (¼ pint, ⅔ cup) double (heavy) cream and reduce again by half. Add the lobster tail, cook for 4 minutes, then remove the pan from the heat. Shell the tail and cut the flesh into 8 slices. Cut a truffle into 8 thin slices. Clean 8 scallops with corals. Strain the sauce.

Prepare 4 pieces of oiled greaseproof (wax) paper. Place 2 slices of lobster on each piece of paper and top them with 2 scallops and 2 slices of truffle. Coat with the sauce and sprinkle with chopped fresh herbs. Close up the papillotes tightly, folding the edges together, and cook them in a preheated oven at 230°C (450°F, gas 8) for a maximum of 5 minutes. Serve in a very hot stainless steel dish so that the papillotes do not collapse.

Purses of lobster with morels

Soak 2 calves' sweetbreads in cold water for 1 hour. Drain and cover with water. Blanch for 5 minutes. Cool in cold water, peel and press them. Put in the refrigerator until the following day.

Rehydrate 50 g (2 oz) dried morels in lukewarm water for 30 minutes. Drain and blanch in boiling water for 3 minutes. Gently brown 2 carrots, 4 shallots and 3 garlic cloves, all very finely sliced, in 25 g (1 oz, 2 tablespoons) butter. Add the diced sweetbreads and braise very gently for 10 minutes. Add 3½ tablespoons dry white wine and reduce. Now add 100 ml (4 fl oz, 7 table-spoons) shellfish stock and 2 seeded, crushed tomatoes. Season with salt and pepper. Cover and cook for 10 minutes. Drain the diced sweetbreads. Purée the contents of the sauté pan in a blender and keep the mixture warm. Set this sauce aside: reheat it when the purses are cooked.

Cook two 900 g (2 lb) lobsters in salted water for 5 minutes, remove the meat and cut into cubes. Add to the sweetbreads. Coarsely chop the morels and add to the lobster mixture.

Make 6 lightly cooked, thin 20 cm (8 in) pancakes. Alternatively, use 6 sheets of brik pastry or filo (phyllo) pastry cut into 20 cm (8 in) squares. Top each pancake or square in turn with a little of the cooled lobster mixture, brush the edge with melted butter and fold the pancake or pastry around the filling to form a neat bundle or purse. Place on a greased baking sheet. Cook the purses in a preheated oven at 200°C (400°F, gas 6) for about 10 minutes or until golden. Serve with the reheated sauce.

Skewered saffron-dressed flat lobster tails

Also known as squat or slipper lobster, there are over 50 species of these lobster-like creatures. They have small claws, but do not have the large, long pincers typical of lobsters. Their shells range from rust-red or chestnut to green-tinged. The powerful ridged tail is wide and the two fine antennae are reduced in size. A more conspicuous pair are widened into shovel shapes, which are useful for digging in search of food. Only the tail is eaten.

Remove the shells from the tails (discard the heads and legs), rinse and blot dry. Marinate the tails in a mixture of 1 pinch saffron threads and 1 chopped garlic clove per 500 g (18 oz) tails, mixed with olive oil, lemon juice, parsley, crumbled thyme, salt and pepper. Thread them on skewers and grill (broil) briefly until the meat is firm and cooked through: time depends on size.

Spit-roast lobster

Plunge a large live lobster head first into boiling salted water for at least 2 minutes to kill it, then skewer it on a spit. Season it with salt, pepper, thyme and powdered bay leaf, then brush with melted butter or oil. Roast it over a dish or roasting pan that contains a few tablespoons of dry white wine and baste frequently while cooking. A lobster weighing about 1.5 kg (3¼ lb) needs to be cooked for 40–45 minutes. Remove the lobster from the spit and arrange it on a long serving dish; serve the juice collected in the pan separately. Spit-roast lobster can be served with a curry or ravigote sauce.

Mussels

To prepare

Mussels are sold alive, cooked, cooked and shelled, smoked and shelled, and preserved in oil or sauce. Live mussels must have come from clean waters, be firmly closed and cooked within 3 days of being caught (discard any with cracked or half-opened shells that do not close when tapped).

The mussels must be completely cleaned of any beard-like filaments and parasites, which may be attached to them, before they are used. This is done by brushing and scraping under running water to remove the beard – the cluster of fine dark hairs by which the shell attached itself to rocks. Pull it firmly away from the shell. The beard should come away in one clump. If the mussels are consumed raw, they must be eaten the same day that they are bought. Cooked mussels may be kept for 48 hours in the refrigerator. Mussels that do not open after cooking should be discarded.

Attereaux of mussels

Prepare the mussels as for *moules marinière* and remove them from their shells. Drain them and roll them in mustard. Thread them on skewers alternating with small button mushrooms. Coat with breadcrumbs and plunge them into very hot fat. Serve with fried parsley and lemon halves.

Croustades à la marinière

Prepare some *moules marinière*. Strain the juice and mix with fresh cream to make a thick velouté sauce. Fill croustades made of puff pastry with the mussels. Coat with the sauce and serve very hot.

Fried mussels

Prepare some *moules marinière*, remove from their shells and leave to cool. Marinate for 30 minutes in olive oil, lemon juice, chopped parsley and pepper. Then dip in frying batter and cook in oil heated to 180°C (350°F). Drain them on paper towels and serve as an hors d'oeuvre (with lemon quarters) or with apéritifs (on cocktail sticks).

Hors d'oeuvre of mussels à la ravigote

Cook some *moules marinière*, remove from their shells and leave them to cool completely in a salad bowl. Prepare a well-seasoned vinaigrette and add to it some chopped hard-boiled (hard-cooked) eggs, parsley, chervil, tarragon and gherkins (pickled cucumbers). Pour over the mussels and stir. Put in a cool place until time to serve.

Iced mussel soup

Place a red (bell) pepper in a preheated oven at 240°C (475°F, gas 9) for a few minutes, to loosen the skin, then peel. Clean 1.5 kg (3¼ lb) mussels and cook over a brisk heat with half a glass of white wine for 2 minutes. Discard any mussels that do not open. Remove the shells and reserve the cooking liquid. Peel and seed 1 cucumber, cut it into dice, then place in a colander and sprinkle with coarse salt; leave to drain. Cut half a bunch of radishes into slices. Shell and skin 500 g (18 oz) broad (fava) beans. Wash and dice 5 mushroom caps (preferably wild) and sprinkle them with lemon juice.

212

Finely slice one half of the peeled red pepper and dice the other half. In a food processor, blend 6 peeled tomatoes, the slices of pepper, the mussel cooking juices, 2 tablespoons olive oil, a little sauce *à l'anglaise* and 10 drops of Tabasco sauce. Add the diced and sliced vegetables, the broad beans and the mussels. Adjust the seasoning. Refrigerate for several hours before serving.

Moules marinière

Trim, scrape and wash some mussels. Peel and chop 1 large shallot per 1 kg (2¼ lb) mussels. Put the chopped shallots in a buttered pan with 2 table-spoons chopped parsley, a small sprig of thyme, half a bay leaf, 200 ml (7 fl oz, ¾ cup) dry white wine, 1 tablespoon wine vinegar and 2 tablespoons butter (cut into small pieces). Add the mussels, cover the pan and cook over a high heat, shaking the pan several times, until all the mussels have opened. Remove the pan from the heat and place the mussels in a large serving dish. Discard any mussels that do not open. Remove the thyme and bay leaf from the saucepan and add 2 tablespoons butter to the liquid. Whisk the sauce until it thickens and pour it over the mussels. Sprinkle with chopped parsley.

Mussel brochettes (1)

Open some mussels over a brisk heat. Discard any that do not open. Remove the mussels from their shells and thread on skewers, alternating them with thin pieces of smoked bacon and tomato. Season with pepper. Cook under a hot grill (broiler) for about 1 minute.

Mussel brochettes (2)

Place some large cleaned mussels in their shells (discard any open shells) in a pan with some finely chopped shallots, chopped parsley, a good pinch of thyme, ground pepper and a little dry white wine. Cook over a high heat until the mussels have opened, then take them out of their shells. (Discard any unopened shells.) Stir a little cold water into some white mustard powder and spread on a plate. Roll the mussels in the mustard, then in breadcrumbs and thread them on to the skewers. Leave for 1 hour. Just before cooking, sprinkle the mussels with a little melted butter; grill (broil) under a medium heat for about 10 minutes.

Mussel croquettes

Prepare a salpicon of *moules marinière* and thinly sliced mushrooms which have been cooked slowly in butter. Add half of its volume of well-reduced béchamel sauce to which some filtered juice from the mussels has been added. Stir the mixture well, over the heat, then spread evenly on a buttered baking sheet and dab the surface with butter to prevent it from forming a crust. Leave to cool completely before making the croquettes.

Divide the cold mixture into portions of 50–75 g (2–3 oz). Roll these out on a floured flat surface and shape them into corks, balls, eggs or rectangles. Dip them in a mixture of egg and oil beaten together and then cover them completely with fine breadcrumbs.

Place the croquettes in a frying basket, plunge into oil heated to 175–180°C (347–356°F), and deep-fry until they are crisp and golden. Drain on paper towels and arrange on a napkin in a pyramid or turban shape. Serve with a white wine sauce.

Mussel-farmers' mouclade

This is a preparation of cultured mussels from the Poitou-Charentes region. They are cooked in white wine with shallots and parsley, usually flavoured with curry or saffron, and coated with their cooking liquid enriched with cream and butter and thickened with egg yolks or cornflour (cornstarch).

Clean and wash 2 kg (4½ lb) mussels, discarding any that are damaged or open. Toss them in a saucepan over a brisk heat until they open. Discard any that do not open. Remove the empty shells and place the ones containing the mussels in a dish; keep hot over a saucepan of boiling water. Strain the juice from the mussels through a fine sieve. Finely chop a garlic clove and a sprig of parsley and blend with 100 g (4 oz, ½ cup) butter. Warm the mussel juice in a saucepan over a gentle heat. Add the flavoured butter, a pinch of curry (or saffron), a pinch of ground celery seed, a dash of pepper and the mussels. Stir well, then simmer for 5 minutes. Sprinkle with 1 teaspoon cornflour (cornstarch), stir well and simmer for 2 minutes. Add 150 ml (¼ pint, ⅔ cup) double (heavy) cream and serve.

Mussel fritots

Prepare some *moules marinière*, remove from their shells, drain and dry. Marinate them for 30 minutes in a mixture of oil, chopped garlic, chopped parsley, lemon juice, a pinch of cayenne pepper, salt and pepper. Then dip them in a light batter and deep-fry until they are golden brown. Drain on paper towels and serve with fried parsley, quarters of lemon and Italian sauce.

Mussel quiche

Cook 450 g (1 lb) mussels and remove them from their shells. Reserve the mussel cooking liquor.

Make a shortcrust pastry (basic pie dough) with 200 g (7 oz, 1¾ cups) plain (all-purpose) flour, 100 g (4 oz, 1 cup) butter, 4 tablespoons water and 3 pinches of salt. Roll out the dough to a thickness of 3 mm (⅛ in) and use it to line a 23 cm (9 in) tart tin (pie pan). Spread the mussels over the base.

Mix 1 egg with 50 g (2 oz, ½ cup) plain flour, 2 egg yolks, 150 ml (¼ pint, ⅔ cup) double (heavy) cream, 250 ml (8 fl oz, 1 cup) milk diluted with some of the mussel cooking liquor, and salt and pepper. Pour the egg mixture over the mussels. Cook the quiche in a preheated oven at 220°C (425°F, gas 7) for 30 minutes and serve with a well-chilled white wine.

Mussels à la bordelaise

Prepare 2 kg (4½ lb) *moules marinière*, drain them, remove one shell from each mussel, and place them in a vegetable dish. Keep hot. Prepare 200 ml (7 fl oz, ¾ cup) meatless mirepoix, moisten it with the strained liquid in which the mussels were cooked, and add 150 ml (¼ pint, ⅔ cup) fish velouté and 2 tablespoons tomato purée (paste). Heat and reduce by one-third, then add the juice of ½ a lemon and whisk in 50 g (2 oz, ¼ cup) butter. Pour this hot sauce over the mussels, sprinkle with chopped parsley and serve.

Mussels à la poulette

Prepare some *moules marinière*, drain them, remove one of the shells from each mussel and place in a dish. Strain the cooking liquid through a fine sieve, reduce by half and add 300 ml (½ pint, 1¼ cups) poulette sauce. Add a little lemon juice, pour over the mussels and sprinkle with chopped parsley.

Mussels in cream

Prepare 2 kg (4½ lb) *moules marinière*, drain them, remove one of the shells from each mussel and place them in a vegetable dish. Keep hot. Strain the cooking liquid through a fine cloth. Prepare 300 ml (½ pint, 1¼ cups) light béchamel sauce, add 200 ml (7 fl oz, ¾ cup) double (heavy) cream and the cooking liquid from the mussels, and reduce by at least one-third. Season with salt and pepper and pour this hot sauce over the mussels.

The béchamel cream sauce may be flavoured with curry or 1 tablespoon chopped onion, softened in butter.

Octopus

Octopus à la provençale

Clean an octopus, remove the eyes and beak, and soak it under running water for a long time. Drain it and beat to tenderize the flesh. Cut the tentacles and body into chunks of the same length. Blanch the pieces in court-bouillon, drain them and pat dry. Then brown in oil in a saucepan, with chopped onion. Season, add 4 peeled, seeded and chopped tomatoes, and simmer for a few minutes. Moisten with ½ bottle of dry white wine and the same quantity of cold water. Add a bouquet garni and a crushed garlic clove. Cook, covered, for at least 1 hour. Sprinkle with chopped parsley and serve in a large bowl.

Ormers (abalones)

Ormers à la cancalaise

Ormers are large single-shelled molluscs found off the Pacific coasts of Asia and Mexico, in the Mediterranean and off the European Atlantic coast. All the muscle is edible and has a chewy texture but unique flavour.

Refrigerate 8 large or 12 medium live ormers for 48 hours to weaken them and remove from their shells while still cold. Remove the beards and set aside. Scrape the ormers under cold running water to remove any black. Refrigerate on a damp cloth for 24 hours. Before cooking, massage gently to tenderize.

Wash and dry the beards, then brown them in 100 g (4 oz, ½ cup) butter. Add 1 peeled and chopped shallot, 1 sliced carrot, 3 finely sliced mushrooms, 3½ tablespoons Coteaux-du-Layon, 1 roasted garlic clove, the stems of ½ bunch of parsley and 2 tablespoons chopped, dried nori. Add 100 ml (4 fl oz, 7 tablespoons) chicken stock. Cover and simmer gently for 1 hour, then strain. (This ormer stock is highly flavoured.)

Blanch 4 unblemished cabbage leaves in boiling salted water. Drain and set aside. Heat 3½ tablespoons oil in a saucepan and briskly fry the leaves of 20 small sprigs of parsley. Drain on paper towels and put to one side. Reheat the ormer stock and thicken with 50 g (2 oz, ¼ cup) butter. Brown the ormers for 2 minutes on each side. Allow to rest for 15 minutes. Deglaze the pan with the stock and 4 teaspoons cider vinegar. Strain through a fine sieve. Reheat the cabbage leaves in a knob of butter and a little water.

Place a perfect warm shell on each plate with a cabbage leaf to one side. Finely shred 2 or 3 ormers and arrange on the cabbage leaf, with some on the shell. Sprinkle with finely chopped parsley, pour some ormer stock on top and garnish with a few leaves of fried parsley.

Oysters

Angels on horseback

Take some oysters out of their shells. Sprinkle them with a little white pepper and wrap each one in a thin slice of bacon. Thread them on skewers and grill (broil) for 2 minutes. Arrange on pieces of hot toast.

Attereaux of oysters

Attereaux are hot hors d'oeuvres of skewered ingredients dipped in a reduced sauce, coated in breadcrumbs and fried.

Poach and drain several large oysters. Cut some mushrooms into thick slices and sauté them in butter. Assemble the attereaux by alternating the oysters with the mushrooms. Dip them in Villeroi sauce made with a fish fumet, coat them with breadcrumbs and plunge them into very hot fat. Serve with fried parsley and lemon halves.

Devilled oysters

Poach, drain and remove the beards of the oysters. Thread the oysters on small kebab skewers, coat with melted butter seasoned with a little cayenne pepper and dip them in fresh white breadcrumbs. Grill (broil) under a low heat and serve with devilled sauce.

Fried oysters Colbert

Shell the oysters and poach them in their own liquid. Drain them, remove the beards and allow to cool. Dip each oyster in milk and coat with flour. Deep-fry in oil and arrange on a napkin. Garnish with lemon quarters and fried parsley. Serve with Colbert butter.

Oyster fritots

Remove the oysters from their shells and poach gently in their own liquor. Drain and dry. Marinate them for 30 minutes in a mixture of oil, chopped garlic, chopped parsley, lemon juice, a pinch of cayenne pepper, salt and pepper. Then dip them in light batter and deep-fry until they are golden brown. Drain on paper towels and serve with fried parsley, quarters of lemon and Italian sauce.

Oyster fritters

Poach the oysters in their own water and let them cool in the cooking liquid. Drain them and dry in a cloth. Leave them to soak for 30 minutes in a mixture of oil, lemon juice, pepper and salt, then dip them in batter. Cook in very hot oil until the fritters are puffed and golden and drain them at once on paper towels. Sprinkle with fine salt and serve with lemon quarters.

Oysters à la Boston

Open 12 oysters; carefully take out the flesh from the shells and drain it. In the bottom of each concave shell, place a little white pepper and a generous pinch of fried breadcrumbs. Replace the oysters in the shells; sprinkle them with grated Gruyère cheese and a few breadcrumbs. Dot each with a small piece of butter. Brown under the grill (broiler) for 6–7 minutes. Serve with buttered fried shrimp or Parmesan cheese straws.

Oysters à la Brolatti

Poach 12 oysters, drain them and remove the beards. Prepare a sauce with 2 chopped shallots tossed in butter, the oyster beards, 2 tablespoons white wine and the strained liquid from the oysters. Reduce to about 3 tablespoons. Thicken the reduced sauces by whisking in 100 g (4 oz, ½ cup) butter. Season with pepper and lemon juice. Strain the sauce and keep it warm. Warm the oyster shells in the oven. Cook the oysters in butter in a covered pan for 1 minute and then return them to their shells. Cover with the sauce and serve.

Oysters à la rhétaise

Open 24 oysters and place in a saucepan with their own strained water, 2 shallots, 1 garlic clove and a knob of butter. Reduce the liquid by half. Put this sauce into a pan with 4 tablespoons single (light) cream, a pinch of cayenne, a pinch of saffron and 2 teaspoons curry powder. Blend together and let it reduce. Add a little lemon juice. Arrange the oysters in individual gratin dishes, cover with the sauce and put under the grill (broiler) for 10 seconds.

Oysters in their shells

Poach the oysters, replace them in their shells and set these firmly into a layer of coarse salt in a baking tin (pan). Brown in a preheated oven at 220°C (425°F, gas 7) for a few seconds (poaching can be omitted). They can then be served in the following ways.

- *à l'américaine* Sprinkle with lemon juice and a pinch of cayenne.
- *à la florentine* Replace in their shells on buttered spinach, then mask with Mornay sauce, sprinkle with grated cheese and brown in the oven.
- *à la polonaise* Sprinkle with chopped hard-boiled (hard-cooked) egg yolk and chopped parsley, then moisten with noisette butter mixed with fried breadcrumbs.

Oyster soup

Open 24 oysters and put them into a sauté pan with the strained liquor from their shells. Add 200 ml (7 fl oz, ¾ cup) white wine. Bring just to the boil and take off the heat as soon as the liquid begins to bubble. Use a draining spoon to transfer the oysters to a plate and set them aside. Skim any scum off the liquid, then whisk in 1 small, finely diced carrot, 1 finely chopped spring onion (scallion) and 3 tablespoons finely crushed water biscuits (crackers) and bring to the boil. Simmer for 1 minute, whisking, then add 200 ml (7 fl oz, ¾ cup) single (light) cream. Gradually whisk in 100 g (4 oz, ½ cup) butter cut into small pieces. The soup should be smooth and hot, but it must not simmer or boil as it will curdle. Replace the oysters and heat for a few seconds. Season with salt and pepper and a pinch of cayenne. Serve at once.

Oysters Robert Courtine

Put 2 chopped shallots in a saucepan with 200 ml (7 fl oz, ¾ cup) champagne. Bring to the boil over a high heat and reduce by half. Let it cool slightly. Open 36 oysters and put them into a saucepan with their strained liquid. Add a few drops of champagne and bring just to the boil. Drain the oysters and pour the liquid into the first pan. Whisk in 200 g (7 oz, generous ¾ cup) butter. Add pepper and the juice of 1 lemon. Adjust the seasoning. Put the oysters into a serving dish or their shells, cover with the sauce and serve at once.

Oysters with cider and winkles

Open 24 oysters and keep the deep halves of the shells. Make a stock with 1 litre (1¾ pints, 4⅓ cups) water, 1 carrot, 2 celery sticks, 1 teaspoon salt and 200 ml (7 fl oz, ¾ cup) cider. Cook 200 g (7 oz) winkles in it for 10 minutes, then take them out of their shells. Skin 2 tomatoes and dice the flesh finely. Poach the oysters in their own water with 6 tablespoons cider. Remove the beards and keep the oysters warm. Chop 2 shallots and cook them in 200 ml (7 fl oz, ¾ cup) cider, then reduce by half. Add 6 tablespoons single (light) cream, reduce again and finish with 50 g (2 oz, ¼ cup) butter cut into small pieces. Add pepper, a few drops of lemon juice and the oysters' cooking liquid. Adjust the seasoning. Snip the leaves from a small bunch of chervil.

Heat the oyster shells, fill them with the oysters and the winkles, and cover with sauce. Sprinkle them with the diced tomato. Glaze them in a preheated oven at 240°C (475°F, gas 9) and just before serving add the chervil leaves.

Oyster velouté soup

Thicken a generous 750 ml (1¼ pints, 3¼ cups) chicken consommé or fish fumet with a white roux made with 40 g (1½ oz, 3 tablespoons) butter and 40 g (1½ oz, 6 tablespoons) plain (all-purpose) flour. Add 450 g (1 lb) skinned fish fillet and simmer gently until the flesh breaks up with a fork. Drain and bone the fish. Reduce the flesh to a purée in a blender or food processor, adding a little cooking liquid. Mix in the rest of the cooking liquid.

Poach 24 oysters in their own juices. Add their cooking liquid to the soup and return to the heat until simmering. Remove from the heat and thicken with 3 egg yolks beaten with 100 ml (4 fl oz, 7 tablespoons) double (heavy) cream. Whisk in 75 g (3 oz, 6 tablespoons) butter. Trim the oysters, steam them quickly to reheat and add them to the soup just before serving.

Poached oysters

Open the oysters and put into a sauté pan. Pour the liquor from the shells over them, straining it through a muslin (cheesecloth) sieve. Bring almost to the boil, removing the pan from the heat as soon as the liquid begins to simmer.

Prawns & shrimps

Bouchées with prawns

Fill some cooked bouchée cases with a ragoût of prawn (shrimp) tails in prawn sauce.

Canapés with shrimps, lobster or langouste

Spread shrimp (or lobster) butter on some round slices of bread. Garnish each canapé with a rosette of shrimp tails (or a medallion of lobster or langouste tail) and a border of chopped parsley or shrimp butter.

Cream of shrimp soup

Prepare 100 ml (4 fl oz, 7 tablespoons) vegetable mirepoix and cook it gently in about 25 g (1 oz, 2 tablespoons) butter. Add 350 g (12 oz, about 2 cups) unpeeled raw shrimps and sauté them. Season with salt and pepper. Moisten with 3 tablespoons white wine and 1 tablespoon brandy that has been ignited. Cook for about 5 minutes. Reserve 12 shrimps for the garnish and purée the rest with the other ingredients in a blender or food processor. Sieve and add 900 ml (1½ pints, 1 quart) milk added to a white roux of 25 g (1 oz, 2 tablespoons) plain (all-purpose) flour. Simmer gently for 5 minutes. Peel the reserved shrimps and garnish the soup with them just before serving.

Cream of prawn, crayfish, lobster, langouste or scampi soups can be made in the same way; peel these larger shellfish before cooking them.

Fried prawns or shrimps

Wash and drain some raw prawns or shrimps and fry them in hot oil for about 1 minute. Drain, season with salt and serve with aperitifs.

Prawn omelette

Bind some peeled (shelled) cooked prawns (shrimp) with prawn sauce and use them to fill an omelette. When serving, pour a thin line of sauce on the plate around the omelette.

Prawn pannequets

Bind some peeled (shelled) cooked prawns (shrimp) with some well-reduced prawn sauce. Prepare some fairly thick savoury pancakes, fill each of them with prawns – about 500 g (18 oz, 3 cups) for 12 pannequets – and roll them up. Arrange them in a buttered dish, brush them with a little melted butter and reheat them in the oven.

Scallop shells of shrimps

Shell some *moules marinière*, and strain the juice. Wash and thinly slice 250 g (9 oz, 3 cups) mushrooms, then sauté briskly in butter with 1 chopped shallot. Prepare a béchamel sauce, add the juice from the mussels and season. Mix all these ingredients, adding 150 g (5 oz, ¾ cup) peeled (shelled) shrimps. Butter 4 scallop shells and distribute the mixture evenly. Sprinkle with fresh breadcrumbs and a little grated Parmesan cheese, baste with melted butter and brown in a preheated oven at 240°C (475°F, gas 9).

Shrimp mousse

Prepare a finely diced mirepoix of vegetables. Toss 350 g (12 oz, 2 cups) shrimps or lobster in melted butter and season with salt, pepper and a little cayenne. Pour brandy over the shellfish and set alight, then just cover with dry white wine. Add the vegetable mirepoix and cook together for 5 minutes. Remove and peel (shell) the shrimps. Reduce the cooking mirepoix, then rub through a sieve (or put through a blender or food processor) with the shrimp flesh. Pound, purée and sieve the shells from half the shrimp and add to the shrimp purée. For every 250 g (9 oz, generous 1 cup) purée obtained, add 5 tablespoons well-reduced fish velouté and 6 tablespoons fish aspic. Cool but do not allow to set. Line a small charlotte mould with fish aspic. Add 100 ml (4 fl oz, 7 tablespoons) half-whisked double (heavy) cream to the shrimp purée, then pour the mixture into the mould. Pour over it a thin layer of aspic and refrigerate for at least 2 hours. Turn out on to a serving dish and garnish with prawns.

Shrimp or prawn mayonnaise

Mix 50 g (2 oz, ⅓ cup) peeled (shelled) cooked shrimps or prawns into 3 tablespoons mayonnaise in a mortar or blender. Sieve the mixture and blend with 200 ml (7 fl oz, ¾ cup) mayonnaise. The sauce can be coloured by adding a drop of cochineal (red food colouring) or a little tomato ketchup.

Shrimp purée

Pound in a mortar some shelled shrimp. Add an equal volume of béchamel sauce mixed with cream and reduce. Adjust the seasoning.

This purée is added to stuffings and sauces for fish and shellfish.

Shrimp velouté soup

Thicken a generous 750 ml (1¼ pints, 3¼ cups) chicken consommé or fish fumet with a white roux made with 40 g (1½ oz, 3 tablespoons) butter and 40 g (1½ oz, 6 tablespoons) plain (all-purpose) flour. Cook 400 g (14 oz, 2⅓ cups) peeled (shelled) shrimps with a mirepoix. Then rub through a sieve or put through a blender or food processor and add this purée to the thickened consommé. Remove from the heat and thicken the soup with a mixture of 3 egg yolks beaten with 100 ml (4 fl oz, 7 tablespoons) double (heavy) cream. Finally, whisk in 65 g (2½ oz, 5 tablespoons) butter or prawn butter, made as for crab butter.

Shrimps in cider

Heat 50 g (2 oz, ¼ cup) butter and a dash of olive oil in a frying pan. As soon as the mixture begins to foam, add some raw shrimps and cover immediately. Stir well. After 3 minutes of cooking, add 100 ml (4 fl oz, 7 tablespoons) dry (hard) cider. Reduce the liquid. Put the shrimps in a cloth. Season with coarse sea salt and pepper and shake well. Eat while still lukewarm with bread and butter, with cider to drink.

Alternatively, prepare a fish stock with 1 litre (1¾ pints, 4⅓ cups) dry cider, 1½ tablespoons coarse sea salt, thyme, bay leaves, 10 black peppercorns and 1 thinly sliced apple. Reduce for 10 minutes. Throw in the raw shrimps and boil for 30 seconds. Put the shrimps in a cloth, season and shake well.

Shrimps sautéed in whisky

Wash, drain and sauté some raw shrimps in oil in a frying pan. Add some pepper, a pinch of cayenne pepper and whisky, Cognac or marc, allowing 6 tablespoons per 500 g (18 oz, 3 cups) shrimps. Flame and serve very hot.

Scallops

To prepare

To open a scallop shell, scrub it thoroughly and, if preferred, place the rounded side on an electric hotplate or in the oven at a low heat for a few minutes before opening it with a knife. Rinse the flesh and halve or slice it as required. Discard the beards or use them in the preparation of a fumet.

Fried scallops Colbert

Quickly poach the white flesh of the scallops in a court-bouillon for 4 minutes, then cut into slices if they are very large. Marinate them with the corals in a mixture of olive oil, garlic and chopped parsley with a little lemon juice, salt and pepper. Leave for 1 hour, turning the ingredients at least once during this time, then drain, dip into batter and fry in plenty of fat. Drain and serve with Colbert butter. (The meat may also be covered in breadcrumbs before frying.)

Mille-feuille of scallops with peppers

Prepare some puff pastry. Roll out thinly and divide into 16 equal rectangles, about 10 × 7 cm (4 × 2½ in). Cook in a preheated oven at 220°C (425°F, gas 7) under golden. Trim the edges and keep warm. Cook 6 peeled and crushed garlic cloves in 250 ml (8 fl oz, 1 cup) whipping cream. Strain, season with salt and pepper and add 25 g (1 oz, 2 tablespoons) butter. Keep warm.

Clean, peel and remove the seeds from 3 red (bell) peppers and 3 green (bell) peppers. Cut into strips and cook in 3 tablespoons olive oil. Sauté 32 walnut halves and 16 scallop corals in butter. Keep these ingredients warm.

Construct 8 mille-feuilles by layering the puff pastry, red pepper, 4 walnut halves, 2 scallop corals, a little garlic cream, green pepper and, finally, a rectangle of puff pastry. Glaze the mille-feuilles with hot melted butter and arrange on a serving dish. Serve with scalloped mushrooms sautéed in butter and beurre blanc.

Nage of scallops with lemon thyme

Remove 2.5 kg (5½ lb) carefully cleaned scallops from their shells. Remove their beards. Wash several times and put in the refrigerator.

Finely snip a bunch of chives and dice the flesh of 1 lemon. Squeeze the juice of 1 lemon. Chop or dice 400 g (14 oz) carrots, 1 medium leek and 300 g (11 oz) celeriac or 2 celery sticks. Bring to the boil 400 ml (14 fl oz, 1¾ cups) fish stock, lightly seasoned with salt and pepper, with 200 ml (7 fl oz, ¾ cup) white wine. Add the vegetables, 4 sprigs lemon thyme and the lemon juice. Bring back to the boil, then reduce the heat. Add the scallops and 100 ml (4 fl oz, 7 tablespoons) double (heavy) cream and simmer gently for another 2 minutes (overcooked, the scallops would become hard). Remove from the heat, discard the thyme sprigs, and stir in the chives and diced lemon. Ladle the nage of scallops into soup bowls, and garnish with chervil or parsley.

Queen scallops and oysters sautéed in Canadian whisky

Remove 12 queen scallops from their shells. Season, then brown on both sides in a frying pan over a high heat. Set aside. Melt 15 g (½ oz, 1 tablespoon) butter in a large saucepan. Add 1 teaspoon chopped shallots and 12 oysters and sauté for 30 seconds. Remove from the heat. Add the scallops and 200 ml (7 fl oz, ¾ cup) Canadian whisky. Flame at once. Using a slotted spoon, remove the scallops and the oysters and keep them warm. Pour 150 ml (¼ pint, ⅔ cup) white wine and 150 ml (¼ pint, ⅔ cup) fish stock into the saucepan, bring to the boil and reduce by half. Add 150 ml (¼ pint, ⅔ cup) crème fraîche and reduce by half again. Incorporate 25 g (1 oz, 2 tablespoons) butter, then 75 g (3 oz, ¾ cup) cornflour (cornstarch). Add salt and pepper to taste and reheat without boiling. Arrange the scallops and oysters on a bed of risotto made with wild rice. Pour over the sauce and garnish with peeled, seeded, chopped tomatoes and chopped chives.

Raw scallops

Open the scallops, remove them from their shells, wash thoroughly (after removing the beards) and pat them dry. Cut the scallops into thin slices and lay them on a cold plate that has been lightly oiled. Brush with olive oil and season with one turn of the pepper mill. Garnish with thin slivers of coral.

Raw scallops with caviar

Open and trim the scallops. In an earthenware dish, mix 2 tablespoons olive oil and 3 tablespoons groundnut (peanut) oil. Slice the white flesh and coral. Dip each slice in the oil mixture, wipe off the excess and put them on a plate, allowing 2 scallops per serving. Season each plate with 3 pinches of salt and 3 turns of the pepper mill. Place 5–6 grains of caviar on each ring and surround the caviar grains with slices of coral meat. Serve with hot buttered toast.

Scallop and chicory cassolettes

Cut 1 kg (2¼ lb) chicory into 1 cm (½ in) segments, wash, drain and sprinkle with lemon juice. Season with salt and sugar, add 2 tablespoons groundnut (peanut) oil and fry for 7–8 minutes in butter without covering the pan. Shell and trim some scallops, put them in a frying pan, season with salt, pepper and a little cayenne, and brown (3–4 minutes), keeping them fairly soft. Arrange them in *cassolettes* or mounds on top of the chicory. Reduce 3 tablespoons port by two-thirds, add the juice of 1 lemon and 50 g (2 oz, 4 tablespoons) butter cut into pieces, then whisk into an emulsion. Add a little lemon zest, pour over the scallops and serve.

Scallop brochettes

Marinate the flesh and corals of 12 good scallops in a mixture of olive oil, garlic and chopped parsley, with a little lemon juice, salt and pepper. Leave for 1 hour, turning the ingredients at least once during this time. Clean 12 small mushrooms.

Remove the seeds from a large sweet (bell) pepper and cut into squares. Cut 200 g (7 oz) smoked brisket into small pieces. Thread all these ingredients on 4 skewers, always placing a piece of meat on either side of the scallop flesh and its coral. Dip into the marinade and grill (broil) for 15–18 minutes under a moderate heat.

Scallop broth with spinach

Cut 12 prepared scallops into slices, 5 mm (¼ in) thick, and place in a buttered frying pan. Add salt and 120 ml (4½ fl oz, ½ cup) fish stock, poach for 2 minutes, then remove and drain. Add 200 ml (7 fl oz, ¾ cup) crème fraîche to the stock and reduce until it is the consistency of a light soup. Add 500 g (18 oz, 3½ cups) chopped fresh spinach and heat for 2 minutes. Then bind with a mixture comprising 100 ml (4 fl oz, 7 tablespoons) double (heavy) cream, 2 egg yolks and the juice of 1 lemon. Then add the scallop slices and adjust the seasoning. Serve in hot dishes garnished with hot roughly chopped tomatoes.

Scallop feuilletés

Open, trim and clean 16 scallops. Sauté them over a brisk heat in a sauté pan with 200 g (7 oz, 1 cup) butter and some freshly ground pepper for 3 minutes, turning them once. Put 2 tablespoons finely chopped shallots into a frying pan with 250 ml (8 fl oz, 1 cup) vermouth and boil to reduce to a syrupy consistency. Add 750 ml (1¼ pints, 3¼ cups) single (light) cream, 1 teaspoon mustard, a little ground pepper and 200 g (7 oz, 2¼ cups) diced mushrooms. Reduce over a brisk heat, then add the scallops, together with the liquid from the sauté pan. Reduce again for 2 minutes.

Roll out 400 g (14 oz) puff pastry and cut it into 8 rectangles about 3 mm (⅛ in) thick. Place 4 scallops on each of 4 rectangles together with a little sauce. Cover with the remaining pieces of pastry. Brush the edges of the pastry with egg yolk and seal each pastry case tightly. Cook in a preheated oven at 230°C (450°F, gas 8) for about 12 minutes. Serve hot, with the remaining sauce.

Scallops au gratin à la dieppoise

Poach the white flesh of 16 scallops very gently for 4 minutes in 500 ml (17 fl oz, 2 cups) fish fumet mixed with 200 ml (7 fl oz, ¾ cup) dry white wine. Cook 1 kg (2¼ lb) small *moules marinière*. Make a white roux with 25 g (1 oz, 2 tablespoons) butter and 25 g (1 oz, ¼ cup) plain (all-purpose) flour and gradually add the fish fumet with 100 ml (4 fl oz, 7 tablespoons) strained cooking stock from the mussels. Add 1 tablespoon chopped mushroom stalks and a bouquet garni to the sauce; check the seasoning and cook gently for 20–25 minutes.

Keep the scallops hot in a covered, lightly buttered gratin dish over a saucepan of hot water. Shell the mussels and keep hot in the rest of their cooking liquor, without boiling. Add 75 g (3 oz, ½ cup) peeled prawns (shelled shrimp). When the sauce is cooked, strain it and add the strained mussels and prawns. Dilute 1 egg yolk with a little of the sauce and whisk it in. Coat the scallops with the sauce, scatter with very fine fresh breadcrumbs, sprinkle with melted butter and brown quickly in a preheated oven at 220°C (425°F, gas 7) or under the grill (broiler).

Scallops in mayonnaise

Line the rounded halves of some scallop shells with a little shredded lettuce seasoned with vinaigrette. Poach the white scallop meat in court-bouillon for 4 minutes, then drain well. Thinly slice the poached white flesh, dip the slices in the vinaigrette, then roll in chopped parsley. Place the slices on the lettuce and cover with mayonnaise. Garnish each scallop with the coral, an anchovy fillet and a few capers or black (ripe) olives.

Scallops Mornay

Poach the white flesh and corals of the scallops. Fill the rounded halves of the shells with Mornay sauce. Slice the flesh and place with the corals, in the shells. Cover with more sauce. Sprinkle with grated cheese, baste with melted butter and brown in a preheated oven at about 240°C (475°F, gas 9).

Steamed scallops

Place the flesh of some scallops and their corals into the basket of a steamer. Slice the flesh if the pieces are very large. Pour a well-spiced court-bouillon into the lower part and steam for 2–3 minutes. Finely sliced vegetables, such as the white part of a leek, fennel or celery, may be placed in the basket and steamed for about 10 minutes, before adding the scallops. Alternatively, the scallops and corals may be put into a dish with a lid, seasoned with salt and pepper and cooked in the oven in their own juice.

Squid

To prepare

Pull the tentacles and head parts away from the body sac. Cut off the tentacles and discard the head. Remove the fine, transparent quill or pen from inside the body sac. Use a little salt to rub the dark membrane from the outside of the body. Rinse well. The tentacles can be chopped. The sac can be sliced into rings or slit and spread flat: scoring the inside of the sac with a sharp knife, without actually cutting right through, prevents it from curling during cooking and gives an attractive appearance.

Fried or sautéed squid

Wash and dry 1 kg (2¼ lb) very small cleaned squid. Put them in a frying pan with 60 ml (2 fl oz, ¼ cup) cold olive oil. Heat and cook over a brisk heat for 10 minutes, turning continually. Season with salt and pepper, cover the pan, reduce the heat and cook for 15 minutes more. Add 2–3 chopped large garlic cloves and 1 tablespoon chopped parsley. Increase the heat and stir briefly. Serve very hot.

Sautéed squid à la basquaise

Wash and dry 500 g (18 oz) ready-cleaned white squid and cut it into strips. Seed and chop 4–5 red and green (bell) peppers, finely chop 4 onions, and peel and finely chop 500 g (18 oz) fresh tomatoes. Fry the peppers in oil, then add the onions, the squid and 1–2 crushed garlic cloves. After cooking for 15 minutes, add the tomatoes and a bouquet garni and season with salt and pepper. Half-cover and cook gently for 10 minutes. Sprinkle with chopped parsley before serving.

Squid à l'andalouse

Wash and dry 1 kg (2¼ lb) white squid flesh and cut it into thin strips. Fry the strips in very hot olive oil. Place 3–4 (bell) peppers in a very hot oven for a few minutes so that the skin swells. Peel, remove the seeds and cut the flesh into thin strips. Peel 3 onions and slice them into rings. Peel 4–5 tomatoes, remove the seeds and crush the pulp. Dice 100 g (4 oz) farmhouse bread and brown in very hot olive oil. Add the strips of pepper to the squid, then the onions and finally the tomatoes. Brown the mixture, add 120 ml (4½ fl oz, ½ cup) very dry white wine and cook for 35–45 minutes over a low heat. Chop and mix together the diced fried bread, a small bunch of parsley and 3–4 large garlic cloves. Add a pinch of saffron, 75 g (3 oz, ¾ cup) ground almonds and 2 tablespoons oil. Pour this mixture over the cooked squid, mix well and adjust the seasoning. Serve piping hot with well-drained rice.

Stuffed squid

Separate the head and tentacles from the bodies of 12 small squid, 10 cm (4 in) long. Remove the quill or pen from inside the bodies and the blackish membranes and skins from the outsides and rinse the squid thoroughly under cold running water. Pat them dry and season with salt and pepper.

Chop the tentacles and brown them in olive oil in a heavy-based saucepan. Add 4 chopped onions and cook gently for 10 minutes until all of the liquid has completely evaporated. Add ½ bunch of parsley, chopped, 50 g (2 oz, ½ cup) fried cubes of bread, 1 chopped garlic clove and a pinch of cayenne pepper. Stuff the squid with this mixture and secure using wooden cocktail sticks (toothpicks). Brown the squid in more olive oil.

Peel 4 large green or red (bell) peppers, or a mixture of both, remove their cores and seeds, then slice them. Peel and roughly chop 8 tomatoes; remove the stones (pits) from 12 black (ripe) olives and halve them, or leave them whole if they are small. Place the vegetables in a casserole, adding seasoning to taste. Arrange the stuffed squid on top. Cover and cook in a preheated oven at 200°C (400°F, gas 6) for 1½ hours, basting frequently. Adjust the seasoning to taste, sprinkle with chopped parsley and serve with rice.

Stuffed squid à la marseillaise

Clean some small squid reserving the tentacles. Chop the tentacles finely with 2 large onions. Soak 100 g (4 oz, 4 slices) stale bread in milk, then squeeze it out. Chop and mix together some garlic and parsley. Brown the tentacles and onions in olive oil, then add 2 peeled and crushed tomatoes. Mix all the ingredients together. Add 2–3 egg yolks, salt, pepper and a pinch of cayenne pepper, and blend well. Fill the squid with this stuffing, sew them up and pack tightly together in an oiled baking dish. Sprinkle with chopped garlic and parsley, add 1 coarsely crushed onion, salt, pepper, 120 ml (4½ fl oz, ½ cup) white wine and an equal amount of hot water. Cover the dish with oiled greaseproof (wax) paper. Start the cooking on the hob (stove top), then transfer the dish to a preheated oven at 180°C (350°F, gas 4) for about 30 minutes. Uncover the dish to reduce the liquid, then sprinkle the squid with olive oil and dried white breadcrumbs and brown under the grill (broiler).

MIXED FISH & SEAFOOD DISHES

Bagration fish soup

Add 225 g (8 oz) skinned fillet of sole, removing any stray bones, to 1 litre (1¾ pints, 4⅓ cups) velouté soup and simmer for 30 minutes. Strain the fish, chop it finely, and return to the velouté. Stir in 3 egg yolks mixed with 100 ml (4 fl oz, 7 tablespoons) cream to bind the soup and adjust the seasoning. Stir in about 50 g (2 oz ¼ cup) butter and hot chopped macaroni. Serve accompanied by grated cheese.

Barquettes à l'américaine

Fill cooked barquette cases with a salpicon of shellfish *à l'américaine*, prepared as for lobster *à l'américaine*, and using a mixture of shellfish and seafood, as preferred. Sprinkle with fried breadcrumbs and bake in a preheated oven at 230°C (450°F, gas 8) until the filling is hot and the breadcrumbs are crisp.

Bouillabaisse

For 8–10 servings, use about 3 kg (6½ lb) fish and shellfish. Place the following ingredients in a large deep flameproof casserole: 300 g (11 oz, 2¾ cups) chopped onions or 100 g (4 oz, 1 cup) leeks and 200 g (7 oz, 1¾ cups) onions, 2 large sliced carrots, and 3 large skinned and finely chopped tomatoes, 3–4 tablespoons crushed garlic, 1 sprig fennel, a small bunch of parsley, 1 sprig thyme, a bay leaf and a piece of dried orange rind.

Add the prepared shellfish, then the firm-fleshed fish cut into uniform pieces with heads, bones and skin removed, as necessary. Moisten with 200 ml (7 fl oz, ¾ cup) olive oil and season with salt and freshly ground pepper. Add a generous pinch of powdered saffron and leave to marinate, covered and in a cool place, for a few hours.

Add sufficient water (or fish stock prepared with the heads and trimmings of the fish) to cover the fish. Cover and boil rapidly for 7–8 minutes. Then add the prepared soft-fleshed fish and continue to boil rapidly for a further 7 minutes. Remove the fish and shellfish and place in a large round dish. Line a soup tureen with dry bread and strain the soup on to it. Sprinkle the soup and the fish with coarsely chopped parsley and serve both at the same time.

Bourride

Bourride is a Provençal fish soup. After cooking, the liquid is strained and bound with aïoli (garlic mayonnaise). The authentic *bourride* from Sète is made with monkfish, but elsewhere whiting, sea perch, grey mullet and red mullet are sometimes mixed together.

Cut 1 kg (2¼ lb) monkfish or mixed fish into pieces and boil rapidly for 20 minutes in a mixture of 1 litre (1¾ pints, 4⅓ cups) each of water and white wine, together with the sliced white part of 1 leek, 2 chopped onions, 2 chopped carrots, 2 chopped garlic cloves, a little dried orange peel, salt and pepper. When the fish is cooked, place each piece on a slice of stale bread and sprinkle with a little saffron. Strain the stock, reduce by half, remove from the heat and blend in some very thick aïoli. Pour the sauce over the fish.

Caldeirada

This is a thick Portuguese soup made from molluscs and fish with white wine, poured over slices of bread glazed with olive oil.

Mix together 1 finely chopped onion, ¼ chopped (bell) pepper, 2 small tomatoes, peeled, seeded and crushed, ½ teaspoon crushed garlic, salt and black pepper from the mill.

Place 12 clams in a heavy-based casserole with 60 ml (2 fl oz, ¼ cup) olive oil. Cover with half the mixture of vegetables, then add 400 g (14 oz) white fish, skinned, filleted and cut into pieces, and 300 g (11 oz) squid, cleaned and cut into strips. Cover with the remaining vegetables and add 200 ml (7 fl oz, ¾ cup) white wine. Bring to the boil, then cover and simmer for 20 minutes. Heat 60 ml (2 fl oz, ¼ cup) olive oil in a frying pan and fry 4 slices of sandwich bread on both sides until golden. Drain on paper towels. Put 1 slice of bread on each plate. Pour a ladle of stock over each slice, then arrange the fish, clams and squid on top. Sprinkle with a generous amount of finely chopped parsley.

Caribbean bouillabaisse

Heat some olive oil in a large saucepan and gently cook 1 large chopped onion, some quartered tomatoes, 1 large crushed garlic clove, and 1 small crushed chilli pepper; add some thyme, grated nutmeg, salt and pepper. Finally add some prepared West Indian fish (such as devil fish and bonito), a small lobster (or a large lobster tail) and 3 crabs. Cover, bring to the boil, and cook for about 20 minutes for fresh; for frozen fish, continue cooking for 15 minutes after they have thawed. Five minutes before cooking is complete, add a little curry powder and 2 generous pinches powdered saffron.

Chaudrée saintongeaise

This is a French fish soup of the Vendée and Saintonge coast, which is made with small skates, soles, small cuttlefish (*casserons*), and sometimes sections of eel and gurnets (gurnard).

Sweat 100 g (4 oz) peeled, chopped garlic, flat-leaf parsley and finely chopped tarragon in 50 g (2 oz, ¼ cup) butter. Season with pepper. Add 500 ml (17 fl oz, 2 cups) white wine, 500 ml (17 fl oz, 2 cups) fish fumet (concentrated fish stock) and a bouquet garni. Simmer for 1 hour.

Fry the following in olive oil in a large sauté pan until golden, adding them one after the other, in this order: 200 g (7 oz) conger eel cut into pieces, 200 g (7 oz) small skate, 200 g (7 oz) sole or céteaux, 200 g (7 oz) brill or plaice, 200 g (7 oz) *casserons* (small cuttlefish) and 200 g (7 oz) live langoustines. Cook in the fish stock for 3–4 minutes each. Then put in a preheated oven at 160°C (325°F, gas 3) for 10 minutes. Thicken the cooking juices with 200 g (7 oz, ¾ cup) butter. Serve with small croûtons roasted in the oven and lightly buttered with garlic butter.

Cotriade

This is a fish soup from the coast of Brittany, prepared with butter or lard (shortening), onions and potatoes. The fish should be selected from the following: sardines, mackerel, sea bream (porgy), angler, hake, conger eel, gurnard and horse mackerel (saurel). For a more delicate dish, do not allow the proportion of oily fish, such as sardines and mackerel, to exceed a quarter of the total weight. If available, 1 or 2 large fish heads may also be included.

Cut 3 good-sized onions into quarters and cook them in a large saucepan with 25 g (1 oz, 2 tablespoons) butter or lard until they are a pale golden colour. Add 3 litres (5 pints, 13 cups) water and 6 peeled sliced potatoes. Flavour with thyme, bay leaf and other herbs. Bring to the boil and cook for about 15 minutes, then add 1.5 kg (3¼ lb) cleaned pieces of fish. Cook for a further 10 minutes. Pour the stock from the resulting soup on to some slices of bread and serve the fish and potatoes separately, accompanied with a sauceboat of vinaigrette.

Fillets of fish en papillotes

Cut out some rectangles of greaseproof (wax) paper large enough to wrap up each fillet (such as sole, whiting, fresh cod, sea bream) folded in two. Spread 1 tablespoon double (heavy) cream in the centre of each papillote and season with salt and pepper. Place on top a fish fillet seasoned with salt and pepper, sprinkled with a little lemon juice and folded in two. Cover with a little cream and scatter with coarsely chopped herbs. Close the papillotes, folding the edges together. Cook in a preheated oven at 230°C (450°F, gas 8) for about 15 minutes.

A little julienne of vegetables cooked in butter may be placed under and over the folded fish fillet. Sliced scallops, peeled blanched prawns (shrimp) and squid rings may be added.

Fillets of fish in cider

Prepare a fish stock, using equal proportions of rough dry (hard) cider and water. Poach the chosen fish fillets or a mixture of fish in this stock, then drain and arrange on the serving dish, keeping them hot. Strain the cooking liquid and reduce by half. To it, add the same volume of double (heavy) cream and reduce a little more. Coat the fillets with the sauce and glaze in a preheated oven at 240°C (475°F, gas 9).

Fish in escabèche

Escabèche is a spicy cold marinade intended for preserving cooked foods and originating in Spain. It is used chiefly for small cooked fish (sardines, mackerel, smelt, whiting, red mullet). The heads are removed (hence the name, from *cabeza*, 'head') then the fish are fried or lightly browned, then marinated for 24 hours in a cooked and spiced marinade. The fish can then be kept for up to a week in a refrigerator.

Gut some small fish (smelt, sand eels, weevers) and remove the heads; clean, wash and wipe the fish. Dip in flour and fry in olive oil until golden. Drain and arrange in an earthenware dish. Slice 1 onion and 1 carrot thinly. Heat the oil used for cooking the fish until it begins to smoke, then fry the onion and carrot and 5–6 unpeeled garlic cloves for a few moments. Remove from the heat and add 150 ml (¼ pint, ⅔ cup) red wine vinegar and 150 ml (¼ pint, ⅔ cup) water. Add a bouquet garni containing plenty of thyme and season with salt, pepper, a pinch of cayenne pepper, and a few coriander seeds. Cook for about 15 minutes, then pour the boiling marinade over the fish and leave to marinate for at least 24 hours. Serve as an hors d'oeuvre.

Fish mousse

Clean 500 g (18 oz) fillets or steaks of either pike, whiting, salmon or sole, or a mixture of white fish and salmon and pound them in a mortar or put in a food processor. Sprinkle with salt and pepper, then blend in 2–3 egg whites, one after the other. Rub this forcemeat through a sieve and refrigerate for 2 hours. Then place the bowl in crushed ice and gradually add 600 ml (1 pint, 2½ cups) double (heavy) cream, stirring the mixture with a wooden spoon. Adjust the seasoning, pour the mousse into a lightly oiled plain mould, and poach gently in a bain marie in a preheated oven at 190°C (375°F, gas 5) for about 20 minutes. Wait about 10 minutes before turning out and serve the mousse warm, coated with a sauce for fish.

Fish soup with mussels

Shred the cleaned white part of 3 leeks, 2 carrots, and 1 celery stick and fry in 100 ml (4 fl oz, 7 tablespoons) olive oil. Add a pinch of saffron, a sprig of thyme, 1 bay leaf, 1 crushed garlic clove and 250 g (9 oz, 1 cup) crushed fresh tomatoes. Add 150 g (5 oz) each of fillets of brill, monkfish, red mullet and weever (sand lance), together with 1.5 litres (2¾ pints, 6½ cups) fish fumet. Simmer for 15 minutes. Season with salt and pepper and add 500 g (18 oz) shelled mussels. Serve piping hot.

Fish velouté soup

Thicken a generous 750 ml (1¼ pints, 3¼ cups) chicken consommé or fish fumet with a white roux made with 40 g (1½ oz, 3 tablespoons) butter and 40 g (1½ oz, 6 tablespoons) plain (all-purpose) flour. Add 675 g (1½ lb) fish and simmer gently until the flesh breaks up with a fork. Drain the fish and bone it if necessary. Reserve about half of the fish and reduce the remainder to a purée in a food processor or blender, adding a little of the cooking liquid. Return the purée to the pan with the rest of the cooking liquid and heat through until it reaches simmering point. Remove from the heat and thicken with a mixture of 3 egg yolks beaten with 100 ml (4 fl oz, 7 tablespoons) double (heavy) cream. Whisk in 75 g (3 oz, 6 tablespoons) butter, then add the reserved fish and serve.

Fish waterzooï

Cut 200 g (7 oz) white part of leeks and the same quantity of celery into fine strips; butter a large flameproof casserole and cover the base with the vegetables; add salt, pepper and a bouquet garni containing 4 sage leaves. Add sufficient fish fumet (or court-bouillon) to cover 2 kg (4½ lb) freshwater fish (about 1.25 litres, 2¼ pints, 5½ cups) and add 100 g (4 oz, ½ cup) butter in small pieces. Cover and cook gently for about 30 minutes, then allow to cool. Meanwhile, clean the fish and cut into sections. Place them in the cold cooking liquid, adding a little more court-bouillon if necessary, partly cover the pan, bring to the boil, and poach for at least 20 minutes. Remove the fish with a slotted fish-slice, discard the bouquet garni and mix 200 ml (7 fl oz,

¾ cup) double (heavy) cream into the cooking liquid. Reduce this sauce, then replace the fish and reheat. Serve from the casserole, accompanied with bread and butter or slices of buttered toast.

Fricassée of sea fish with Bellet zabaglione

To serve 6, you will need 800 g (1¾ lb) young turbot, 1.5 kg (3¼ lb) John Dory, 4 slices of monkfish, 2 red mullet, 4 scampi and 500 ml (17 fl oz, 2 cups) white Bellet wine or a good Provençal wine. Fillet the turbot and the John Dory. Wash the fillets and season with salt and pepper. Heat 3 table-spoons olive oil and 40 g (1½ oz, 3 tablespoons) butter in a large frying pan. When the mixture foams, add all the fish and the scampi. Add a large chopped shallot and cook for a few seconds. Add about 100 ml (4 fl oz, 7 tablespoons) Bellet wine. Remove the red mullet, fillet them and replace in the pan. Add 3 tablespoons concentrated fish stock and finish cooking. Arrange the fish on a dish and keep hot.

Make a zabaglione by whisking together 8 egg yolks and 400 ml (14 fl oz, 1¾ cups) white Bellet wine over hot water until thick and foamy. Season with salt and pepper and add 500 ml (17 fl oz, 2 cups) hot double (heavy) cream. The zabaglione should be hot and foamy, but must not boil. Adjust the seasoning. Coat the fricassée with the zabaglione. Sprinkle with fresh chervil and serve with lightly cooked (al dente) French (green) beans, with a knob of butter on top.

Marinated fish à la grecque

Gently cook 100 g (4 oz, 1 cup) finely chopped onions in 150 ml (¼ pint, ⅔ cup) olive oil without browning them. Add 150 ml (¼ pint, ⅔ cup) white wine, 150 ml (¼ pint, ⅔ cup) water and the strained juice of 1 lemon. Add 2 finely shredded (bell) peppers, 1 crushed garlic clove and a bouquet garni (consisting of parsley, a sprig of thyme, a bay leaf and a sprig of fresh fennel). Season with salt and pepper and boil for 15 minutes. Pour piping hot over the prepared selected fish, allow to cool and keep in the refrigerator. This quantity of sauce is sufficient for 500 g (18 oz) fish. Suitable fish include small species, such as small sardines and red mullet.

Marinated sea bass, salmon and scallops

Peel and grate 1 large piece of fresh root ginger. Soak for 2 or 3 days in 100 ml (4 fl oz, 7 tablespoons) olive oil. Thinly slice 250 g (9 oz) sea bass, 250 g (9 oz) fresh salmon fillet and 4 shelled scallops. Arrange decoratively on 4 plates. Season with 1 teaspoon each sea salt and pepper. Sprinkle ½ bunch of fresh dill, very finely chopped, on top. Allow to marinate for 1 hour. Then add 1 tablespoon ginger oil (or olive oil marinated with sliced fresh root ginger) and a dash of lemon juice and serve.

Marseille bouillabaisse

Scale, clean and remove the head of 2 kg (4½ lb) of several kinds of whole fish (conger eel, sea bream, red gurnard, monkfish, whiting, scorpion fish, John Dory). Cut into pieces. Fry 1 onion, 1 garlic clove, 2 leeks and 3 celery sticks, all peeled and finely chopped, in 7 tablespoons of oil until golden. Add the fish heads and trimmings. Cover with water, bring to the boil and simmer for 20 minutes. Strain the mixture through a sieve and press to obtain as much of the cooking juices as possible. Crush 3 peeled tomatoes. Peel and chop 1 onion, 2 garlic cloves and 1 fennel bulb and fry in oil in a saucepan until golden. Add the stock, tomatoes and bouquet garni. Add the scorpion fish, red gurnard, monkfish, conger eel, sea bream, 10 little crabs (*étrilles brossées*) and a few strands of saffron. Cook over a high heat. Then add the John Dory and whiting. Cook for another 5–6 minutes.

Make a *rouille* to accompany the bouillabaisse. Moisten a slice of bread with a little of the stock and squeeze it. Pound it with 3 garlic cloves and 1 chopped red chilli. Add 1 egg yolk, then 250 ml (8 fl oz, 1 cup) olive oil while whisking this *rouille* like a mayonnaise.

Cut a baguette into slices and toast lightly or brown in the oven. Arrange the fish and trimmings on a large dish, pour the bouillon into a soup tureen, and serve with the *rouille* and croûtons.

Matelote à la canotière

Butter a frying pan and make a bed of 150 g (5 oz, 1 cup) sliced onions and 4 crushed garlic cloves. Add 1.5 kg (3¼ lb) mixed or individual freshwater fish (carp, eel) cut into equal-sized pieces, a large bouquet garni and 1 litre (1¾ pints, 4⅓ cups) dry white wine. Bring to the boil. Add 100 ml (4 fl oz, 7 tablespoons) brandy and flame. Cover and gently simmer for 25 minutes. Drain the fish pieces, placing them in another frying pan, and retain the stock.

To the fish add 125 g (4½ oz, 1½ cups) cooked button mushrooms and 125 g (4½ oz, ¾ cup) small glazed onions. Reduce the fish stock by two-thirds and bind with beurre manié – for 1 litre (1¾ pints, 4⅓ cups) stock, bind with 50 g (2 oz, ½ cup) plain (all-purpose) flour kneaded with 50 g (2 oz, ¼ cup) butter. Finally, add a further 150 g (5 oz, ⅔ cup) butter.

Pour the sauce over the fish and simmer gently. Serve the *matelote* plain, with rice, or garnished with gudgeons fried in breadcrumbs, or whitebait, and crayfish cooked in a court-bouillon.

Meurette of fish

Meurette is a term for certain dishes cooked in red wine sauce, such as a matelote of river fish (for example eel, carp and pike). Clean 1.4 kg (3 lb) freshwater fish (such as small carp, young pike, small eels, perch and trout) and cut them into pieces. Brown them in butter in an flameproof casserole, then flame them with marc (use at least 1 liqueur glass). Shred 1 carrot, 1 onion and 1 shallot and add them to the casserole. Stir thoroughly. Cover the contents of the casserole with red Burgundy wine, add a small crushed garlic clove and a bouquet garni, and season with salt and pepper. Cover and simmer very gently for about 20 minutes. Rub some small croûtons of bread with garlic and fry them in butter. Thicken the sauce with 1 tablespoon beurre manié, adjust the seasoning and serve garnished with the fried croûtons.

Paella

Cut a chicken weighing about 1.4 kg (3 lb) into 8 pieces and season them with salt and pepper. Place the crushed backbone and the giblets in a stewpan, cover with water, season with salt and pepper, bring to the boil and skim. Peel and chop 2 onions, cut the white part of a leek and a celery stick into fine strips and chop 3 garlic cloves. Add all the vegetables with a bouquet garni. Wait until the stock comes to the boil again, then simmer for 1 hour.

Wash 500 g (18 oz) prepared squid, cut into thin strips and put in a saucepan with some cold water. Bring to the boil, leave to boil for 5 minutes, then cool and set aside.

Heat 4 tablespoons olive oil in a deep frying pan with a metal handle (or use a paella pan) and fry the chicken pieces in it until they turn golden. Drain them. Gently reheat the same oil and add 250 g (9 oz) *chorizo* cut into round slices, then the squid, 2 sweet (bell) peppers, seeded and cut into thin strips, and 2 chopped onions. Add a pinch of saffron and leave to soften, uncovered, for 5–6 minutes. Add 6 large tomatoes (peeled, seeded and crushed) and reduce for 5 minutes, still uncovered.

Measure the volume of 400 g (14 oz, 2 cups) long-grain rice, tip it into the pan and mix everything together. Place the chicken pieces on top, then add

12 scraped and washed mussels, 12 Venus clams (if available), a handful of brushed and washed cockles and 8–12 langoustines. Strain the giblet stock and measure two and a half times the volume of the rice, then pour into the pan. Cover with foil, bring to the boil over the heat, then cook in a preheated oven at 220°C (425°F, gas 7) for 25–30 minutes. Add 250 g (9 oz, 1¾ cups) frozen peas, stirring them into the mixture, and leave to cook for a further 5 minutes. Turn off the oven and leave the paella there for about 10 minutes before serving, to allow the rice to finish swelling.

Pochouse

Also known as *pattchouse*. A Burgundy *matelote* (fish stew) made from a selection of pike, gudgeon, eel, perch or carp; it should also include burbot, which is now very rare. The Bresse *pochouse* often includes tench, carp and catfish. *Pochouse* is cooked with white wine and thickened with beurre manié.

Butter a flameproof casserole generously and completely cover the bottom with 2–3 large peeled sliced onions and 2 carrots cut into rings. Clean 2 kg (4½ lb) freshwater fish and cut into uniform pieces: use 1 kg (2¼ lb) eels (skinned) and 1 kg (2¼ lb) burbot, tench, pike or carp. Place the pieces of fish in the casserole with a bouquet garni in the centre. Cover with dry white wine and add 2 crushed garlic cloves. Add salt and pepper, cover, bring to the boil, reduce the heat and allow to simmer for about 20 minutes.

Meanwhile, dice 150 g (5 oz) unsmoked streaky bacon and blanch for 5 minutes in boiling water. Strain. Glaze 20 small (pearl) onions. Clean and slice 250 g (9 oz, 3 cups) mushrooms and sprinkle with lemon juice. Toss the bacon and mushrooms in butter in a sauté pan. Strain the pieces of fish and add them to the sauté pan, together with the onions.

Thicken the cooking liquid from the fish with 1 tablespoon beurre manié, strain and pour into the sauté pan. Simmer for a few minutes. Add 200 ml

(7 fl oz, ¾ cup) crème fraîche. Boil, uncovered, for 5 minutes to reduce. Pour into a deep serving dish and garnish with garlic-flavoured croûtons.

Ragoût à la cancalaise

Remove the beards from some oysters and poach in their own liquid or a well-seasoned fish fumet. Add some peeled prawns (shelled shrimp) and bind all the ingredients together with normande sauce. This ragoût is used for filling pies, tarts and vols-au-vent. It can also accompany whole fish or fish fillets, such as whiting, sole or brill.

Scallop shells of fish à la Mornay

Mix some cooked fish – allow about 450 g (1 lb) for 4 people – with 300 ml (½ pint, 1¼ cups) Mornay sauce and some chopped parsley. A mixture of white fish and prawns (shrimp) or salmon can be used. Season to taste. Fill the scallop shells with this mixture. Sprinkle with grated Gruyère cheese, add a few knobs of butter and brown in a preheated oven at 240°C (475°F, gas 9).

Scallop shells of fish à la provençale

Mix 400 g (14 oz) cooked fish (white fish, tuna, shellfish or a mixture) with 400 ml (14 fl oz, 1¾ cups) well-seasoned Provençal sauce to which 1 table-spoon capers has been added. Distribute the mixture evenly among the scallop shells and sprinkle with some grated cheese according to taste. Baste each scallop shell with ½ teaspoon olive oil and heat in the oven.

Seafood bouchées

Prepare and cook some savoury bouchée cases. Prepare a seafood ragoût. Warm the bouchée cases in the oven (if prepared in advance), fill with the hot seafood ragoût, cover with the bouchée tops and serve immediately.

Seafood brochettes

Prepare a marinade using olive oil, plenty of lemon juice, finely chopped herbs and garlic, fresh crumbled thyme, salt and pepper. Marinate an assortment of seafood for 30 minutes: oysters poached for 1 minute in their liquor, mussels opened by heating in the oven, raw scallops, lobster tails, large peeled prawns (shrimp) and scampi. Thread on to skewers without draining, alternating with very small mushrooms (pierced through the bottom of the cap) and blanched cubed bacon (optional). Grill (broil) under a high heat.

Seafood croûtes

Cut some slices of bread and remove the crusts. Lightly fry in butter and coat with a cheese béchamel sauce. Place on these slices shellfish (oysters, mussels, clams), cooked in white wine, as for *moules marinière*, and coat them with a sauce made with their cooking stock. Sprinkle with fresh breadcrumbs, moisten with melted butter, and brown in a preheated oven at 220°C (425°F, gas 7). Peeled prawns (shelled shrimp) may be added to the shellfish.

Seafood Dartois

Prepare 400 g (14 oz) puff pastry. Poach 8 langoustines or scampi in a court-bouillon for 5 minutes. Prepare 8 scallops and poach in a small casserole for 6–7 minutes with 100 ml (4 fl oz, 7 tablespoons) white wine, 150 ml (¼ pint, ⅔ cup) single (light) cream, 1 good-sized shallot (chopped), salt and pepper. Drain the langoustines, shell the tails and cut into sections. Drain the scallops, reserving the liquor, and dice. Add 50 g (2 oz, ⅓ cup) shelled shrimps to the langoustines and scallops and gently heat the seafood together in butter. Add some Calvados or marc brandy and set it alight. Pour the reserved cooking juices from the scallops over the mixture and thicken with 1 tablespoon beurre manié. Adjust the seasoning, allow to cool completely.

Roll and cut the pastry into two rectangular strips of equal size and thickness. Spread one of the strips with the seafood filling, leaving a border of 1 cm (½ in) all round the edge. Place the second pastry strip on top and seal the edges. Cook in a preheated oven at 220°C (425°F, gas 7) for about 20–25 minutes.

Seafood flan

Bake a flan case (pie shell) blind. Prepare a seafood ragoût using small or cut up shellfish (such as oysters, mussels and cockles). Blend the shellfish with a fairly thick normande sauce and fill the flan case with the mixture. Sprinkle with toasted breadcrumbs and a little melted butter and brown in a preheated oven at 240°C (475°F, gas 9).

Seafood omelette

Beat some eggs with chopped parsley and chervil, salt and pepper and make 2 flat omelettes. Put one on to a round ovenproof dish and cover it with a ragoût of mussels, prawns (shrimp), small clams or other shellfish, poached and bound with prawn sauce. Cover with the second omelette. Coat with a cream sauce flavoured with prawn butter and glaze in a hot oven.

Seafood ragoût

Peel and chop 2 shallots and 1 large onion. Clean 800 g (1¾ lb) mussels and 12 langoustines. Dip 5 or 6 tomatoes into boiling water to loosen their skins, peel them, remove their seeds and crush the pulp.

Place the mussels in a pan with 200 ml (7 fl oz, ¾ cup) dry white wine, 1 bouquet garni and half the chopped shallots and onion. Season with pepper. Cover the pan and cook until the shells just open, then remove the mussels and strain the cooking liquid through fine muslin (cheesecloth).

Place the flesh of 15 scallops and the strained mussel liquid in a saucepan, cover and poach very gently for 5 minutes. Remove the scallops from the liquid. Remove the mussels from their shells.

Sauté the langoustines in oil in a flameproof casserole. When red, add some pepper and the remaining shallots and onion; cook until golden. Add a liqueur glass of warm brandy and flame. Add the crushed tomatoes and the cooking liquid; cover, cook very gently for 5–6 minutes, then remove and drain the langoustines. Continue cooking the tomatoes for 10 minutes.

Meanwhile, shell the langoustine tails, crush the shells and add them to the casserole to flavour the mixture. Cut the langoustine tails into chunks and slice the scallop flesh. Heat 50 g (2 oz, ¼ cup) butter in a sauté pan until it foams, then add the langoustines, scallops, mussels and 100 g (4 oz) peeled (shelled) shrimps. Press the tomato sauce through a fine sieve, add 200 ml (7 fl oz, ¾ cup) double (heavy) cream, adjust the seasoning and reduce until the mixture just starts to thicken. Pour over the seafood.

Seafood risotto

Clean and cook 2 litres (3½ pints) mussels and 1 litre (1¾ pints) cockles or clams separately in white wine seasoned with spices and herbs. Drain the shellfish and remove from their shells. Put them in a casserole with 200 g (7 oz) peeled prawn (shelled shrimp) tails and 4 shelled scallops, previously poached in white wine and sliced. Prepare 400 ml (14 fl oz, 1¾ cups) fish velouté sauce, using a white roux and the combined cooking liquids. Cook this sauce for 25 minutes, or until very smooth; add 6 tablespoons double (heavy) cream and reduce. Then mix in 40 g (1½ oz, 3 tablespoons) butter and press through a sieve. Pour the sauce over the shellfish and keep hot without boiling. Meanwhile, prepare a risotto à la piémontaise and arrange it in a large border in a deep dish. Pour the seafood mixture into the centre.

Seafood zephyr

Wash 2 litres (3½ pints) mussels and open them; shell 300 g (11 oz) shrimps. Reserve 6 mussels and 12 shrimps and finely chop the remainder together.

Prepare a soufflé: mix together over a low heat 50 g (2 oz, ¼ cup) butter and 65 g (2½ oz, ⅔ cup) plain (all-purpose) flour, mix in 500 ml (17 fl oz, 2 cups) cold milk and bring to the boil. Add 5 egg yolks, then the chopped seafood. Whisk 5 egg whites to stiff peaks and fold lightly into the mixture. Butter a 20 cm (8 in) soufflé dish and empty the mixture into it, three-quarters filling it. Level the surface by shaking the dish. Cook in a preheated oven at 190°C (375°F, gas 5) for about 20 minutes or until almost cooked.

Meanwhile, mix ½ egg yolk with 25 g (1 oz, ¼ cup) grated Gruyère cheese. Dip the reserved mussels and shrimps in the egg yolk mixture. When the soufflé is almost cooked, increase the oven temperature to 240°C (475°F, gas 9) and rapidly scatter these mussels and shrimps over the top of the soufflé, together with a little grated cheese. Brown for about 5 minutes and serve immediately.

Shellfish pilaf

Dice 150 g (5 oz) cooked crab, lobster or langouste meat. Shell 150 g (5 oz) cooked shrimps and toss in butter. Cook 500 ml (17 fl oz, 2 cups) *moules marinière* (or use cockles or clams), allow them to cool in the cooking juices, then remove the shells and keep warm. Strain and measure the cooking juices and dilute with boiling water to obtain 680 ml (23 fl oz, 2¾ cups) liquid. Wash and drain 300 g (11 oz, 1½ cups) long-grain rice. Heat 4 tablespoons olive oil in a frying pan; add the rice and stir. When it is transparent, add the diluted mussel juice, salt and pepper; cover and cook for 15 minutes. Then add the shellfish meat (bound with lobster butter or langouste butter made by the same method), the shrimps and the mussels. Serve piping hot.

Soupe oursinade

Clean 2 kg (4¼ lb) rockfish and small green crabs and cut the fish into pieces of about 5 cm (2 in). Make a roux with 50 g (2 oz, ¼ cup) butter and 75 g (3 oz, ¾ cup) plain (all-purpose) flour. Pour 150 ml (¼ pint, ⅔ cup) olive oil into a large saucepan. Clean and finely slice 1 leek, 1 fennel bulb and 1 celery stick; peel and crush the cloves from 1 small head (bulb) of garlic; peel and finely slice 2 or 3 onions. Put all the vegetables into the hot oil and cook over a low heat, adding 3 sprigs of parsley.

When the vegetables are soft, add the fish and the crabs and turn the heat up to its maximum. Add 1 sprig of thyme, 3 bay leaves, 5 fresh tomatoes (peeled, seeded and coarsely chopped) and 100 g (4 oz, ½ cup) tomato purée (paste). Cook all these ingredients for about 10 minutes, until their juices run. Add the roux, then stir in 1 bottle white wine and finish with 4 litres (7 pints, 4 quarts) water. Bring to the boil. Add salt and pepper and cook, covered, over a moderate heat (or in a preheated oven at 180°C, 350°F, gas 4) for 30 minutes.

Then put everything through a vegetable mill or blender. Bring the soup to the boil again and add the liquid and corals from 24 sea urchins, 300 ml (½ pint, 1¼ cups) double (heavy) cream and 100 g (4 oz, ½ cup) prawn butter. Boil for 5 minutes, then pour the soup through a fine strainer and serve immediately.

Terrine de l'océan

Scale, gut and clean a 1 kg (2¼ lb) turbot, a 1 kg (2¼ lb) pike, 500 g (18 oz) fresh salmon and 2 large red mullet. Lift out the fillets and ensure that no bones remain. Reserve the trimmings.

Cut an 800 g (1¾ lb) lobster in half, seal it in 40 g (1½ oz, 3 tablespoons) slightly salted butter, then remove the shell and put it to one side. Thoroughly clean 1 kg (2¼ lb) mussels and cook in a covered pan until they open (discard any that do not). Remove the flesh and retain the cooking juices.

Prepare the forcemeat as follows: wash 500 g (18 oz) leeks and finely slice the white parts; chop 2 garlic cloves and 4 shallots. Soften all these vegetables in 40 g (1½ oz, 3 tablespoons) slightly salted butter. Add 200 g (7 oz, 3 cups) coarsely chopped sorrel, then the leaves of a sprig of tarragon. Use a coarse grater to shred the fillets of pike and then the lobster flesh. Blend in the leek and sorrel mixture. Season with salt and pepper; add a pinch of *quatre épices* or 'four spices', 2 tablespoons mustard and 3 whole eggs. Mix thoroughly, then add the mussels.

Now prepare the terrine: line a white porcelain ballotine mould with bards, leaving the ends hanging over the side of the dish, and brush with egg white, then spread in it the first layer of forcemeat and cover with the fillets of turbot and salmon. Add a second layer of forcemeat, then the flesh and corals of 1 kg (2¼ lb) scallops, pointing the corals towards the centre of the mould. Chop 1 large truffle and sprinkle over the scallops, then add another layer of forcemeat, then the red mullet fillets and finally the rest of the forcemeat. Put a bay leaf in the centre.

Dissolve 7 g (¼ oz, 1 envelope) powdered gelatine in 4 tablespoons water; pour over the terrine. Fold down the bards to seal the top of the terrine, cover and cook in a bain marie in a preheated oven at 190–200°C (375–400°F, gas 5–6) for 1¼ hours.

Prepare an aspic with the fish trimmings, the shell of the lobster, the juice of the mussels, the green parts of the leeks and some gelatine. Pour this over the terrine when it has cooled. Keep cool until just before serving. To serve, stand the mould in a little hot water, then turn it out on to a serving dish. Garnish with lettuce leaves and parsley. Serve some herb-flavoured mayonnaise separately.

BASIC RECIPES
& CLASSIC
ADDITIONS

Aspics & glazes

Fish aspic

Prepare a strong fumet: put 1 kg (2¼ lb) white fish trimmings (bones and heads of brill, hake, whiting, sole or turbot), 2 onions, 150 g (5 oz) mushroom parings, 2 shredded carrots, a large bouquet garni, salt, pepper, 7 tablespoons dry white wine (or red wine when cooking salmon, salmon trout or carp) and 2 litres (3½ pints, 9 cups) cold water in a large saucepan. Bring to the boil and then simmer for 30 minutes. Dissolve 45–75 g (1½–3 oz, 6–12 envelopes) gelatine, depending on the degree of firmness required for the aspic, in a little water. Chop up 2 whiting fillets. Mix the dissolved gelatine with the whiting flesh and 2 or 3 egg whites. Strain the fish fumet, pressing the liquid out of the ingredients, and pour it back into the clean saucepan. Add the whiting mixture and bring to the boil, stirring continuously. When it boils, stop stirring and simmer for 30 minutes. Gently strain through a fine cloth and flavour the aspic with champagne or sherry.

Meat aspic

Brown 1 kg (2¼ lb) leg of beef and 500 g (18 oz) knuckle of veal, cut into pieces, 1 calf's foot, 500 g (18 oz) veal bones and 250 g (9 oz) bacon rind, trimmed of fat, in a preheated oven at 200°C (400°F, gas 6). Peel and shred 2 onions, 4 carrots and 1 leek. Place all these ingredients in a stockpot together with a large bouquet garni, 1 tablespoon salt and pepper. Add 3 litres (5 pints, 13 cups) water and bring to the boil. Skim, then add a ladleful of very cold water and simmer for 5 hours. Carefully strain the liquid through a strainer lined with muslin (cheesecloth), let it cool completely and put it in the refrigerator so that the fat which solidifies on the surface can be removed easily. Clarify the stock with 200 g (7 oz) lean beef, 2 egg whites and a small bouquet of chervil and tarragon.

The aspic can be flavoured with Madeira, port, sherry or with any other liquor. If this is done, the flavouring is added just before straining the aspic. White aspic is obtained in a similar fashion, but the meat and bones are not browned. Game aspic is obtained by adding to meat aspic 1.25 kg (2¾ lb) game carcasses and trimmings, which have been previously browned in the oven, and several juniper berries.

Chicken aspic is obtained by adding to meat aspic either a whole chicken or 1.5 kg (3¼ lb) chicken carcasses and giblets that have both been browned in the oven.

Meat glaze

Remove all the fat from a brown stock. When it is as clear as possible, boil it down by half. Strain through a muslin cloth (cheesecloth), then boil it down again and strain. Continue this process until it will coat the back of a spoon, each time reducing the temperature a little more as the glaze becomes more concentrated. Pour the meat glaze into small containers, cool, cover and keep them in the refrigerator.

A similar method is used with a poultry or game stock to obtain a poultry or game glaze.

Boil down a fish fumet to a syrupy consistency, then decant it and strain it through muslin to obtain a light-coloured fish stock used to enhance the flavour of a fish sauce or to pour over fish before putting it in the oven.

Batters

Blinis à la française

Blend 20 g (¾ oz, 1½ cakes) fresh (compressed) yeast or 1 teaspoon dried yeast with 50 g (2 oz, ½ cup) sifted strong plain (bread) flour with 500 ml (17 fl oz, 2 cups) warmed milk and leave to rise for 20 minutes in a warm place. Then mix in 250 g (9 oz, 2¼ cups) sifted strong plain flour, 4 egg yolks, 300 ml (½ pint, 1¼ cups) warm milk and a generous pinch of salt. Mix the ingredients well. Leave the batter to rest for a minimum of 1 hour. At the last moment, add 4 stiffly whisked egg whites and 100 ml (4 fl oz, 7 tablespoons) whipped cream. Make small thick pancakes by frying quantities of the batter in butter in a small frying pan, turning them over after a few minutes.

Coating batter

This batter is suitable for coating food before deep-frying. Sift 200 g (7 oz, 1¾ cups) plain (all-purpose) flour into a bowl. Add 2 teaspoons baking powder, 2 tablespoons groundnut (peanut) oil, a pinch of salt and 250 ml (8 fl oz, 1 cup) warm water. Mix the ingredients thoroughly and beat until smooth, then leave the batter to rest in a cool place for at least 1 hour. Just before using, fold in 2 stiffly whisked egg whites.

Fritter batter (1)

Sift 250 g (9 oz, 2¼ cups) plain (all-purpose) flour into a bowl. Heat 200 ml (7 fl oz, ¾ cup) water until just lukewarm. Make a well in the flour and add 150 ml (¼ pint, ⅔ cup) beer, the water and a generous pinch of salt to the middle of it. Mix, drawing the flour from the sides to the centre. Add 2 tablespoons groundnut (peanut) oil and mix. Leave to rest for 1 hour. Stiffly beat 2 or 3 egg whites and fold into the batter. Do not stir or beat.

Fritter batter (2)

Put 250 g (9 oz, 2¼ cups) sifted plain (all-purpose) flour in a mixing bowl. Make a well in the centre and add 1 teaspoon salt, 2 eggs and 300 ml (½ pint, 1¼ cups) groundnut (peanut) oil. Whisk the eggs and oil together, incorporating a little of the flour. Add 250 ml (8 fl oz, 1 cup) beer and, stirring well, gradually incorporate the rest of the flour. Allow to stand for about 1 hour. A few minutes before using the batter, whisk 3 egg whites stiffly and fold into the batter using a wooden spoon or rubber spatula.

Pancake batter

Mix 500 g (18 oz, 4½ cups) plain (all-purpose) flour with 5–6 beaten eggs and a large pinch of salt. Then gradually add 1 litre (1¾ pints, 4⅓ cups) milk or, for lighter pancakes, 500 ml (17 fl oz, 2 cups) milk and 500 ml (17 fl oz, 2 cups) water. The batter may also be made with equal quantities of beer and milk, or the milk may be replaced by white consommé. Finally, add 3 tablespoons oil, either one with little taste, such as groundnut (peanut) oil or sunflower oil or, if the recipe requires it, use olive oil; 25 g (1 oz, 2 tablespoons) melted butter may also be added. Leave the batter to stand for 2 hours. Just before making the crêpes, dilute the batter with a little water – about 100–200 ml (4–7 fl oz, ½–¾ cup).

Pannequets

Make a batter with 250 g (9 oz, 2¼ cups) plain (all-purpose) flour, a pinch of salt, 3 beaten eggs, 250 ml (8 fl oz, 1 cup) milk, 250 ml (8 fl oz, 1 cup) water and 1 tablespoon melted butter. Prepare some fairly thick pancakes. Pile them in a covered dish and keep hot over a saucepan of boiling water.

Butters

Anchovy butter

Soak 100 g (4 oz) canned or bottled salted anchovies to remove the salt. Purée the fillets in a blender, season and, if liked, add a dash of lemon juice. Work into 225 g (8 oz, 1 cup) softened butter. This butter is used for vol-au-vents, canapés and hors d'oeuvres and to accompany grilled (broiled) fish.

Beurre manié

To thicken 500 ml (17 fl oz, 2 cups) stock or sauce, work together 25 g (1 oz, 2 tablespoons) butter and 25 g (1 oz, 4 tablespoons) plain (all-purpose) flour. Add lumps of this paste to the boiling liquid and whisk over the heat for 2 minutes, whisking each time before adding the next portion.

Caviar butter

Blend 100 g (4 oz) pressed caviar, work into 225 g (8 oz, 1 cup) softened butter and then press through a sieve. This butter is used to garnish canapés or various cold hors d'oeuvres and to flavour some fish sauces.

Colbert butter

Add 1 tablespoon chopped tarragon and 1 tablespoon meat glaze to 200 g (7 oz, ¾ cup) maître d'hôtel butter.

Crab butter

Blend 225 g (8 oz) crabmeat (cooked in court-bouillon and with all cartilage removed). Work into 225 g (8 oz, 1 cup) softened butter. This butter is used for canapés, cold fish or hors d'oeuvres and in fish and shellfish sauces.

Crayfish butter

Pound in a mortar (or crush in a processor) 250 g (9 oz) chopped and cooked crayfish shells and trimmings. Add to 225 g (8 oz, 1 cup) softened butter in a bain marie. Melt the butter mixture slowly but thoroughly. Place some muslin (cheesecloth) over a bowl containing iced water. Pour the melted butter on to the cloth and wring so that the butter goes into the bowl. Place in the freezer or refrigerator to set the butter quickly. As soon as the butter has set, remove from the bowl and blot it dry. Crayfish butter is used for preparing canapés, soups, stuffings, shellfish dishes and sauces.

Garlic butter (with cooked garlic)

Boil 8 large peeled garlic cloves in salted water for 7–8 minutes, dry and purée. Work into 225 g (8 oz, 1 cup) softened butter. Garlic butter is used to complete sauces, and in garnishes for cold hors d'oeuvres.

Garlic butter (with raw garlic)

Crush 2–4 garlic cloves and add to 225 g (8 oz, 1 cup) softened butter. Mix well. A little finely chopped parsley and grated lemon zest can be added to complement the raw garlic.

Horseradish butter

Grate 100 g (4 oz) horseradish. Work it into 225 g (8 oz, 1 cup) softened butter in a blender, then sieve. It is used in the same way as garlic butter.

Langoustine butter

Prepare as for crab or prawn butter using the meat of the langoustine cooked in court-bouillon. A stronger butter may be made by following the method for crayfish butter if the meat of the langoustine is used for another purpose.

Lobster butter

This is prepared in the same way as prawn butter using the meat and eggs of the lobster cooked in court-bouillon. It is used for the same purposes.

Maître d'hotel butter

Work 2 tablespoons finely chopped parsley, 1–2 dashes lemon juice and a pinch of salt into 225 g (8 oz, 1 cup) softened butter. This butter is served with grilled (broiled) fish, fish fried in an egg-and-breadcrumb coating, and various steamed or boiled vegetables.

Mustard butter

Add 2 tablespoons tarragon mustard to 225 g (8 oz, 1 cup) softened butter and season. A hard-boiled (hard-cooked) egg yolk, some chopped herbs and a dash of lemon juice may also be added. Use as for anchovy butter.

Prawn butter

Blend 225 g (8 oz) shelled prawns (shrimp). Work into 225 g (8 oz, 1 cup) softened butter. This butter is used to garnish canapés, cold fish or hors d'oeuvres, and to complete fish and shellfish sauces.

Sardine butter

Sardine butter is prepared as for anchovy butter, using the filleted and skinned canned fish.

Condiments & seasonings

Cranberry compote

Combine 500 g (18 oz, 2¼ cups) caster (superfine) sugar, the grated zest of ½ a lemon and 200 ml (7 fl oz, ¾ cup) water in a saucepan; slowly bring to the boil, then boil for 5 minutes. Add 1 kg (2¼ lb) washed and stalked cranberries and cook over a high heat for 10 minutes. Remove the fruit from the liquid with a perforated spoon, allow to drain a little and place in a dish. Reduce the syrup by one-third if the compote is to be eaten straight away, or by half if it is to be kept for a few days in the refrigerator. Pour the syrup over the fruit and allow to cool for 1 hour.

This compote may be served as a condiment for savoury dishes as well as for a fruit dessert.

Cranberry sauce

Cook 250 g (9 oz, 2 cups) cranberries with 250 ml (8 fl oz, 1 cup) water until the fruit is tender. Add 175 g (6 oz, ¾ cup) sugar, stir until it dissolves, then bring to the boil and remove from the heat.

Curry powder

This is a useful spice mixture and enough to season 600–900 ml (1–1½ pints, 2½–3¾ cups) sauce or a dish to yield 4–6 portions. Place 1 cinnamon stick, 4 cloves, 4 green cardamoms, 2 tablespoons cumin seeds and 4 tablespoons coriander seeds in a small saucepan. Roast the spices gently, shaking the pan frequently, until they are just aromatic. Remove from the pan and cool, then grind to a powder. Mix in 2 teaspoons ground fenugreek, ½ teaspoon ground turmeric and ½ teaspoon chilli powder.

Preserved lemons

Wash 1 kg (2¼ lb) untreated lemons, wipe and cut into thick round slices (or quarter small lemons lengthways.) Dust with 3 tablespoons fine salt and leave to discharge their juices for about 12 hours. Drain, place in a large jar and cover completely with olive oil. Leave in a cool place for 1 month before use. Close the jar firmly after opening and keep in a cool place away from light.

Dressings & mayonnaise

Aïoli

Peel 4 large garlic cloves (split them in two and remove the germ if necessary). Pound the garlic with 1 egg yolk in a mortar or blend them. Season and, while pounding or blending, very gradually add 250 ml (8 fl oz, 1 cup) olive oil, as for a mayonnaise. The sauce is ready when it is thick and creamy. The bulk of the sauce may be increased by adding 2 teaspoons mashed boiled potato.

Anchovy mayonnaise

Add 1 teaspoon anchovy essence (paste) or 4 puréed anchovy fillets to 300 ml (½ pint, 1¼ cups) mayonnaise. Mix well.

Caviar mayonnaise

Pound 25 g (1 oz) caviar in a mortar and add 3 tablespoons mayonnaise. Continue to pound. Rub the mixture through a fine sieve and blend with 200 ml (7 fl oz, ¾ cup) mayonnaise.

Mayonnaise

Ensure that all the ingredients are at room temperature. Put 2 egg yolks, a little salt and white pepper, and a little vinegar (tarragon, if required) or lemon juice in a medium bowl; 1 teaspoon mustard can also be added. Stir quickly with a wooden spoon or whisk. As soon as the mixture is smooth, use a tablespoon to blend in about 300 ml (½ pint, 1¼ cups) olive oil. Add the oil drop by drop, with a few drops of vinegar, taking care to beat the sauce against the sides of the bowl. The whiteness of the sauce depends on this continued beating. As it increases in volume, larger quantities of oil can be added in a thin trickle and also more vinegar or lemon juice. It is essential to add the ingredients slowly and sparingly to avoid curdling.

Vinaigrette

Dissolve a little salt in 1 tablespoon vinegar. Add 3 tablespoons oil and some pepper. The vinegar can be replaced by another acid, such as lemon, orange or grapefruit juice, in which case, the ratio is half fruit juice to half oil.

Other flavourings, such as herbs, mustard or garlic, may be added to taste. The mixture may also be placed in a screw-top jar and shaken vigorously to form an emulsion. For a creamy dressing, replace the oil with crème fraîche.

Flavourings, fillings & accompaniments

Duchess potato

Cut 500 g (18 oz) peeled potatoes into thick slices or quarters. Boil them briskly in salted water. Drain, put in a warm oven for a few moments to evaporate excess moisture, and press through a sieve. Put the purée into a saucepan and dry off for a few moments on the hob (stovetop), turning with a wooden spoon. Add 50 g (2 oz, ¼ cup) butter and season with salt, pepper and a little grated nutmeg. Mix in 1 egg and 2 yolks.

This mixture is easier to pipe while hot: it may be piped for borders or into swirls on a greased baking sheet for duchess potatoes proper. Brush the cooled swirls of potato with beaten egg and brown them in a hot oven.

Alternatively, spread the purée on a buttered baking sheet, leave until cold and shape as indicated in the recipe.

Mushroom essence

Clean and dice about 450 g (1 lb) open-cap cultivated mushrooms, then place them in a saucepan and season with salt. Add a little white wine and water.

Bring to the boil, stirring, then reduce the heat and cover the pan tightly. Cook for about 20 minutes, until the mushrooms are greatly reduced. Strain the liquor through a sieve, pressing or squeezing the mushrooms dry. Boil the liquor to reduce it to a full-flavoured essence.

Pommes Anna

Peel 1 kg (2¼ lb) potatoes and cut into thin even round slices. Wash, wipe and season with salt and pepper. Slightly brown 75 g (3 oz, 6 tablespoons) butter in a special casserole (or in a sauté pan) and arrange the potatoes in circular layers, making sure that they are evenly coated with butter, then compress them into a cake with a wooden spatula. Cover and cook in a hot oven for 25 minutes. Quickly turn the whole cake over on to a flat dish and slide it back into the casserole to brown the other side.

Russian salad

Boil and finely dice some potatoes, carrots and turnips; boil some French (green) beans and cut into short pieces. Mix together equal quantities of these ingredients and add some well-drained cooked petits pois. Bind with mayonnaise and pile up in a salad bowl. Garnish with a julienne of pickled tongue and truffles and add some finely diced lobster or langouste meat.

For a more elaborate dish, the ordinary mayonnaise can be replaced by thickened mayonnaise and the salad is poured into mould lined with aspic and garnished with slivers of truffle and pickled tongue. Chill in the refrigerator for 4 hours and remove from the mould just before serving.

Spinach in cream

Wash, trim, parboil and dry some spinach. Arrange it in a warm vegetable dish and pour heated crème fraîche or cream sauce over. Stir before serving.

Forcemeats

Fish cream forcemeat

Pound 1 kg (2¼ lb) boned and skinned whiting or pike in a mortar (or purée in a blender). Then press through a fine sieve. Whisk 4 egg whites lightly with a fork and add them to the fish purée a little at a time. Season with 4 teaspoons salt and a generous pinch of ground white pepper. Press through the sieve a second time, place in a terrine, and chill for 2 hours. Remove the terrine from the refrigerator and place in a bowl of crushed ice. Then work in 1.5 litres (2¾ pints, 6½ cups) double (heavy) cream using a wooden spoon. (It is essential to keep the cream and the pâté as cold as possible to prevent curdling.)

Fish forcemeat for mousses and mousselines

Skin and bone 1 kg (2¼ lb) fish (pike, whiting, salmon, sole or turbot) and season with 4 teaspoons salt, a generous pinch of pepper and grated nutmeg. Pound the fish in a mortar, add 4 lightly whisked egg whites (one by one), transfer to a blender and then press through a fine sieve. Put the resulting purée in a terrine, smooth out with a wooden spatula and chill for at least 2 hours. Place the terrine in a bowl of crushed ice or ice cubes and incorporate 1.25 litres (2¼ pints, 5½ cups) double (heavy) cream, working it in gently with a spatula. Refrigerate until needed. This forcemeat can also be used for quenelles and to garnish large braised fish or fillets of sole or turbot.

Forcemeat for fish

Crumble 250 g (9 oz, 9 slices) crustless bread into milk. Sauté 75 g (3 oz, ⅔ cup) chopped onions and 150 g (5 oz, 1⅔ cups) chopped button mushrooms in 25 g (1 oz, 2 tablespoons) butter. Add a small handful of chopped parsley and cook for a few minutes. Meanwhile, add 4 tablespoons white wine to 3 chopped shallots in a pan and reduce. Mix the shallots into the other vegetables. Squeeze out the bread and place in a terrine. Add the vegetable mixture and work together. Bind with 2 egg yolks and season with salt and pepper and, if liked, a generous pinch of grated nutmeg and ½ a garlic clove, chopped.

Frangipane panada

Mix 125 g (4½ oz, 1¼ cups) plain (all-purpose) flour and 4 egg yolks in a saucepan with a wooden spoon, then add 90 g (3½ oz, ⅓ cup) melted butter, ½ teaspoon salt, some pepper and a pinch of nutmeg. Thin the mixture with 250 ml (8 fl oz, 1 cup) boiled milk, poured in gradually. Cook for 5–6 minutes, beating vigorously with a whisk. Pour into a buttered dish, smooth the surface, cover with buttered paper and leave to cool.

Godiveau lyonnais (pike forcemeat)

Pound together in a mortar 500 g (18 oz) trimmed diced beef suet, 500 g (18 oz) frangipane panada and 4 egg whites (these ingredients may first be put through a blender). Add 500 g (18 oz) pike flesh and season. Work vigorously with a spatula, then with a pestle. Rub through a fine sieve, place in an earthenware dish and work with a spatula until smooth. The forcemeat is shaped into quenelles and poached in salted water as a garnish for pike.

Matignon mixture

For the *au maigre* (meatless) version, cook 125 g (4½ oz, 1¼ cups) sliced carrots, 50 g (2 oz, ½ cup) chopped celery, and 25 g (1 oz, ¼ cup) sliced onions gently in butter. Add salt, a sprig of thyme, half a bay leaf and a pinch of sugar. When the vegetables are very soft, add 6 tablespoons Madeira and boil to reduce until nearly all the liquid has evaporated. For the *au gras* version (with meat), add 100 g (4 oz, ½ cup) lean diced bacon to the mixture with the onions.

Mirepoix with meat

Peel and finely dice 150 g (5 oz) carrots and 100 g (4 oz) onions. Cut 50 g (2 oz) celery and 100 g (4 oz) raw ham (or blanched streaky bacon) into fine strips. Heat 25 g (1 oz, 2 tablespoons) butter in a saucepan and add the ham and vegetables, together with a sprig of thyme and half a bay leaf. Stir the ingredients into the butter, cover and cook gently for about 20 minutes until the vegetables are very tender.

Mushroom duxelles

Clean and trim 250 g (9 oz, 3 cups) button mushrooms and chop them finely, together with 1 onion and 1 large shallot. Melt a large knob of butter in a frying pan, add the chopped vegetables, salt and pepper. Cook over a brisk heat until the vegetables are brown and the water from the mushrooms has evaporated. If the duxelles is for use as a garnish, add 1 tablespoon cream.

Prawn forcemeat

Cook 125 g (4½ oz, ¾ cup) prawns or shrimps in some salted water. Pound them in a mortar with 100 g (4 oz, ½ cup) butter and then press the mixture through a fine sieve. Add to this mixture half its weight of finely sieved hard-boiled (hard-cooked) egg yolks. Mix together well.

Ratatouille niçoise

Trim the ends of 6 courgettes (zucchini) and cut them into rounds (do not peel them). Peel and slice 2 onions. Cut the stalks from 3 green (bell) peppers, remove the seeds and cut them into strips. Peel 6 tomatoes, cut each into 6 pieces and seed them. Peel and crush 3 garlic cloves. Peel 6 aubergines (eggplants) and cut them into rounds. Heat 6 tablespoons olive oil in a cast-iron pan. Brown the aubergines in this, then add the peppers, tomatoes and onions, and finally the courgettes and the garlic. Add a large bouquet garni containing plenty of thyme, salt and pepper. Cook over a low heat for about 30 minutes. Add 2 tablespoons fresh olive oil and continue to cook until the desired consistency is reached. Remove the bouquet garni and serve very hot.

Shellfish forcemeat

This is a mousseline forcemeat made with crayfish, lobster or crab meat. Allow 4 egg whites, 1.5 litres (2¾ pints, 6½ cups) double (heavy) cream, 1 tablespoon salt and a generous pinch of white pepper for each 1 kg (2¼ lb) shellfish meat.

Smoked herring or sardine forcemeat

Make a white roux with 1 tablespoon butter and 2 tablespoons flour. Add 100 ml (4 fl oz, 7 tablespoons) warm milk and cook for about 10 minutes, stirring continuously with a wooden spoon. Remove from the heat when very thick. Add 1 whole egg and 2 egg yolks. Put either 1 large smoked herring fillet (soaked in a little milk to remove some of the salt if necessary) or 4 medium sardines in a blender and reduce to a purée. Incorporate this into the roux and cook for 3–4 minutes. Press through a sieve. This forcemeat is used as a filling for croustades, *dartois* and small pastry cases.

Vegetable macédoine

Peel and dice 250 g (9 oz) each of new carrots, turnips, French (green) beans and potatoes. Prepare 500 g (18 oz, 3½ cups) shelled peas. Add the carrots and turnips to a pan of boiling salted water. Bring back to the boil and add the beans, then the peas and finally the potatoes. Keep on the boil but do not cover. When the vegetables are cooked, drain and pour into a serving dish and add butter, cream or mayonnaise (keep the cooking water for a soup base). Sprinkle with chopped herbs.

Vegetable mirepoix

This mirepoix is cooked in the same way as mirepoix with meat, but the ham or bacon is omitted and the vegetables are shredded into a brunoise.

Pastry & dough

Bouchée cases

Dust the working surface with flour and roll out some puff pastry to a thickness of about 5 mm (¼ in). Using a round, crinkle-edged pastry (cookie) cutter, 7.5–10 cm (3–4 in) in diameter, cut out circles of pastry and place them on a damp baking sheet, turning them over as you do so. Use a 7.5–10 cm (3–4 in) ring cutter to stamp out rings of pastry. Brush the edge of the pastry bases with beaten egg and place the rings on top. Chill the cases for about 30 minutes. Bake in a preheated oven at 220°C (425°F, gas 7) for 12–15 minutes. Using the point of a knife, cut out a circle of pastry from inside each bouchée, lift it out and set aside to use as a lid. If necessary remove any soft pastry inside the case. The bouchées are now ready to be filled according to the recipe.

Brioche dough

Soften 225 g (8 oz, 1 cup) butter at room temperature. Crumble 7 g (¼ oz, ½ cake) fresh (compressed) yeast and stir in 1 tablespoon warm water. In a separate container stir 1 tablespoon sugar and a pinch of salt into 2 tablespoons cold milk. Sift 250 g (9 oz, 2¼ cups) strong plain (bread) flour, make a well in the centre, and add the yeast mixture and 1 lightly beaten egg. After working in a little flour, add the sugar and salt mixture, and another lightly beaten egg. Continue to work the dough until it becomes smooth and elastic. It should stretch easily. Mix a third of the dough with the softened butter, then add the second and finally the remaining third of the dough to the mixture.

Put the dough in a 2 litre (3½ pint, 9 cup) container, cover with a cloth, and leave to rise in a warm place until it has doubled in volume. Then separate the dough into 3 pieces, knead lightly and leave to rise again. Leave to rest for a few hours in a cool place: the dough is now ready to be shaped and baked.

• *Standard brioche dough* This is prepared in exactly the same way, but the quantity of butter is reduced to 175 g (6 oz, ¾ cup).

• *Pâte levée pour tartes* This yeasted brioche dough is used for tarts and flans. Prepare as for brioche dough, but use 250 g (9 oz, 2¼ cups) plain (all-purpose) flour, 7 g (¼ oz, ½ cake) fresh (compressed) yeast, ½ teaspoon salt, 2 teaspoons caster (superfine) sugar, 2 eggs, 100 g (4 oz, ½ cup) butter and 6 tablespoons milk.

Choux paste

To make about 40 small buns, 20 larger buns or éclairs, measure 250 ml (8 fl oz, 1 cup) water or milk and water (in equal proportions) into a saucepan. Add a large pinch of salt and 65 g (2½ oz, 5 tablespoons) butter cut into small pieces. Heat gently until the butter melts, then bring to the boil. As soon as the mixture begins to boil, take the pan off the heat, add 125 g (4½ oz,

1 cup) plain (all-purpose) flour all at once and mix quickly. Return the saucepan to the heat and cook the paste until it thickens, stirring: it takes about 1 minute for the paste to leave the sides of the saucepan. Do not overcook the mixture or beat it vigorously as this will make it greasy or oily. Remove from the heat and cool slightly. Beat in 2 eggs, then 2 more eggs, one after the other, continuing to beat hard until a smooth glossy paste is obtained. Use as required.

Flan case, baked blind

Prepare 350 g (12 oz) pastry dough (short or shortcrust, sweet, fine lining or puff) and roll out to a thickness of 3 mm (⅛ in). Grease and flour a 28 cm (11 in) pie plate or flan ring and line it with the pastry, pressing firmly around the edges to ensure that it stays in place and taking care not to stretch the pastry. Leave a thicker edge of pastry at the top so that it does not shrink while it is being baked. Trim off the excess pastry by rolling the rolling pin around the rim of the plate or by trimming with a sharp knife. Prick the bottom with a fork and completely cover the pastry with lightly buttered greaseproof (wax) paper or foil, greased side down. To keep the base of the flan flat, sprinkle the surface of the paper with baking beans or dried peas. Bake in a preheated oven at 200°C (400°F, gas 6) for about 10 minutes. Remove the paper or foil and baking beans, glaze the crust with beaten egg, and return to the oven for 3–4 minutes, or until the pastry is cooked and dried out. The flan case (pie shell) may then be filled.

Pasta dough

Sift 500 g (18 oz, 4½ cups) strong plain (bread) flour into a bowl and make a well in the middle. Dissolve 2 teaspoons salt (or less to taste) in 2 tablespoons water, put it in the middle of the flour, then add 3 beaten eggs and 6 egg yolks.

Gradually work the liquids into the flour to make a firm dough. Knead the dough thoroughly, working it with the heel of the palm until the dough is smooth and firm. Wrap the dough in a cloth or cling film (plastic wrap) and leave it in a cool place, but not the refrigerator, for 1 hour so it loses its elasticity, then use according to the recipe.

Puff pastry

Put 500 g (18 oz, 4½ cups) plain (all-purpose) flour on a board in a circle, making a well in the middle. Since flours differ, the exact proportion of water to flour is variable. Into the centre of this circle put 1½ teaspoons salt and about 300 ml (½ pint, 1¼ cups) water. Mix and knead until the dough is smooth and elastic. Form into a ball and leave to stand for 25 minutes.

Roll out the dough into square, mark a cross in the top and roll out the wedges to form an evenly thick cross shape. Put 500 g (18 oz, 2¼ cups) softened butter in the middle of this dough. (The butter should be softened with a wooden spatula until it can be spread easily.) Fold the ends of the dough over the butter in such a way as to enclose it completely. Leave to stand for 10 minutes in a cold place, until rested and firmed slightly.

The turning operation (called *tournage* in French) can now begin. Roll the dough with a rolling pin on a lightly floured board in such a way as to obtain a rectangle 60 cm (24 in) long, 20 cm (8 in) wide and 1.5 cm (⅝ in) thick. Fold the rectangle into three, give it a quarter-turn and, with the rolling pin at right angles to the folds, roll the dough out again into a rectangle of the same size as the previous one. Again fold the dough into three and leave to stand for about 15 minutes and chill if too sticky. Repeat the sequence (turn, roll, fold) a further 4 times, leaving the dough to stand for about 15 minutes after each folding. After the sixth turn, roll out the dough in both directions and use according to the recipe.

Puff pastry croustades

Sprinkle the worktop with flour and roll out puff pastry to a thickness of
1–2 cm (½–¾ in). Using a pastry (cookie) cutter, cut rounds 7.5–10 cm
(3–4 in) in diameter. With a smaller cutter, make a circle centred on the first,
with a diameter 2 cm (¾ in) smaller, taking care not to cut right through the
pastry: this smaller circle will form the lid of the croustades. Glaze with egg
yolk and place in a preheated oven at 230°C, (450°F, gas 8). As soon as the
crust has risen well and turned golden, take the croustades out of the oven.
Leave until lukewarm, then take off the lid and, with a spoon, remove the soft
white paste inside. Leave the croustades to cool completely.

Alternatively, roll the pastry to a thickness of only 5 mm (¼ in) and cut
half of it into circles 7.5–10 cm (3–4 in) in diameter, and the rest into rings of
the same external diameter and 1 cm (½ in) wide. Brush the base of the rings
with beaten egg and place them on the circles; glaze with beaten egg and cook.

Shortcrust pastry

Sift 225 g (8 oz, 2 cups) plain (all-purpose) flour into a bowl and stir in a
pinch of salt, if required. Cut 50 g (2 oz, ¼ cup) chilled butter and 50 g (2 oz,
¼ cup) chilled lard or white vegetable fat (shortening) into small pieces, then
lightly rub into the flour until the mixture resembles breadcrumbs. Sprinkle
3 tablespoons cold water over the mixture, and mix in with a roundbladed
knife. The mixture should form clumps: press these together into a smooth
ball. Chill the pastry for 30 minutes. Roll out and use as required.

Timbale case

Butter a large timbale or charlotte mould. Garnish the inside with little shapes
of pasta dough (slightly moistening them so that they will adhere to the
pastry used to line the mould).

Prepare 400 g (14 oz) lining pastry and roll it out into a circle 20 cm (8 in) in diameter and 5 mm (¼ in) thick. Sprinkle lightly with flour and fold in half, then bring the ends into the centre until they meet. Roll out again to smooth away the folds. Place this round of pastry in the mould and press it firmly against the base and sides without disturbing the pasta-dough decorations. Cut off any excess pastry.

Line the pastry case (shell) with buttered paper (buttered side inwards), then fill it up with dried beans. Place a circle of paper on top of the dried beans (which should be heaped into a dome) and then, on top of this, a round sheet of pastry 1 cm (½ in) thick. Join the edges of the pastry together by pressing them between the fingers, then make the rim of the pie by pinching this border with pastry pincers.

Moisten the lid with water and garnish with little shapes (leaves, rosettes, fluted rings) cut from a thin sheet of pastry. Make a chimney in the centre of the lid. Brush with egg and bake in a preheated oven at 190°C (375°F, gas 5) for 35–40 minutes.

Take the timbale out of the oven, cut round the lid with a sharp-pointed knife, then remove it. Take out the paper and dried beans and brush the inside of the pastry case with egg. Put the timbale back in the oven with the door open, to dry for a few minutes, then remove it, turn it out of the mould on to a wire rack and keep it hot together with the lid. Fill as desired and replace the lid. Serve immediately.

Vol-au-vent case

Prepare 500 g (18 oz) fine puff pastry. Divide it in half and roll out each half to a thickness of 5 mm (¼ in). Cut out 2 circles, 15 cm (6 in) in diameter. Place 1 pastry circle on a slightly dampened baking sheet. Using a 12–13 cm (4¾–5 in) round cutter, remove the centre of the second circle. Dampen the top of the pastry circle and place the outer ring from the second one on top. Turn the ring over as you place it on the circle so that the slightly floury underside is uppermost.

Roll the central circle of pastry from the ring to the same size as the vol-au-vent. Dampen the border of the vol-au-vent and place this third layer on top. Glaze the top with beaten egg top then use a small knife to score around the inside of the border. This marks the lid covering the well in the vol-au-vent; scoring it without cutting through completely makes it easier to remove when cooked. Mark a pattern on top of the lid by lightly scoring it in a criss-cross pattern.

Bake in a preheated oven at 220°C (425°F, gas 7) for about 15 minutes until well-risen and golden-brown. After taking it out of the oven, place the vol-au-vent on a wire rack; carefully cut out the lid without breaking it, place it on the wire rack, and remove the soft pastry from the inside of the vol-au-vent. Keep hot. Reheat the filling, fill the case with it, place the lid on top and serve very hot.

Rice dishes

Pilaf rice

Sweat some very finely chopped onions in butter without browning. Add the unwashed rice and stir until it becomes transparent. Add 1½ times its volume boiling water. Season with salt and add a bouquet garni. Put greaseproof (wax) paper over the rice and cover with a lid. Cook for 16–18 minutes in a preheated oven at 200°C (400°F, gas 6). Remove from the oven and allow to stand, covered, for 15 minutes. Add butter and stir to separate the grains.

Rice à la créole

Thoroughly wash 500 g (18 oz, 2½ cups) long-grain rice and pour it into a sauté pan. Add salt and enough water to come 2 cm (¾ in) above the level of the rice. Bring to the boil and continue to boil rapidly with the pan uncovered. When the water has boiled down to the same level as the rice, cover the pan and cook very gently until the rice is completely dry (about 45 minutes). The second cooking stage may be carried out in a cool oven.

Risotto à la milanaise

Heat 40 g (1½ oz, 3 tablespoons) butter or 4 tablespoons olive oil in a saucepan and cook 100 g (4 oz, ¾ cup) chopped onions very gently, without browning. Then add 250 g (9 oz, 1¼ cups) rice and stir until the grains become transparent. Add twice the volume of stock, a ladleful at a time, stirring with a wooden spoon and waiting until all the liquid has been absorbed before adding more. Adjust the seasoning, add a small bouquet garni, then add 200 ml (7 fl oz, ¾ cup) thick tomato fondue, 500 g (18 oz) pickled ox (beef) tongue, ham and mushrooms (in equal proportions, all chopped), and a little white truffle. Keep the risotto hot without allowing the rice to cook further.

Risotto à la piémontaise

Prepare the rice as for risotto *à la milanaise*, but omit the tomato fondue, tongue, ham and mushrooms, adding instead 75 g (3 oz, ¾ cup) grated Parmesan cheese and 25 g (1 oz, 2 tablespoons) butter. Some saffron may also be added.

Sauces & purées

Allemande sauce

(from Carême's recipe) Prepare some velouté; pour half of it into a saucepan with an equal quantity of good chicken consommé containing some mushroom skins and stalks but no salt. Place the pan on a high heat and stir with a wooden spoon until it boils. Then cover the pan and simmer gently for about 1 hour to reduce the sauce; skim off the fat and return it to a high heat, stirring with the wooden spoon so that it does not stick to the pan. When the sauce is thoroughly reduced and well thickened it should leave a fairly thick covering on the surface of the spoon. When poured, it should make a coating similar to that of redcurrant jelly at its final stage of cooking.

Remove the saucepan from the heat and make a liaison of 4 egg yolks mixed with 2 tablespoons cream. Put this through a sieve and add a knob of unsalted butter, the size of a small egg, cut up into small pieces. Pour this a little at a time into the velouté, taking care to stir with the wooden spoon to thicken as the liaison blends in. When completely thickened, place the allemande on a moderate heat, stirring all the time, and as soon as it has begun to bubble slightly, remove from the heat and add a dash of grated nutmeg. When well blended, press through a sieve.

Allemande sauce based on fish stock

Using a wooden spatula, mix together 2 or 3 egg yolks (according to size) and 400 ml (14 fl oz, 1¾ cups) rich fish stock in a heavy-based saucepan over a low heat. Then stir in 500 ml (17 fl oz, 2 cups) velouté. Bring to the boil, whisking constantly to prevent the sauce from sticking, and reduce until it coats the spatula. Check seasoning. Cut 50 g (2 oz, ¼ cup) butter into small pieces and mix into the sauce. Place in a bain marie, topping up the water from time to time.

Anchovy purée

Add 2 tablespoons desalted anchovies to 150 ml (¼ pint, ⅔ cup) well-reduced béchamel sauce and mix in a blender. Then rub the mixture through a sieve. Stir in some heated butter just before using. This anchovy purée may be used in fritters, vol-au-vent and rissoles.

Anchovy purée (for cold dishes)

Desalt 75 g (3 oz) anchovies, remove the fillets and reduce them to a purée in a mortar or in a blender with 4 hard-boiled (hard-cooked) egg yolks and 40 g (1½ oz, 3 tablespoons) butter. Add 1 tablespoon chopped herbs. Mix well.

This purée is used to stuff hard-boiled eggs, artichoke hearts and fish (red mullet), for serving cold.

Anchovy purée (for hot dishes)

Desalt 75 g (3 oz) anchovies, remove the fillets and pound them into a purée in a mortar or with a blender. Add to this purée 150 ml (¼ pint, ⅔ cup) thick béchamel sauce and, if desired, 2–3 sieved or pounded hard-boiled (hard-cooked) egg yolks and some coarsely chopped herbs.

This purée is used to fill bouchées, tartlets or rissoles to be served hot.

Anchovy sauce (cold)

Thoroughly desalt 6–8 anchovy fillets by soaking them in milk. Drain, wipe and purée them in a blender with 1 tablespoon capers, 100 ml (4 fl oz,

½ cup) oil, the juice of ½ a lemon and salt and pepper. Serve as a dip with an assortment of raw vegetables – small artichokes, cauliflower florets, small sticks of carrot and seeded cucumber, thin slices of green or red sweet (bell) peppers, small quarters of fennel or raw mushrooms – or with fish poached in a court-bouillon, either hot or cold.

Anchovy sauce (hot)

Add 2 tablespoons anchovy butter to 200 ml (7 fl oz, ¾ cup) béchamel sauce. Check the seasoning. This sauce can be served hot with any fish poached in a court-bouillon.

Anchoyade

Peel 3 garlic cloves and scrape them on the prongs of a fork over a plate. Rinse and chop the leaves of 6 sprigs of parsley. Remove the salt from 10 anchovies and fillet them or use drained canned anchovy fillets. Add them to the garlic and shred them, using 2 forks. Make the sauce by incorporating 100 ml (4 fl oz, 7 tablespoons) olive oil into the anchovy paste, whisking all the time. Still whisking, add the chopped parsley and a few drops of vinegar.

Andalusian sauce

Add 5 teaspoons very reduced and rich tomato fondue to 75 g (3 oz, ⅓ cup) mayonnaise. Finally, add 75 g (3 oz, ½ cup) sweet (bell) peppers, seeded and very finely diced.

Bâtarde sauce

Mix 20 g (¾ oz, 1½ tablespoons) melted butter, 20 g (¾ oz, 3 tablespoons) plain (all-purpose) flour and 250 ml (8 fl oz, 1 cup) salted boiling water. Whisk the mixture vigorously, adding 1 egg yolk mixed with 1 tablespoon ice-cold water and 1 tablespoon lemon juice. Over a very low heat, gradually incorporate 100 g (4 oz, ½ cup) butter cut into small pieces, stirring constantly. Season with salt and pepper, and strain if necessary. This sauce is served with boiled vegetables and fish.

Béarnaise sauce

Put 1 tablespoon chopped shallots, 2 tablespoons each of chopped chervil and tarragon, a sprig of thyme, a piece of bay leaf, 2½ tablespoons vinegar, and a little salt and pepper in a pan. Reduce by two-thirds, then allow to cool slightly. Mix 2 egg yolks with 1 tablespoon water, add to the pan and whisk over a very low heat. As soon as the egg yolks have thickened, add 125 g (4½ oz, ½ cup) butter in small pieces, a little at a time, whisking continuously. Adjust the seasoning, adding a dash of cayenne pepper if desired, and a little lemon juice. Add 1 tablespoon each of chopped chervil and tarragon and mix. The sauce can be kept in a warm bain marie until required, but it must not be reheated once it has cooled.

Béchamel sauce

Gently heat 500 ml (17 fl oz, 2 cups) milk with 1 bay leaf, a thick slice of onion and 1 blade of mace. Remove from the heat just as it boils, cover and set aside for at least 30 minutes. Strain the milk and discard the flavourings.

Melt 40 g (1½ oz, 3 tablespoons) butter over a low heat in a heavy based saucepan. Add 40 g (1½ oz, 6 tablespoons) flour and stir briskly until the mixture is smoothly blended, without allowing it to change colour. Gradually stir in the milk and bring to the boil, beating well to prevent any lumps from forming. Season with salt and pepper and (according to the use for which the sauce is destined) a little grated nutmeg. Simmer the sauce gently for 3–5 minutes, stirring from time to time.

Bercy sauce or shallot sauce for fish

Peel some shallots and chop them very finely. Add to a good wine vinegar and season with salt and pepper. This sauce is traditionally served with oysters or raw mussels.

Beurre blanc

Put 5–6 chopped shallots in a saucepan with 250 ml (8 fl oz, 1 cup) wine vinegar, 325 ml (11 fl oz, 1⅓ cups) fish stock and ground pepper; reduce by two-thirds. Cut 225 g (8 oz, 1 cup) very cold butter (preferably slightly salted) into small pieces. Remove the pan from the heat and add all but one piece of the butter all at once, beating briskly with a whisk until smooth. Finally, add the last piece of butter and mix it in gently, stirring and turning the pan so that the sauce is not frothy. Season with salt and pepper. Pour the sauce into a warmed sauceboat and place in a lukewarm bain marie until required.

Beurre blanc nantais

Follow the instructions for beurre blanc, adding 1 tablespoon double (heavy) cream at the same time as the butter.

Blond roux

Make a white roux, but cook it gently for 10 minutes, stirring constantly, until it becomes a golden colour.

Bordelaise sauce

(From a recipe by Carême) Place in a saucepan 2 garlic cloves, a pinch of tarragon, the seeded flesh of 1 lemon, 1 small bay leaf, 2 cloves, 1 glass of Sauternes and 2 teaspoons Provençal olive oil. Simmer gently. Skim off all the fat from the mixture and mix in enough espagnole sauce to provide sauce for an entrée and 3–4 tablespoons light veal stock. Reduce the mixture and add ½ a glass of Sauternes while still simmering. Strain the sauce when it is the right consistency. Just before serving add a little butter and the juice of ½ a lemon.

Bourguignonne sauce for fish

Prepare a fish stock using 1 litre (1¾ pints, 4⅓ cups) red wine, the bones and trimmings of the fish to be used in the dish, a medium chopped onion, a small bouquet garni, a handful of mushroom peelings, salt and pepper. Strain, reduce by half and thicken with some beurre manié according to taste.

Brandade sauce à la provençale

This sauce is not made with salt cod, but it is served with poached salt cod. Put 2 tablespoons thin allemande sauce, 3 egg yolks, a pinch of grated nutmeg, a pinch of fine pepper, a pinch of crushed garlic, the juice of 1 large lemon and a pinch of salt into a saucepan. Stir continuously over a low heat until the sauce is smooth and velvety. Remove from the heat and add (a tablespoon at a time) about 250 ml (8 fl oz, 1 cup) good Aix olive oil. Just before serving, add the juice of 1 lemon and 1 tablespoon chopped blanched chervil.

Brown chaud-froid sauce for fish

Mix 500 ml (17 fl oz, 2 cups) demi-glace and 500 ml (17 fl oz, 2 cups) greatly reduced and clarified fish or game fumet (it must have the consistency of wobbly jelly). Gradually pour the hot mixture over 16 egg yolks and add 200 g (7 oz, ¾ cup) butter, whisking all the time.

Brown roux

Make a white roux, but cook it very gently for 15–20 minutes, stirring constantly, until it becomes a light brown colour.

Butter sauce

Proceed as for bâtarde sauce, but use 25 g (1 oz, 2 tablespoons) butter and 25 g (1 oz, ¼ cup) plain (all-purpose) flour mixed to a roux. Do not thicken with egg yolk. This sauce is served with fish and boiled vegetables.

Cambridge sauce

Thoroughly desalt 6 anchovies, then remove the bones. Blend together 3 hard-boiled (hard-cooked) egg yolks, the anchovy flesh, 1 teaspoon capers and a small bunch of tarragon and chervil. Add 1 teaspoon English mustard to the mixture and season with pepper. Thicken with groundnut (peanut) oil or sunflower oil, as for mayonnaise, then add 1 tablespoon vinegar. Adjust the seasoning. Add chopped chives and parsley.

Caper sauce

To accompany boiled fish, add 2 tablespoons pickled capers, well drained, to 250 ml (8 fl oz, 1 cup) hollandaise sauce or butter sauce.

Cardinal sauce

Heat 200 ml (7 fl oz, ¾ cup) cream sauce and 100 ml (4 fl oz, 7 tablespoons) fish stock and reduce by half. Add 100 ml (4 fl oz, 7 tablespoons) cream and bring to the boil. Remove from the heat and add 50 g (2 oz, 4 tablespoons) lobster butter. Season with a little cayenne and strain through a conical strainer. Garnish with a spoonful of chopped truffles, unless the recipe already contains them.

Chambertin sauce

Peel and dice 2 carrots and 2 onions. Soften them with 20 g (¾ oz, 1½ table-spoons) butter in a shallow frying pan. Add a bouquet garni, 100 g (4 oz,

1¼ cups) chopped mushrooms (including stalks and peelings), ½ a chopped garlic clove, 250 g (9 oz) trimmings from white fish, salt and pepper. Moisten with 500 ml (17 fl oz, 2 cups) Chambertin and cook for at least 20 minutes in a covered pan. Remove the lid and reduce by a third. Pass through a conical strainer and bind with 1 tablespoon beurre manié.

Chambord sauce

This is a classic sauce for large fish, such as carp, salmon or sole, that are to be cooked whole. Prepare a genevoise sauce using the braising stock of the fish that is being cooked and dilute it with red wine to the full quantity. This sauce is used to coat the fish.

Chantilly sauce

Dilute 200 ml (7 fl oz, ¾ cup) very thick suprême sauce with 100 ml (4 fl oz, 7 tablespoons) whipped cream.

Choron sauce

Dilute 200 ml (7 fl oz, ¾ cup) béarnaise sauce with 2 tablespoons tepid tomato purée which has been well reduced and sieved. It is essential to use a very concentrated purée.

Crayfish sauce

(from Carême's recipe) Wash 50 medium-sized crayfish. Cook them with ½ a bottle of champagne, a sliced onion, a bouquet garni, a pinch of coarsely ground pepper and a little salt. When the crayfish have cooled, drain them and strain the cooking liquor through a silk strainer. Boil down by half, then add 2 tablespoons white sauce. Reduce again to the desired consistency and add ½ a glass of champagne. After reducing again, strain the sauce through a sieve. Just before serving, add a little glaze and best butter, then the shelled crayfish tails. Add to the sauce crayfish butter made with the pounded crayfish shells.

Cream sauce

Add 100 ml (4 fl oz, 7 tablespoons) double (heavy) cream to 200 ml (7 fl oz, ¾ cup) béchamel sauce and boil to reduce by one-third. Remove from the heat and add 25–50 g (1–2 oz, 2–4 tablespoons) butter and 60–100 ml (2–4 fl oz, ¼–scant ½ cup) double cream. Stir well and strain. This sauce is served with vegetables, fish, eggs and poultry.

Curry or Indian sauce

Cook 4 large sliced onions slowly in 5 tablespoons ghee, butter or oil. Add 1 tablespoon each of chopped parsley and chopped celery, a small sprig of thyme, ½ a bay leaf, a pinch of mace, salt and pepper. Sprinkle with 25 g (1 oz, ¼ cup) flour and 1 generous tablespoon good-quality curry powder and stir. Then add 500 ml (17 fl oz, 2 cups) chicken, fish or vegetable stock, stir and bring to the boil, stirring. Reduce the heat, cover the pan and cook slowly for about 30 minutes. A quarter of the chicken stock can be replaced by coconut milk for a coconut-flavoured curry. Rub the sauce through a sieve, add 1 teaspoon lemon juice and 5 tablespoons cream, and reduce a little. Adjust the seasoning to taste.

Demi-glace sauce

Boil down to reduce by two-thirds a mixture of 500 ml (17 fl oz, 2 cups) espagnole sauce and 750 ml (1¼ pints, 3¼ cups) clear brown stock. Remove from the heat, add 3 tablespoons Madeira and strain. A handful of sliced mushroom stalks may be added during cooking.

Devilled sauce

Mix 150 ml (¼ pint, ⅔ cup) dry white wine with 1 tablespoon vinegar, then add 1 tablespoon finely chopped shallots, a sprig of thyme, a small piece of bay leaf and a generous pinch of pepper. Reduce the sauce by two-thirds, then add 200 ml (7 fl oz, ¾ cup) demi-glace and boil for 2–3 minutes. Strain through a sieve. Just before serving, add 1 teaspoon chopped parsley and check the seasoning, adding a little cayenne pepper if liked. Alternatively, omit straining the sauce and add 1 tablespoon butter or beurre manié.

Diplomat sauce

Add 2 tablespoons truffle parings or chopped mushroom stalks to 200 ml (7 fl oz, ¾ cup) fish fumet and reduce by half. Make 75 g (3 oz) white roux and add 750 ml (1¼ pints, 3¼ cups) fish stock (use the cooking liquid of the fish specified in the recipe). Strain the reduced fumet and add it, together with 200 ml (7 fl oz, ¾ cup) double (heavy) cream, to the sauce. Reduce again by half. Add 50 g (2 oz, ¼ cup) lobster butter, 4 tablespoons double cream, 1 tablespoon brandy and a pinch of cayenne pepper. Strain. If the sauce is served separately, add to it 1 tablespoon diced lobster flesh (cooked in a court-bouillon) and 1 tablespoon diced truffles.

Duxelles sauce

Make 4 tablespoons mushroom duxelles. Add 100 ml (4 fl oz, 7 tablespoons) white wine and reduce until nearly dry. Add 150 ml (¼ pint, ⅔ cup) demi-glace sauce and 100 ml (4 fl oz, 7 tablespoons) sieved tomato sauce. Boil for 2–3 minutes, pour into a sauceboat and sprinkle with chopped parsley.

Alternatively, the duxelles may be moistened with 150 ml (¼ pint, ⅔ cup) consommé and 100 ml (4 fl oz, 7 tablespoons) sieved tomato sauce and thickened with 1 tablespoon beurre manié.

Espagnole sauce (1)

(From Carême's recipe) Put 2 slices of Bayonne ham into a deep saucepan. Place a noix of veal and 2 partridges on top. Add enough stock to cover the veal only. Reduce the liquid rapidly, then lower the heat until the stock is reduced to a coating on the bottom of the pan. Remove it from the heat. Prick the noix of veal with the point of a knife so that its juice mingles with the stock. Put the saucepan back over a low heat for about 20 minutes. Watch the liquid as it gradually turns darker.

To simplify this operation, scrape off a little of the essence with the point of a knife. Roll it between the fingers. If it rolls into a ball, the essence is perfectly reduced. If it is not ready, it will make the fingers stick together.

Remove the saucepan from the heat and set it aside for 15 minutes for the essence to cool. (It will then dissolve more readily.) Fill the saucepan with clear soup or stock and heat very slowly.

Meanwhile prepare a roux: melt 100 g (4 oz, ½ cup) butter and add to it enough flour to give a rather liquid consistency. Put it over a low heat, stirring from time to time so that gradually the whole mixture turns a golden colour. As soon as the stock comes to the boil, skim it, and pour 2 ladles into a roux. When adding the first ladleful of stock, remove the roux from the heat, then replace it and stir in the second ladleful until the mixture is perfectly smooth. Now pour the thickened sauce into the saucepan with the veal noix. Add some parsley and spring onions (scallions), ½ bay leaf, a little thyme, 2 chives and some mushroom trimmings. Leave to simmer, stirring frequently. After 1 hour skim off as much of the fat as possible, then 30 minutes later, skim off the fat again.

Strain through a cloth into a bowl, stirring from time to time with a wooden spoon so that no skin forms on the surface, as easily happens when the sauce is exposed to the air.

Espagnole sauce (2)

Make a brown roux with 25 g (1 oz, 2 tablespoons) butter and 25 g (1 oz, ¼ cup) plain (all-purpose) flour. Add 1 tablespoon mirepoix, 50 g (2 oz, ⅔ cup) chopped mushrooms and 1 kg (2¼ lb) crushed tomatoes. Stir in 2.25 litres (4 pints, 10 cups) brown stock and simmer gently for 3–4 hours, skimming the sauce occasionally. Pass through a very fine sieve, or preferably strain through muslin (cheesecloth), when cold.

Financière sauce (1)

(from Carême's recipe) Put some shredded lean ham, a pinch of mignonette (coarsely ground white pepper), a little thyme and bay leaf, some shredded mushrooms and truffles, and 2 glasses of dry Madeira into a saucepan. Simmer and reduce over a gentle heat. Add 2 tablespoons chicken consommé and 2 tablespoons well-beaten espagnole sauce. Reduce by half, press through a fine sieve, strain, then heat again, stirring in 3 tablespoons Madeira. Reduce to the desired consistency and serve in a sauceboat.

When this sauce is intended for a game entrée, the chicken consommé is replaced by game fumet. Add a little butter just before serving.

Financière sauce (2)

(modern recipe) Make 200 ml (7 fl oz, ¾ cup) Madeira sauce, adding 100 ml (4 fl oz, 7 tablespoons) truffle essence while it is reducing. This sauce is usually used to bind the financière garnish.

Fines herbes sauce

Make 250 ml (8 fl oz, 1 cup) demi-glace sauce or brown stock and add 2 tablespoons chopped parsley, chervil and tarragon. Reduce, press through a very fine sieve, add a few drops of lemon juice and adjust the seasoning.

Genevoise sauce

Crush 500 g (18 oz) salmon trimmings. Peel and dice a large carrot and a large
onion. Cut 10 parsley sprigs into small pieces. Sauté the vegetables and
parsley in 15 g (¼ oz, 1 tablespoon) butter for 5 minutes over a low heat. Add
a sprig of thyme, ½ bay leaf, pepper and the fish trimmings. Cook very slowly
in a covered saucepan for 15 minutes. Add a bottle of red wine (Chambertin
or Côtes-du-Rhône) and a little salt to the pan juice. Boil down slowly for
30–40 minutes. Strain the sauce, then thicken it with 1 tablespoon beurre
manié (1 tablespoon anchovy butter may also be stirred in). Adjust the
seasoning to taste.

Gooseberry sauce

Cook 500 g (18 oz) gooseberries in a saucepan with 500 ml (17 fl oz, 2 cups)
water and 6 tablespoons sugar. When the pulp becomes very soft, strain and
serve piping hot. If the gooseberries are very ripe and sweet, add a few drops
of lemon juice.

Gribiche sauce

Thoroughly pound or mash the yolk of a hard-boiled (hard-cooked) egg and
gradually add 250 ml (8 fl oz, 1 cup) oil, beating constantly and keeping the
mixture smooth as for a mayonnaise. As it thickens, add 2 tablespoons
vinegar, salt, pepper, 1 tablespoon each of capers, chopped parsley, chervil
and tarragon, and the white of the hard-boiled egg cut into julienne.

Green sauce

For 400 ml (14 fl oz, 1¾ cups) sauce, prepare 300 ml (½ pint, 1¼ cups)
mayonnaise and 100 ml (4 fl oz, 7 tablespoons) purée of green herbs
(spinach, watercress, parsley, chervil and tarragon), blanched for 1 minute in

boiling water, cooled under the tap, thoroughly dried and then pounded in a mortar. Mix the 2 preparations together and rub through a sieve.

Use the sauce as for a mayonnaise, especially to accompany cold poached fish, such as salmon.

Hollandaise sauce

Pour 4 tablespoons water into a pan with a pinch of salt and a pinch of ground pepper. Place the base of the saucepan in a bain marie of hot water; do not allow the water to approach boiling point, but keep it hot. In another saucepan, melt 500 g (18 oz, 2¼ cups) butter without letting it get too hot. Beat 5 egg yolks with 1 tablespoon water and pour into the pan containing the warmed water. With the pan still in the bain marie, whisk the sauce until the yolks thicken to the consistency of thick cream; add the melted butter slowly, whisking all the time, and then add 2 tablespoons water, drop by drop. Adjust the seasoning and add 1 tablespoon lemon juice. The sauce can be strained.

Hungarian sauce

Peel and chop some onions and fry them in butter, without browning them. Season with salt and pepper and sprinkle with paprika. For 6 tablespoons cooked onion add 250 ml (8 fl oz, 1 cup) white wine and a small bouquet garni. Reduce the liquid by two-thirds. Pour in 500 ml (17 fl oz, 2 cups) velouté sauce (with or without butter enrichment). Boil rapidly for 5 minutes, strain through a strainer lined with muslin (cheesecloth) and finish with 50 g (2 oz, ¼ cup) butter.

Italian sauce

Clean and chop 250 g (9 oz, 2 generous cups) button mushrooms, 1 onion and 1 shallot. Heat 5 tablespoons olive oil in a saucepan, add the chopped vegetables and cook over a high heat until the juices from the mushrooms are completely evaporated. Add 150 ml (¼ pint, ⅔ cup) stock, 6 tablespoons tomato purée (paste), salt, pepper and a bouquet garni and cook gently for 30 minutes. Just before serving, add 1 tablespoon diced lean ham and 1 tablespoon chopped parsley.

Lobster sauce

Prepare 300 ml (½ pint, 1¼ cups) fish fumet made with white wine. Reduce the fumet by two-thirds, let it cool and add 4 egg yolks; whisk over a low heat until thick and light. Melt 250 g (9 oz, 1 cup) butter and blend it into the sauce, whisking constantly. Add 2 tablespoons lobster butter. Still whisking, season with salt and pepper and add the juice of ½ a lemon. At the last moment, a little diced lobster meat can be added.

Mornay sauce

Heat 500 ml (17 fl oz, 2 cups) béchamel sauce. Add 75 g (3 oz, ¾ cup) grated Gruyère cheese and stir until all the cheese has melted. Take the sauce from the heat and add 2 egg yolks beaten with 1 tablespoon milk. Bring slowly to the boil, whisking all the time. Remove from the heat and add 2 tablespoons double (heavy) cream (the sauce must be thick and creamy). For browning at a high temperature or for a lighter sauce, the egg yolks are omitted. If the sauce is to accompany fish, reduced fish stock is added.

Mushroom stock

Bring 6 tablespoons water with 40 g (1½ oz, 3 tablespoons) butter, the juice of ½ a lemon and 1 scant tablespoon salt to the boil. Add 300 g (11 oz, 3½ cups) mushrooms and boil for 6 minutes. Drain and retain the cooking stock to flavour a white sauce, fish stock or marinade.

Mushroom purée

Prepare 200 ml (7 fl oz, ¾ cup) béchamel sauce. Add 6 tablespoons double (heavy) cream and stir over a brisk heat until reduced by a third. Clean and chop 500 g (18 oz, 6 cups) mushrooms. Press through a sieve or blend in a food processor. Place the purée in a shallow frying pan and stir over a brisk heat until the vegetable juice has evaporated. Add the béchamel, a pinch of salt, a little white pepper and a dash of grated nutmeg. Stir over the heat for a few minutes. Remove from the heat and blend with 50 g (2 oz, ¼ cup) butter.

Mussel sauce

Prepare 500 g (18 oz) small *moules marinière* with 300 ml (½ pint, 1¼ cups) white wine; remove from their shells and keep hot. Strain the cooking liquid and reduce to 2 tablespoons. Cool until lukewarm, then beat in 2–3 egg yolks, then 100 g (4 oz, ½ cup) butter and a few drops of lemon juice. Add the mussels and adjust the seasoning.

Mustard sauce with butter

Prepare 200 ml (7 fl oz, ¾ cup) hollandaise or butter sauce. Add 1 tablespoon mustard and strain. This sauce is served with boiled or grilled (broiled) fish.

Mustard sauce with cream

Mix 1 part Dijon mustard with 2 parts double (heavy) cream. Season with a little lemon juice and some salt and pepper. Whisk thoroughly until the sauce becomes slightly mousse-like.

Nantua sauce

Make 200 ml (7 fl oz, ¾ cup) béchamel. Add an equal volume of strained crayfish cooking liquor and single (light) cream. Boil to reduce by one-third.

While boiling, beat in 100 g (4 oz, ½ cup) crayfish butter, 1 teaspoon brandy and a tiny pinch of cayenne pepper. Rub through a very fine sieve.

Noisette butter

Gently heat some butter in a frying pan until it is golden and gives off a nutty smell. Serve scalding hot with lambs' or calves' sweetbreads, fish roe, vegetables (boiled and well drained), eggs or skate poached in stock. Noisette butter is known as meunière butter when lemon juice is added.

Normande sauce

In a heavy-based saucepan heat 200 ml (7 fl oz, ¾ cup) fish velouté sauce and 6 tablespoons each of fish fumet and mushroom essence, and reduce by one-third. Mix 2 egg yolks with 2 tablespoons double (heavy) cream, add to the pan and cook gently until thickened. Do not boil. Just before serving, add 50 g (2 oz, ¼ cup) butter cut into small pieces and 3 tablespoons double cream. If necessary, pass the sauce through a very fine strainer.

An alternative method is as follows: mix 2 tablespoons mushroom peelings with 200 ml (7 fl oz, ¾ cup) fish velouté; add 6 tablespoons double cream and boil down by half. Then add 50 g (2 oz, ¼ cup) butter cut into pieces and 4 tablespoons double cream. Strain through a very fine sieve.

Oyster sauce

Open and poach 12 oysters. Prepare a white roux with 20 g (¾ oz, 1½ table-spoons) butter and 20 g (¾ oz, 3 tablespoons) flour, then moisten with 6 tablespoons oyster cooking liquid, 6 tablespoons milk and 6 tablespoons single (light) cream. Adjust the seasoning. Bring to the boil and cook for 10 minutes. Pass through a sieve. Add the debearded and sliced oysters and a pinch of cayenne.

Portuguese sauce

Cook 2 finely chopped onions in 1 tablespoon olive oil until soft. Peel, seed and crush 4 tomatoes and add to the onions with 2 crushed garlic cloves. Bring to the boil, cover and cook slowly for 30–35 minutes, stirring from time to time, until the tomatoes reduce to a pulp. Moisten with 150 ml (¼ pint, ⅔ cup) stock and season with ground pepper. Leave to cook for 10 minutes. Bind with 2 teaspoons beurre manié and sprinkle with chopped parsley.

Poulette sauce

Whisk 2 or 3 egg yolks with 400 ml (14 fl oz, 1¾ cups) fish fumet. Heat for about 10 minutes, whisking, adding lemon juice (from ½–1 lemon) and 50 g (2 oz, ¼ cup) butter. Remove from the heat when the sauce coats the spoon. Keep the sauce warm in a bain marie, stirring from time to time.

Prawn sauce

Add ½ teaspoon anchovy essence (extract) to 250 ml (8 fl oz, 1 cup) English butter sauce. Mix 40 g (1½ oz, ¼ cup) peeled (shelled) cooked prawns (shrimp) with the sauce and season with a pinch of cayenne pepper.

Prawn sauce (for fish)

Blend 200 ml (7 fl oz, ¾ cup) normande sauce with 2 tablespoons prawn butter. Season with a pinch of cayenne pepper and press through a sieve or mix in a blender. If the sauce is to be served separately, add to it 1 tablespoon peeled (shelled) cooked prawns (shrimp) just before serving.

Provençal sauce

Heat 2 tablespoons olive oil in a heavy-based saucepan. Soften in it without browning 3 tablespoons peeled and chopped onions, then add 800 g (1½ lb,

3 cups) peeled, seeded and crushed tomatoes and cook gently for about 15 minutes. Add a crushed garlic clove, a bouquet garni, 200 ml (7 fl oz, ¾ cup) dry white wine and 200 ml (7 fl oz, ¾ cup) meat stock. Leave to cook, covered, for 15 minutes, then adjust the seasoning, remove the lid and reduce the sauce by half. Add some fresh chopped parsley or basil just before serving.

Ravigote sauce

Prepare 120 ml (4½ fl oz, ½ cup) plain vinaigrette with mustard. Add ½ teaspoon chopped tarragon, 1 teaspoon chopped parsley, 1 teaspoon fines herbes, 2 teaspoons chervil, 1 finely chopped small onion and 1 tablespoon dried and chopped capers.

Rémoulade sauce

Make some mayonnaise with 250 ml (8 fl oz, 1 cup) oil, replacing, if desired, the raw egg yolk with 1 hard-boiled (hard-cooked) egg yolk rubbed through a fine sieve. Add 2 very finely diced gherkins, 2 tablespoons chopped herbs (parsley, chives, chervil and tarragon), 1 tablespoon drained capers and a few drops of anchovy essence (extract) (optional).

Rouille

Rouille is a Provençal sauce whose name (meaning rust) describes its colour, due to the presence of red chillies and sometimes saffron. The chillies are pounded with garlic and breadcrumbs (or potato pulp), then blended with olive oil and stock. Rouille is served with bouillabaisse, boiled fish and octopus. Lemon juice and fish liver may be added. Pound 2 small red chillies and 1 garlic clove in a mortar (soak dried chillies first for a few hours in cold water). Add 1 teaspoon olive oil if liked (this is not essential and may change the taste). Pound 2 scorpion-fish livers (optional) and 1 small potato, cooked either in the bouillabaisse or in a little fish fumet, and add the chillies. When the mixture is smooth, gradually blend it with some strained broth from the bouillabaisse (use enough to make it up to 7 times the original volume).

Russian sauce

Mix equal quantities of caviar and the finely sieved creamy parts (liver) of lobster. Add the caviar mixture to some mayonnaise: use 1 part mixture to 4 parts mayonnaise. This sauce may be seasoned with a little mild mustard.

Sauce à l'anglaise

(from Carême's recipe) Chop 4 hard-boiled (hard-cooked) egg yolks very finely and mix them in a saucepan with some fairly thick velouté of the kind used as a sauce for an entrée. Then add a dash of pepper, some grated nutmeg, the juice of 1 lemon and a little anchovy butter.

Sauce à la grecque for fish

Heat a finely sliced ¼ celery heart and 3 finely sliced onions in 3 tablespoons olive oil. Add a bouquet garni (including fennel), 6 tablespoons white wine and 12 coriander seeds. Boil down by two-thirds. Add 6 tablespoons thin velouté sauce and the same quantity of single (light) cream. Boil down by one-third. Blend in 50 g (2 oz, ¼ cup) butter and strain before serving.

The velouté sauce may be replaced by an equal volume of strained fish fumet and 1 tablespoon beurre manié, added in small knobs to the boiling liquid, which is whisked for 1–2 minutes.

Sauce à la russe

(from Carême's recipe) Chop and blanch 1 tablespoon parsley, chervil and tarragon, drain it, and mix with a fairly thick velouté sauce. Just before serving, add 1 tablespoon fine mustard, 1½ teaspoons caster (superfine) sugar, a pinch of finely ground pepper and some lemon juice.

Shrimp purée

Pound in a mortar some shelled shrimp. Add an equal volume of béchamel sauce mixed with cream and reduced. Adjust the seasoning. This purée is added to stuffings and sauces for fish and shellfish.

Sorrel fondue

Peel and finely chop 1 small onion. Cook in 50 g (2 oz, 4 tablespoons) butter until soft, without browning. Add 675 g (1½ lb) trimmed, shredded sorrel and mix well. Cover and cook gently for 5 minutes. Add salt and pepper, stir well and cover. Cook for a further 5 minutes or until the sorrel is reduced to a pulp. Press through a sieve or purée in a blender. The fondue may be flavoured with garlic, lemon juice and a bouquet garni, if required.

Suprême sauce

Prepare a velouté with a white roux, comprising 40 g (1½ oz, 3 tablespoons) butter and 40 g (1½ oz, 6 tablespoons) plain (all-purpose) flour and 750 ml (1¼ pints, 3¼ cups) well-seasoned and well-reduced chicken consommé. Add 500 ml (17 fl oz, 2 cups) white chicken stock and reduce it by at least half. Add 300 ml (½ pint, 1¼ cups) crème fraîche and reduce to about 600 ml (1 pint, 2½ cups), when it should coat the spoon. Remove from the heat and stir in 50 g (2 oz, ¼ cup) butter. Strain through a very fine sieve and keep warm.

Tartare sauce

Make some mayonnaise, replacing the raw egg yolk with hard-boiled (hard-cooked) egg yolk. Add finely chopped chives and chopped spring onion (scallions). Alternatively, a mixture of raw egg yolk and hard-boiled egg yolk can be used and chopped mixed herbs can replace the chives and onion.

Tomato fondue

Peel and chop 100 g (4 oz, ¾ cup) onions. Peel, seed and finely chop 800 g (1¾ lb) tomatoes. Peel and crush 1 garlic clove. Prepare a bouquet garni rich in thyme. Soften the onions in a heavy-based saucepan with 25 g (1 oz, 2 tablespoons) butter, or 15 g (½ oz, 1 tablespoon) butter and 2 tablespoons olive oil, or 3 tablespoons olive oil. Then add the tomatoes, salt and pepper, the garlic and bouquet garni. Cover the pan and cook very gently until the tomatoes are reduced to a pulp. Remove the lid, stir and continue cooking, uncovered, until the fondue forms a light paste. Adjust the seasoning, strain through a sieve and add 1 tablespoon chopped parsley or herbs.

Tomato sauce

Cut 100 g (4 oz, 6 slices) streaky (slab) bacon into small dice. Blanch, drain and lightly cook in 3–4 tablespoons oil. Add 100 g (4 oz, ¾ cup) each of diced carrots and diced onion. Cover and lightly fry for 25–30 minutes. Sprinkle in 50 g (2 oz, ½ cup) sifted plain (all-purpose) flour and lightly brown. Add 3 kg (6½ lb) fresh tomatoes, peeled, seeded and pounded, 2 crushed garlic cloves, a bouquet garni and 150 g (5 oz) blanched lean ham. Add 1 litre (1¾ pints, 4⅓ cups) white stock. Season , add 1½ tablespoons sugar and bring to the boil while stirring. Cover and leave to cook very gently for 2 hours. Strain into a basin. Pour tepid melted butter on the surface to prevent a skin from forming.

Velouté sauce

Stir 2.75 litres (4¾ pints, 12 cups) white veal, fish or chicken stock into a pale blond roux made with 150 g (5 oz, ⅔ cup) butter and 150 g (5 oz, 1¼ cups) plain (all-purpose) flour. Blend well together. Bring to the boil, stirring until the first bubbles appear. Cook the velouté very slowly for 30 minutes, skimming frequently. Strain through a cloth. Stir until it is completely cold.

Velouté may be prepared either in advance or just before it is required. As the white stock used for making it is seasoned and flavoured, it is not necessary to add other flavourings. An exception is made for skins and trimmings of mushrooms, which may be added when available, this addition making the sauce more delicate.

Vénitienne sauce

(from Carême's recipe) Boil together in a saucepan 2 tablespoons allemande sauce, a generous pinch of chopped tarragon blanched and drained in a fine silk strainer, 1 tablespoon chicken glaze, a little Isigny butter, a pinch of grated nutmeg and a few drops of good tarragon vinegar.

Véron sauce

Prepare a reduced herb mixture as for a béarnaise sauce. Then add 200 ml (7 fl oz, ¾ cup) normande sauce and 2 tablespoons very concentrated brown veal stock or fish glaze. Season with a pinch of cayenne, rub through a sieve and add 1 tablespoon snipped chervil or tarragon.

Villageoise sauce

Slice 400 g (14 oz, 2½ cups) onions and cook gently for 20 minutes with a piece of butter – about 50 g (2 oz, ¼ cup). Add 300 ml (½ pint, 1¼ cups) very thick béchamel sauce, then 200 ml (7 fl oz, ¾ cup) veal or poultry stock and a little mushroom essence. Continue to cook over a low heat, stirring constantly. Strain the sauce and thicken it with an egg yolk. Away from the heat, beat in 40 g (1½ oz, 3 tablespoons) butter cut in small pieces.

Victoria sauce for fish

Prepare 250 ml (8 fl oz, 1 cup) white wine sauce. Add 2 tablespoons lobster butter, a dash of cayenne, and 2 tablespoons diced lobster flesh and truffles.

Villeroi sauce

Prepare 200 ml (7 fl oz, ¾ cup) allemande sauce, dilute with 4 tablespoons white stock flavoured with little mushroom essence, then reduce until it coats the spoon. Put through a strainer and stir until the sauce is barely tepid.

Vincent sauce

Make a mayonnaise with 1 egg yolk, 1 teaspoon white mustard, 1 tablespoon white wine vinegar, 250 ml (8 fl oz, 1 cup) oil, salt and pepper. Blanch chives, chervil, watercress, sorrel and parsley for 1 minute in boiling water (a little mint, sage or burnet may also be added). Rub the mixed herbs through a sieve and add 1 generous tablespoon of the resulting purée to the mayonnaise. Mix in 1 finely chopped hard-boiled (hard-cooked) egg and adjust the seasoning.

Waterfisch sauce (cold)

Prepare a vegetable julienne as for hot waterfisch sauce; moisten with 200 ml (7 fl oz, ¾ cup) of the court-bouillon used to cook the fish that the sauce is to accompany and simmer until evaporated. Dissolve 2 leaves or 7 g (¼ oz, 1 envelope) gelatine in 200 ml (7 fl oz, ¾ cup) fish court-bouillon, add the vegetable julienne while hot, then allow to cool. Mix with 1 tablespoon each of chopped gherkins, chopped sweet red (bell) pepper and capers.

Waterfisch sauce (hot)

Cut into very fine strips 50 g (2 oz) carrots, 25 g (1 oz) white part of leeks, 25 g (1 oz) celery, 25 g (1 oz) Hamburg parsley roots and 2 teaspoons grated orange zest. Place the julienne in a saucepan, moisten with 200 ml (7 fl oz, ¾ cup) dry white wine and boil until all the liquid has evaporated. Add 200 ml (7 fl oz, ¾ cup) fish court-bouillon made with white wine and reduce completely once again. Prepare 500 ml (17 fl oz, 2 cups) hollandaise sauce and mix the vegetables into it, together with 1 tablespoon blanched, chopped, parsley sprigs. Keep hot in a bain marie until ready to serve.

White roux

Melt the butter in a heavy-based saucepan, then clarify it. Add the same weight (or a little more) of sifted plain (all-purpose) flour – up to 125 g (4½ oz, 1 cup) flour for 100 g (4 oz, ½ cup) butter. To make 1 litre (1¾ pints, 4⅓ cups) béchamel sauce, the roux should contain 75 g (3 oz, ¾ cup) flour and the same weight of butter; to make 1 litre (1¾ pints, 4⅓ cups) velouté sauce, use 50–65 g (2–2½ oz, ½–⅔ cup) flour and the same weight of butter.

Mix the butter and flour, stirring constantly with a wooden spoon and covering the whole bottom of the saucepan, so that the roux does not colour unevenly and become lumpy. Continue to cook in this way for 5 minutes, until the mixture begins to froth a little. Take the pan off the heat and leave it to cool until time to add the liquid (milk, white stock, fish stock). To prevent lumps from forming this must be poured boiling on to the cold roux. Use a whisk to mix the roux and heat gradually while whisking constantly. (Alternatively, the cold liquid may be whisked gradually into the warm roux.)

White sauce

Make 100 g (4 oz, ½ cup) pale blond roux using 50 g (2 oz, ¼ cup) butter and 50 g (2 oz, ½ cup) plain (all-purpose) flour. Blend in 1 litre (1¾ pints, 4⅓ cups) white stock (fish, chicken or veal). Bring to the boil and cook gently for 1½ hours, skimming from time to time.

White wine sauce

Boil 150 ml (¼ pint, ⅔ cup) fish fumet made with white wine, until reduced by two-thirds. Allow to cool slightly and add 2 raw egg yolks. Whisk over a gentle heat, as for hollandaise sauce. As soon as the yolks thicken to a creamy consistency, whisk in, a little at a time, 150 g (5 oz, ⅔ cup) clarified butter. Season; add ½ teaspoon lemon juice and some mushroom skins and stalks if wished. Rub through a fine sieve and reheat, but do not boil.

Stocks & consommés

Brown veal stock

Bone 1.25 kg (2¾ lb) each of shoulder and knuckle of veal. Tie them together with string and brush with melted dripping. Crush 500 g (18 oz) veal bones as finely as possible. Brown these ingredients in a large flameproof casserole or saucepan. Peel and slice 150 g (5 oz) carrots and 100 g (4 oz) onions, then add them to the pan. Cover and leave to sweat for 15 minutes. Add 250 ml (8 fl oz, 1 cup) water and reduce to a jelly-like consistency. Repeat the process. Add 3 litres (5 pints, 13 cups) water or white stock and bring to the boil. Skim and season. Leave to simmer very gently for 6 hours. Skim off the fat and strain through a fine sieve or, better still, through muslin (cheesecloth).

Chicken consommé

Proceed as for simple beef consommé, but replace the lean beef by a small chicken and 3 or 4 giblets browned in the oven, and the shin of beef (beef shank) by 800 g (1¾ lb) veal knuckle. For clarification, proceed as for clear beef consommé, using 4 or 5 chopped chicken giblets instead of the chopped beef. The chicken may then be used for croquettes or patties.

Chicken stock

Chop 450 g (1 lb) chicken wings, 1 carrot, 1 leek, 1 celery stick and 1 onion. Simmer in 1.5 litres (2¾ pints, 6½ cups) water for 20 minutes, then strain.

Court-bouillon eau de sel

This is the easiest kind of court-bouillon to prepare as it consists only of salted boiling water – use 15 g (½ oz, 1 tablespoon) coarse sea salt per 1 litre (1¾ pints, 4⅓ cups) water. It is not usually flavoured, but a little thyme and a bay leaf may be added if desired.

Court-bouillon with milk

Add 1 finely shredded onion, a sprig of thyme, salt and pepper to equal quantities of milk and water (the court-bouillon should cover the food that is to be cooked). It is used principally for cooking flatfish, such as brill or turbot, or smoked or salted fish, such as smoked haddock or salt cod (in the latter case, do not add salt).

Court-bouillon with wine

For every 2.5 litres (4¼ pints, 11 cups) water, add 500 ml (17 fl oz, 2 cups) dry white wine, 50 g (2 oz, ⅓ cup) grated carrot, 50 g (2 oz, ⅓ cup) grated onion, a sprig of thyme, a piece of bay leaf, 25 g (1 oz, 2 tablespoons) coarse salt and possibly a small celery stick, chopped, and a sprig of parsley (although these have a strong flavour). Add 2 teaspoons peppercorns 10 minutes before the end of the cooking time.

The wine should be chosen for its fruity flavour. The amount of wine can be increased if the amount of water is reduced by the same quantity. Red wine may also be used, especially if the court-bouillon is to be used to make an aspic jelly, which will then have a pale pink colour. Court-bouillons with white wine are used for cooking shellfish and fish of all types. Court-bouillons with red wine are used for cooking lean white-fleshed fish such as bass, which are served cold.

Fish consommé

For 5 litres (8½ pints, 5½ quarts) consommé use 1.5 kg (3¼ lb) pike, 575 g (1¼ lb) white fish bones, 1 kg (2¼ lb) turbot heads, 300 g (11 oz) onions, 200 g (7 oz) leeks, 75 g (3 oz, 1 cup) parsley sprigs, 25 g (1 oz) celery, a sprig of thyme, a bay leaf, 2 tablespoons salt and 600 ml (1 pint, 2½ cups) dry white wine.

Proceed as for simple beef consommé, but chop the onions and leeks finely and boil slowly for 45 minutes only. Strain the stock through a sieve. To clarify the consommé, use 1.5 kg (3¼ lb) whiting or chopped pike, 150 g (5 oz) leeks, 50 g (2 oz, ¾ cup) parsley sprigs, and 4 egg whites. Proceed as for clear beef consommé, but cook very slowly and only for about 30 minutes; finally strain the consommé.

Fish fumet (or good stock)

Crush 2.5 kg (5½ lb) bones and trimmings of white fish (sole, lemon sole, whiting, brill, turbot). Peel and thinly slice 125 g (4½ oz, 1½ cups) onions and shallots; clean and thinly slice 150 g (5 oz, 1⅔ cups) mushrooms or mushroom stalks and trimmings; squeeze the juice from ½ a lemon; tie 25 g (1 oz) parsley sprigs into a bundle. Put all the ingredients in a saucepan and add a small sprig of thyme, a bay leaf, 1 tablespoon lemon juice and

1 tablespoon coarse sea salt. Moisten with 2.5 litres (4¼ pints, 11 cups) water and 500 ml (17 fl oz, 2 cups) dry white wine (or red for some recipes). Bring to the boil, then skim and boil very gently for 30 minutes. Strain through muslin (cheesecloth) and leave to cool.

Fish stock

Make fish stock as for fish fumet. For a less refined result, the wine may be replaced by the same quantity of water.

Lemon or vinegar court-bouillon

For every 3 litres (5 pints, 13 cups) water, allow 250 g (9 oz, 1¼ cups) sliced carrots, 150 g (5 oz) onions (quartered, and, if desired, studded with a clove), 1 sprig thyme, a bay leaf, 1–2 parsley sprigs, 25 g (1 oz, 2 tablespoons) coarse sea salt, either the juice of 2 lemons or 200 ml (7 fl oz, ¾ cup) vinegar, and finally 2 teaspoons peppercorns (added 10 minutes before the end of the cooking period).

This court-bouillon can be used when the natural colour of the fish is to be preserved, for example, when cooking salmon or salmon trout, and also when cooking shellfish, as it makes the shell turn bright red.

Light brown stock

Scald 150 g (5 oz) fresh pork rind and 125 g (4½ oz) knuckle of ham for 4–5 minutes. Bone 1.25 kg (2¾ lb) lean stewing beef (leg or blade) and cut into cubes, together with the same amount of knuckle of veal. Peel 150 g (5 oz) carrots and 150 g (5 oz) onions, cut into slices, then brown on the hob (stove top) in a large flameproof casserole with all the meat, 500 g (18 oz) crushed veal or beef bones and the pork rind. Add 1 bouquet garni, 1 garlic clove, 500 ml (17 fl oz, 2 cups) water and reduce to a jelly-like consistency.

Add another 500 ml (17 fl oz, 2 cups) water and reduce to a jelly again. Add 2.5–3 litres (4¼–5 pints, 11–13 cups) water and 2 teaspoons coarse salt; bring to the boil and simmer very gently for 8 hours. Skim off the fat and strain through a fine sieve or, better still, through muslin (cheesecloth).

Simple beef consommé

Chop 2 kg (4½ lb) lean beef and 1.5 kg (3¼ lb) shin of beef (beef shank) (with bone) and place in a stockpot. Add 7 litres (12 pints, 7½ quarts) cold water and bring to the boil, then skim. Season with coarse salt. Add 3 large carrots, 400 g (14 oz) turnips, 100 g (4 oz) parsnips, 350 g (12 oz) leeks tied in a bundle, 2 celery sticks, sliced, 1 medium onion stuck with 2 cloves, 1 garlic clove, 1 thyme sprig and ½ bay leaf. Simmer very slowly so that boiling is hardly perceptible for 4 hours. Remove the meat and strain the stock. Remove the surplus fat carefully and adjust the seasoning.

White chicken stock

Prepare this in the same way as for ordinary white stock, but add a small chicken (which can be used afterwards in another recipe) or use double the quantity of giblets.

White stock

Bone an 800 g (1¾ lb) shoulder of veal and a 1 kg (2¼ lb) knuckle of veal, then tie them together with string. Crush the bones. Place the bones, meat and 1 kg (2¼ lb) chicken giblets or carcasses in a saucepan. Add 3.5 litres (6 pints, 3½ quarts) water, bring to the boil and skim. Add 125 g (4½ oz) sliced carrots, 100 g (4 oz) onions, 75 g (3 oz) leeks (white part only), 75 g (3 oz) celery and 1 bouquet garni. Season. Simmer gently for 3½ hours. Skim off the fat and strain through a very fine sieve or, better still, through muslin (cheesecloth).

INDEX

Index

Picture acknowledgements

Cabanne P. et Ryman C. *Coll. Larousse* colour plates 1, 13, 14, 15; **Magis J.-J.** *Coll. Larousse* colour plates 5, 7; **Magis J.-J.** *La Photothèque culinaire* colour plates 4, 6, 8, 10, 11, 12; **Miller G.** *Coll. Larousse* colour plate 2; **Sudres J.-D.** *Coll. Larousse* colour plates 3, 9, 16.

Editorial Director **Jane Birch**
Executive Editor **Nicky Hill**
Design Manager **Tokiko Morishima**
Editorial team **Anne Crane, Lydia Darbyshire, Bridget Jones, Cathy Lowne**
Index **Hilary Bird**
Cover design **Tokiko Morishima**
Senior Production Controller **Ian Paton**
Picture Research **Jennifer Veall**
Typesetting **Dorchester Typesetters**